Fundamentals
of
News Reporting

Fundamentals of News Reporting
(Second Edition)

Ralph S. Izard
Hugh M. Culbertson
Donald A. Lambert

Ohio University

With foreword by Wes Gallagher

KENDALL/HUNT PUBLISHING COMPANY
DUBUQUE, IOWA

Copyright © 1971, 1973 by Ralph S. Izard, Hugh M. Culbertson
and Donald A. Lambert

Library of Congress Catalog Card Number: 70-145615

ISBN 0—8403—0329—7

All rights reserved. No part of this publication may be reproduced, stored in a retrieval system, or transmitted, in any form or by any means, electronic, mechanical, photocopying, recording, or otherwise, without the prior written permission of the copyright owner.

Printed in the United States of America

Contents

Foreword vii

A Note from the Authors xi

Chapter 1. A Matter of Judgment: What Is News? 1

Chapter 2. Qualities of Effective Newswriting 27

Chapter 3. The Language of News 43

Chapter 4. Structuring the News Story 64

Chapter 5. Spot News: Immediate Description 88

Chapter 6. Reporting What Others Say 101

Chapter 7. Tools for Gathering Information 118

Chapter 8. The Specialist at Work: Beat Reporting 142

Chapter 9. Rewriting: The Second Effort 156

Chapter 10. Humanizing the News 167

Chapter 11. The Journalist and the Law 182

Chapter 12. Beyond the Fundamentals 194

Appendix 1. The Mechanics of Copy Preparation 218

Appendix 2. The Associated Press Stylebook 224

Index 275

Foreword

Today we live in a world in which controversial public issues multiply like rabbits. There is little consensus in any field of human endeavor, whether it be science, politics, business or academic life. As the voices of partisanship have become more strident, their owners have become more intolerant of other people's views. Intolerance breeds prejudice, and prejudice breeds extremism. Compromise is a dirty word. Nonnegotiable demands are the "in" thing.

In such a society, humanity needs a clear, cold light to illuminate the problems of the day and thereby challenge men to solve them. Such a light will not come from the partisans. Most public advocates demonstrate their high respect for the truth by using it sparingly. This light must come from the journalist with no ax to grind except the practice of his profession.

This era is one of great opportunity for the young journalist because there never has been greater need for calm journalistic voices. Someone must be the spokesman of sanity in this schizophrenic nuclear era.

The role of the objective journalist will never be easy. He will not win popularity. He will sometimes alienate his friends. He will be attacked by all sides. Reporting will be much more difficult because objective reporting demands more effort. Like the priest or minister, the objective reporter is called upon to use his conscience and reason instead of his emotions.

The youth of today is supposed to be turned against materialism and the establishment. It is supposed to be turned against the status quo. If this is true, objective journalism should have great appeal. It will put you against the establishment, whether that be the establishment of the right or the left. It will put you against prejudice which is ruthless against its enemies. It will put you against the advocates of any cause who yell loudly for objective reporting but who really want propagandists for their own side. The rewards will be the same as those received by the judge who finds his verdict upheld by a higher court or a scientist who struggles for years to achieve sometimes impossible goals. There will be the satisfaction of providing an essential information service to the society.

The objective reporter seeks to be *fair*. He or she seeks to be fair to the readers by being accurate and perceptive enough to gather all available facts. I emphasize *all* because there is no room in this world for Simple Simon or lazy reporting. He presents the warts and the blemishes along with the favorable items. He does not omit facts to strengthen a case, nor quote out of context.

This does not mean a story should be a simple recital of opposing views. On the contrary, every statement, every fact should be questioned and put in the proper perspective. Nothing should be accepted at face value. If the speaker is ambiguous, this should be pointed out. If he has said something previously which contradicts his latest statement, this should be carried as well. It may be, and frequently is, that the weight of the story will be on one side or other because that is where the weight of the evidence is. But this does not make a story unobjective.

I have tried to tell AP reporters that there is no reason why an intelligent reader should believe that the reporter is right just because he is called an expert or is experienced. The reader or listener in this era has grown increasingly skeptical and cynical, particularly about the views of "experts" or public figures. The reader or listener can be convinced only by logical presentation of facts. And he is quick to recognize an unfair presentation. Journalistic carelessness reinforces the reader's doubts, just as a careless phrase on the air by a commentator can prejudice his delivery in the eyes of viewers. One error, one careless phrase, one misspelled name can destroy a story. Of course, all journalists are going to stub their toes occasionally. But it is one thing to be undone by events even though you may be painstaking. It is quite another to be undone by reportorial arrogance or carelessness.

The courts can protect freedom of the press and communication media but they cannot inspire public confidence in journalism. This can come only from journalism's own performance.

Journalistic performance depends on high standards of newswriting. The good reporter knows his craft and uses it to achieve effective and meaningful communication with his readers. Good reporters must have a broad educational background and a constant dedication to the best copy they can produce. That means they know how to spell, they know proper grammar, they know style, they know how to organize a story, they know how to use a direct quote, and they know the language and how to use it properly. These are factors

FOREWORD

stressed by all news-gathering organizations, for the problems of the press, television, radio and magazines are the same. The media must communicate, and they must maintain credibility.

Reading this book will not make anyone a great writer, but the individual who carefully studies and masters through practice and experience the fundamentals of news reporting—here or elsewhere—will have taken a giant step toward being a professional journalist—a necessity for a democratic society.

Wes Gallagher
President and General Manager
The Associated Press
50 Rockefeller Plaza
New York, N.Y. 10020

A Note from the Authors

The specific point of this book is to provide the beginning news reporter with cogent, specific and professional advice about news reporting and the ways in which the newspaper story is written. It is based on the assumption that the reader comes with little or no prior knowledge about this specialized form of communication and seeks to explain both the standard practices and the "whys" behind those standard practices.

No effort is made to cover the whole range of journalism or even of newswriting. The reader will find that included here are only the bare bones, the fundamentals. The carpenter must first acquire his hammer, saw, level and rule; then he must learn to use them with professional skill. Likewise, the journalist must obtain a knowledge of the language and of the specialized form of writing he is dealing with before he can learn to use them effectively. Only continued and long-term practice in the use of these fundamentals will provide the professional polish required before one can call himself a seasoned reporter.

Reading this book will not produce a polished reporter as from the head of Zeus or Joseph Pulitzer. The journalism student must supplement its content with material from professors or practicing journalists, from reading other books and his daily newspaper and, most importantly, from actual experience in reporting and writing. Perhaps in no field does the adage that "practice makes perfect" have more validity than in news writing.

We have sought to stress both the collection of information and the writing style used in passing that information along to the readers. This, we feel, is proper, for it is not enough to be a good writer and poor in collecting information, or vice versa. Newspaper writing, no matter how pleasing the literary quality, is worthless unless it contains information which the reader wants or needs. Likewise, no amount of information has value to a newspaper or its readers unless the reporters are able to transmit that information in an effective, clear manner.

Within the discussion of writing, emphasis has been placed on qualities of good writing regardless of its specific type, as well as good newspaper writing. We do not feel that good news writing can be, or should be, divorced from the broad spectrum of composition in general. Of secondary emphasis have been discussions of how to write specific types of news stories within the overall guidelines which define the good newspaper story. This broad emphasis represents a feeling that the fundamentals of news reporting vary little from medium to medium. Although this book is concerned primarily with newspapers, the reporter who has a firm grasp of the basics of news reporting should be able to shift to other media with a change only in the techniques of presentation, not in the reporting process. Thus, knowledge of the fundamentals outlined here should be of benefit to the electronic or magazine reporter, as well as the public relations or advertising man whose duties include writing.

On a more specific level, the reader will find that there are a number of themes which appear throughout this book. Among these recurrent themes are the following which the authors consider very important:

1. That the good reporter is not satisfied with doing a good job; he wants constant improvement.

2. That the good reporter always is thinking about his readers, both in terms of writing style and in information presented.

3. That the good reporter consistently stresses accuracy, clarity, completeness and speed.

4. That although there are guidelines for newspaper writing, the reporter's judgment is crucial. He can break or bend any rule except that of accuracy if the circumstances are right.

5. That although there are guidelines, these are not restricting for the good reporter. They may limit his writing techniques, but they never limit the possibilities for literary and informational quality.

In seeking to provide professional orientation to this book, the three authors have called upon both academic and professional aspects of their backgrounds: Donald A. Lambert spent almost 10 years with the Erie, Pa., Morning News, working, at various times, as general assignment reporter, city hall reporter, columnist and editorial page editor; he received his academic training at the Pennsylvania State University. Hugh M. Culbertson has degrees in agricultural journalism and communication from Michigan State University and the University of Wisconsin. His professional experience includes four years as a science writer for the Michigan Cooperative Extension

NOTE FROM THE AUTHORS xiii

Service. Ralph S. Izard is a former general assignment reporter and education editor for the Charleston, W. Va., Daily Mail and staff writer for the Associated Press. His academic training was at West Virginia University and the University of Illinois.

It is appropriate at this point that we pause to express appreciation to some of those from whom we learned much about journalism. This book would not have been possible without the inspiration and knowledge, expressed both on the job and in the classroom, of the following people: the late W. Benton Jones, longtime managing editor, Erie Morning News; Larie Pintea, present managing editor, Erie Morning News; the late Dr. Verling C. Troldahl, professor of communication, Michigan State University; the late Earl C. Richardson, former newspaper editor and longtime Cooperative Extension Service editor, Michigan State University; Paul A. Atkins, professor of journalism, West Virginia University; the late Vint Jennings, managing editor, Charleston Daily Mail; and Rex Woodford, executive news editor, Charleston Daily Mail.

And special thanks for specific contributions to the second edition of this book must go to the following: Tom Price and Katie Sowle, for providing an expert discussion of journalistic law; Byron Scott, for the example of how journalists must translate scientific jargon; Wes Gallagher, for some excellent thoughts on objectivity in the foreword; Duane W. Bowler, editor, Billings, Montana, Gazette, for some excellent examples of rewriting; and Linda Holland, for providing any kind of help when it was needed.

If at times the language of this book tends to be rather evangelical, we do not apologize for it. The role of the news reporter, regardless of his medium, will continue to be an increasingly important one in the coming years. We cannot help but be impressed by the need for reporters who have talent and wisdom, and who are willing to put out the kind of effort necessary to achieve quality. Although there is much that is good in mass media content today, there are many examples of poor reporting and bad writing. Thus, attending to the mass media can be an emotional experience: exhilarating if the quality is good, frustrating if it is poor. We believe in the potential of the media, and we hope that this book will make some contribution toward their continued improvement.

RIZ
H.M.C.
D.A.L.

Fundamentals of News Reporting

CHAPTER 1

A Matter of Judgment: What Is News?

The newspaper reader is a man in a hurry. Studies show he will often spend less than a half hour on his daily paper. He's almost certain to skip a particular story unless he sees some reason for reading it. It follows that the newspaper which makes a habit of ignoring reader interests will soon go bankrupt.

Each day, editors must select a few dozen, or perhaps a few hundred, events among literally millions all over the world. Of these chosen few stories, only a dozen or so make the front page. The remainder get varied play on inside pages.

The news judgment process is a complex one—so complex that it has baffled and worried journalism critics and scholars for decades. In the early 1920s, Walter Lippmann realized that newsmen must somehow simplify the whole business to survive. Wrote Lippmann:

> Without standardization, without stereotypes, without routine judgments, without a fairly ruthless disregard for subtlety, the editor would soon die of excitement... The thing could not be managed at all without systematization, for in a standardized product there is economy of time and effort, as well as a partial guarantee against failure.[1]

A 1942 reporting text expressed some doubt that news judgment is tangible enough to be learned. These authors felt it was an open question whether news judges are born rather than made. However, they emphasized that a serious effort to define news should strengthen a reporter's intuitive news judgment—whatever that may be.[2]

About ten years later, another journalism text sharply criticized those who feel news judgment is an instinctive ability which one can't learn. Noting that news judges disagree, this author insisted that "the apprentice news editor can learn to be an astute judge of news, and that such a learning process can benefit from a sound theory of what makes news."[3]

Only in the 1960s did scholars begin probing the news judgment process with much precision. In this chapter, we will review some lessons from these studies.

First, we pause to emphasize that reporters as well as editors judge the news. It's true that editors assign reporters to cover stories and decide which items go where in the paper. However, reporters must often help for at least three reasons:

1. In covering a beat, the reporter will often run into a new, unexpected story lead. His city editor may never get wind of such leads unless the reporter thinks enough of them to pursue them further.

2. Because he is close to a story, a reporter will normally be in a good position to judge how it will develop and how vigorously it should be pursued. Thus intelligent editors often ask reporters for news judgment advice.

3. In writing a story, the reporter must decide what facts merit lead play, what facts may go near the end, and which ones should simply be left out. Such "within story" news judgment is discussed in Chapter 4.

What Is News?

Many authors have tried to define news in a sentence or a paragraph. Such definitions help little because they tend to falsely imply that news is a static object rather than a complex process involving many parts (news source, editor, reporter, and the "news hole" or available space, to name a few) which influence each other.

To quote one early text, news was "anything timely that is interesting and significant to readers in respect to their personal affairs or their relation to society, and the best news is that which possesses the greatest interest and significance for the greatest number."[4]

Most such definitions (including the one above, with its emphasis on timeliness) stress *change* as an essential element of news. Current or possible future changes that affect a person and his environment make up the real stuff of news.

This emphasis on change, along with the conflict and turmoil that go along with it, comes in for much criticism. For example, the authors, who were in constant contact with college students during the late 1960s, often became angered at mass media portrayals of the American college campus. In focusing on riots and unrest, newsmen seemed to ignore the large number of students who went along as usual—working hard, having a good time, and striving for change in unspectacular ways.

A MATTER OF JUDGMENT

Such news selection gives a seemingly distorted view of campuses and our young people. And distortion is a serious matter because most people—including legislators who vote on college budgets—have little or no direct contact with the campus. In the same vein, very few people are eye witnesses to events in Washington, Peking and countless other places that shape our world. We *must* depend on the mass media for a balanced account.

It also seems apparent that certain things merit attention partly because they don't change. President Johnson's 1968 Commission on Civil Disorders implied that race relations remained static in the United States for centuries, and the media ignored them. Society might have changed its ways more effectively, and with less pain, had media attention come before the "explosions" of the late 1950s and 1960s.[5]

In replying to this kind of criticism, many newsmen would doubtless argue that magazines and specialized sections within the paper (for example, business and campus news sections) should describe the status quo so as to put change in perspective. The regular news columns might then report primarily change.

This argument has some merit. However, current discussions of interpretive reporting (see Chapter 12) suggest that the newsman must put events in perspective as he reports them. The distinction between interpretation and straight news reporting is not as clear as it once seemed. Certainly this issue will receive lively debate for years to come.

Before looking at what is assumed to make a good news story, we present a model of mass communication developed in the late 1950s by MacLean and Westley.[6] This model will help organize the rest of the chapter.

A model like this one is not a profound device that provides ready-made answers. It's simply a diagram calling attention to aspects of a process which cry out for study.

The news process begins at the left side of this diagram with X's or objective events to be reported. A house burns down, with the fire lasting 52 minutes and flames shooting 93 feet into the air. Looters steal 200 television sets during a ghetto uprising. These are factual events.

In the model, the reporter may be viewed as a "nonpurposive communicator" (C). To call him nonpurposive is simply to say that he has no ax to grind, no reason to report the facts other than as

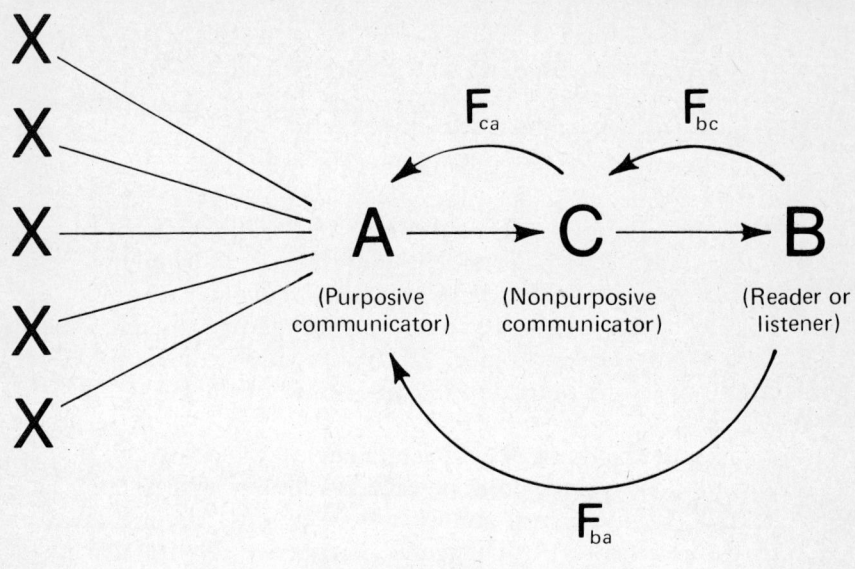

Figure 1-A.

they are. His purpose is to serve the reader (B) by describing events (X's) so the reader has an accurate understanding of these events.*

The reporter (C) must usually rely on witnesses and experts to help reconstruct and interpret events. These "middle men" or A's are called "purposive communicators" because they often have axes to grind, preferences and just plain lapses which color their reports. Somehow the reporter must arrive at the truth despite A's failings. This may require discounting reports here, correcting for probable bias there and so on.

A may be a company's public relations director putting out information on a plant disaster. Such an A (purposive source) will normally try to give C (the newsman) a picture of X's which makes the company look favorable.

---

*Westley and MacLean note that *institutions*, rather than *individuals*, sometimes play the A, C and B roles. For example, A may sometimes be a company and/or its public relations department. C can denote an entire newspaper editorial staff or a wire service staff. The precise definition of A, C and B will vary from one situation or analysis to the next. The above diagram represents a somewhat simplified version of the model as originally presented. For simplicity, lines indicating occasional direct observation of X's (objective events) by C (the nonpurposive communicator) and B (the reader or listener) are omitted here. The model is given, as altered, courtesy of the authors and Journalism Quarterly.

A MATTER OF JUDGMENT

In other cases, a source may have much less obvious reasons for reporting incompletely or inaccurately. An eyewitness at a tragic automobile accident may miss certain details simply because he couldn't bear to watch constantly. Also, the mishap's great speed may have contributed to inaccurate perception.

In an attempt to make their employers or clients better known and more popular, public relations men often lose sight of news judgment—of what interests the public. An example may clarify this. We will first analyze a press release sent to Montana papers in May 1965 by Montana State College.

Bozeman—Beginning in September, ROTC training will be optional at Montana State College as the school follows a trend set by other educational institutions around the country.

Optional ROTC (Reserve Officers Training Corps) means students no longer will be required to take two years of military training, as freshmen and sophomore males with no prior service have done practically since MSC opened its doors in 1893.

This paragraph, in addition to being made up of one very long, hard-to-read sentence, lacks the evidence and careful attribution needed to make it news. Officers of the Army and Air Force, like most bureaucrats, almost always make optimistic public statements about their projects. As a result, the reader learns very little here.

While the new program is certain to cut down on the number of students entering basic ROTC, officers of the Army and Air Force detachments believe their programs will flourish and continue to provide officers in sufficient quality and quantity to meet the needs of their respective services.

Basically, ROTC has worked like this in the past. All male students have taken either the basic Air Force or Army course for two years.

Then they could, if qualified, enter the advanced program their final two years. When the graduate received his diploma he was commissioned a second lieutenant.

The program really won't change much, except that it's optional and students will do better financially than past cadets. All advanced cadets receive monthly stipends much like scholarships. They are furnished a uniform and receive $40 per month for participating in the program. The total of all benefits for other than scholarship students is about $1,000 for the last two years.

To say without attribution that the Army and the Air Force offer some of the "best" scholarships amounts to editorializing. One could get around this by defining the scholarships as "among the largest offered as to dollar-value" or something of that sort.

ROTC scholarship programs have been instituted through Federal sources. The Army and Air Force now offer some of the best scholarships available at Montana State.

However, "best" is not synonymous with "largest." ROTC scholarships obviously have strings attached, and many students may prefer smaller stipends which leave more time for studying and other activity.

The sentence beginning with "Annual" exemplifies another form of puffery. To say that annual increases in the number of scholarships are expected is vague—it's not clear who does the expecting or whether the increase is limited to Montana State. The assertion that scholarships will go to students with a "bent for study, hard work and leadership ability" adds very little to the story, as it's hard to see what else might be considered (except perhaps financial need). And the phrase "basic course" needs clarification for many readers.

The release's last eight paragraphs, beginning with "In addition to the academic work, etc.," have no spot news value. They represent an obvious attempt to plug ROTC. The paragraphs on the Air Force drill team, the Army's Scabbard and Blade, and flight training at Gallatin Field do contain concrete facts which some editors may keep in the story. However, the last four paragraphs offer virtually no information new to someone with even a cursory knowledge of ROTC (one exception might be the asser-

Here is the scholarship program the MSC detachments are making known to present and future students:

Students successfully completing the basic course will be eligible to compete for scholarships worth about $2,000 to in-state cadets and about $2,500 to those from out-of-state.

Tuition, books, fees, supplies and equipment, plus a retainer fee of $50 per month, will be paid by either service.

Scholarships are available from both services for the next school year on a competitive basis. Annual increases in the number of scholarships are expected and students with a bent for study, hard work and leadership ability have an excellent chance to be awarded a scholarship at the completion of their basic course.

The Army and Air Force have announced new two-year programs to afford opportunity for commissions to junior college graduates, transfer students, and other students who have at least two years schooling remaining of undergraduate or graduate work.

Under the new plan, a qualified student can attend six weeks field training between the sophomore and junior year with pay and then enter the advanced course. Selection for field training is on a national basis depending on requirements existing at the time. Hence, students have no guarantee of being able to compete for a commission in two years.

In addition to the academic work, for which the students receive regular college credit, the ROTC units sponsor popular extra-curricular activities.

The Air Force has a precision drill team, intra-mural athletic teams and the Arnold Air Society, which is an honorary and social organization. A coed auxiliary known as Angel Flight is sponsored by the Arnold Air Society.

The Army has Scabbard and Blade, similar to the Arnold Air Society, and a special

A MATTER OF JUDGMENT 7

tion that the military is relying more and more on ROTC officers). Further, the press release contains several high-sounding but almost meaningless phrases which few newsmen would use. Examples include *integral part of the college curriculum, degrees and academic rank commensurate with other institutional departments, ROTC is so important, attract the top-notch college student, There's no better way to attract high-caliber college graduates, selected leading colleges and universities,* and *greatest single source of officer procurement.*

forces unit which trains in cross-country skiing, rock climbing and land navigation.

Both Army and Air Force cadets who are qualified may train in light planes at Gallatin Field near Bozeman. Each cadet who successfully completes the flight instruction program receives an FAA private pilot's license and is eligible for further flight training upon being commissioned. All expenses incidental to flight training and ground school are paid by the government.

ROTC programs are an integral part of the college curriculum and department personnel hold degrees and academic rank commensurate with other institutional departments. The Armed Forces provide the instructional personnel for the programs, while the College provides classrooms and equipment and pays related expenses.

Some people may wonder why ROTC is so important and why the government hopes to attract the top-notch college student. The service branches are depending more and more upon the college ROTC program for officers. The services require a degree as prerequisite for a commission. There's no better way to attract high-caliber college graduates than at the source—the college itself.

ROTC is offered at selected leading colleges and universities throughout the nation and is the greatest single source of officer procurement.

High school graduates, college students and others desiring more information about the reserve officers training corps may contact either Lt. Col. Aaron C. Brown, professor of military science and tactics, or Lt. Col. Frank S. Raggio, professor of aerospace studies, Montana State College, Bozeman.

Now let's see what happened when an editor (C or nonpurposive source) went to work on this release. The following version was prepared by editor Duane W. Bowler for use in the Billings Gazette.

BOZEMAN—ROTC is going Op (for optional) at Montana State College.

No more hut-too, hut-too for the unwilling undergraduate. Joe Bobcat will join the Reserve Officers Training Corps if he wants to—and if ROTC wants him.

The New Op order starts in September. It has some angles not found in the pre-Op days that have existed since MSC was founded in 1893.

MSC now will offer, not command, careers in both Army and Air Force ROTC programs. For those who make the grade, some of the best scholarships—money—are available.

Aspirants for Army and Air Force second lieutenant commissions will drill for two school years with the hope of being selected.

Once basic is over, the junior male may compete for scholarships worth about $2,000 to in-state and $2,500 to out-of-state cadets.

Either service will pay him tuition, books, fees, supplies and equipment—plus a retainer of $50 per month.

Students who transfer to MSC from junior colleges and the like won't have to do the two years of drilling under the Big Sky. They can qualify for competition by six weeks field training.

Op ROTC also has its fringe benefit—social prestige.

The Air Force has its precision drill team, intramural athletics and the Arnold Air Society—the flyboys' equivalent of Scabbard and Blade. AND a coed auxiliary known as Angel Flight.

The Army has its Scabbard and Blade and a special forces unit that trains in cross-country skiing, rock climbing and land navigation.

Qualified Air Force cadets get to fly and so do those of the Army. They train, at government expense, at Gallatin Field. Completion gets them a FAA private pilots' license and a ticket for further training after commissioning.

It's the new look for Op ROTC after nearly 70 years of compulsory wearing of the khaki at land grant colleges.

Many a former student at MSC can recall the fate of a classmate (or himself) who had to take ROTC basic as a senior because he skipped too many drills in his first glorying at campus life.

The rewritten version is little more than one-third as long as the original. While more attribution is needed, the rewrite man has lost very little information—perhaps none interesting enough to make an impression on many readers.

Perhaps surprisingly, the rewrite probably has more promotional impact than the press release used verbatim, though promotion was not the rewrite man's goal. The newspaperman has written in a readable, interesting way—basically because he kept his *audience* in mind. The press-release author, however, apparently became so concerned with pleasing his *employer* that he forgot the reading public.

In developing the model, Westley and MacLean criticize a widespread assumption that news flow is a one-way street (source to reporter to audience). They emphasize that any communication process requires feedback in which readers and listeners "turn around" and talk to speakers and writers. Hence the need for the "feedback loops" (F_{bc}, F_{ca}, and F_{ba}).

The news judgment process depends to a much greater degree on feedback within the news system than most books suggest. Specifically:

F_{bc} = feedback from reader to reporter. Many successful journalists do wander in the hustings, talking to ordinary citizens, to figure out what issues are salient, and how the winds of public opinion blow. Some papers, like the Minneapolis Star-Tribune, survey their readers regularly.

F_{ca} = feedback from reporter to news source. As he covers a running story or works a beat, the reporter will talk a great deal with his news sources, and his news judgment is apt to depend partly on his relationship with them. We will say more on this later.

F_{ba} = feedback from reader to news source. Often a purposive news source like a politician will do a public opinion poll to gauge public reactions. Such polls may sometimes be newsworthy in themselves. However, this line of feedback is basically outside the reporting process and will get scant attention here.

The Westley-MacLean Model makes it clear that news judgment depends largely on how a reporter views his readers (B's) and his news sources (A's).

Most authors assume news judgment hinges almost entirely on how the judge views his audience. Contemporary American standards of journalism suggest the editor must serve the reader and only the reader. Practically, it's the reader who buys papers. And ethically, it's the editor's job to protect and help readers by shedding light on events.

Such a view may be very sound *theoretically*. However, *in practice*, the reporter's relations with news sources often influence his judgment. As we'll show later in this chapter, it takes a great deal of discipline and expertise to ignore or shut out reporter-source relationships in making news judgments IF the reporter feels this should be done.

We now consider the question of what distinguishes a front page story from one that winds up at the bottom of page 17 or in the "round file." At this point, our emphasis will be on news value as viewed by readers (B's).

News Elements

Reporters often talk of finding a "peg" on which to hang a story. That is, what, specifically, does a story have that makes it likely to catch a reader's eye? The answer depends partly on what angle the reporter chooses to emphasize, and on how he organizes the story.

Journalism texts generally list about 8-12 key news attributes. There is considerable debate on just how much use the practicing newsman makes of such traits. Certainly he doesn't have time to measure each story painstakingly on a dozen separate yardsticks.

Granting that, few observers have come up with clearer ways of talking about news judgment. Beginners can sharpen their ability by making a conscious effort to weigh stories on the various news elements. After a time it becomes second nature for a person to use the elements, quickly and perhaps unconsciously, in assessing a given story.

There is no universally accepted list of elements, and we will simply discuss 10 of the more popular ones.

Proximity. Other things being equal, an event in the reader's home town generally seems more interesting than one in Madagascar. In fact, a great many Americans seemingly want to ignore events in distant lands. This desire has long been widespread in the United States, especially during times of actual and threatened war.

A study of news flow in Oregon sheds some light on the importance and limitations of proximity as a news element.[7] In general, Oregon editors gave more space to nearby events than to faraway ones. This lawful relationship proved particularly valid when applied to within-state news for larger papers aimed at statewide circulation. Most smaller papers had fairly small circulation areas, and their coverage tended to drop off rather abruptly at the boundaries of these areas.

At first glance proximity seems like a very objective measure—one that can be expressed in miles. However, recent authors have suggested it's partly psychological. In an experiment, University of North Carolina students guessed that Chapel Hill (home of the university) was much closer to Atlanta than to Philadelphia. On the map, Chapel Hill was equally far from the two cities. Yet identification with the South apparently made Atlanta seem closer.[8]

For a given reader, a story may have high psychological but low physical proximity or vice versa. For example, the death of a woman's son 10,000 miles away in battle is very close, psychologically, to her. Also, a story about a next door neighbor whom one has never met may be quite distant psychologically. In such cases, psychological distance surely takes precedence over physical distance in news judgment.

Timeliness. Traditionally, timeliness may very well have been the most respected of news elements. Reporters regard a beat on the competition as a major badge of honor. In fact, a day-old story simply is not considered news by many editors unless some new angle comes along.

In a 1961 study, 92 per cent of all wire stories run in 23 Minnesota papers were published on the day they were received. Few stories were kept for more than one day on the chance that new developments might bring them back to life.[9]

Recent talk about interpretive reporting seems to indicate some realization that timeliness can be overdone as a news element. Certain events surely deserve to be reported even though they are not timely, partly because they help people understand matters of current interest.

For example, many if not most people in western nations have a deep and abiding interest (perhaps often a morbid curiosity) about Nazi Germany. Certain government documents which shed light on the horrors and inner workings of Nazism weren't made available to historians until the mid or late 1960s. The events described in such documents are surely newsworthy today, even though they happened 25 to 50 years ago. (Of course, the release of the documents itself may be timely. This would add value to such a story.)

It's often said that radio and television have taken over much of the spot news function long reserved for papers. As a result, the newspaper special edition has nearly disappeared, and the newspaperman supposedly can concentrate more and more on reporting in depth.

However, many editors doubt that the electronic media can even do a good spot news job in a 15-minute or half-hour show. As a result, speed remains important in the newspaper business.

Novelty. There's an old saying that it is really news when a man bites a dog. Such an event is *rare*. Perhaps more important, it's startling and *unexpected*. Too much emphasis has sometimes been placed on the bizarre and unexpected, just as it has on timeliness. However, when kept in perspective, novelty is certainly a legitimate news element.

In this country, people tend to think of government as very big, cold and impersonal. It's quite novel when an individual citizen stands up to fight the system and gets its goat to the point where it allegedly fights back as in the following Washington Post story.[10]

Russell T. Forte's war with the Prince George's County Commissioners has escalated. Forte contends the Commissioners have bent zoning regulations all out of shape to allow a commercial parking lot next to his backyard in Chillum in retaliation for his political activities against them.

Forte has been busy politically, all right.

1. Forte is aligned with County citizen groups which have been loudly criticizing the Commissioners over an array of planning and zoning decisions.

2. Last autumn, Forte filed a suit in Circuit Court charging the Commissioners with misusing public funds for "political propaganda" purposes.

Forte's suit came at the height of another in the County's long series of battles over a home rule charter. There were two slates of charter-writing candidates, with Forte supporting one slate and the Commissioners the other. If the candidates Forte supported won, the Commissioners would have little to say about the drastic governmental reorganization that a home rule charter could bring if adopted by the voters in 1970.

Well, the Commissioners won the court fight but their candidates lost the election; partly, various people claim, because of all the noise Forte caused.

3. To cap it all off, Forte has not merely accused the Commissioners of retaliation against him on the parking lot issue, he has filed another court suit to overturn the zoning exception that allows the lot.

Novelty has meaning only when defined in terms of the reader's expectations. In 1969, one of the authors heard a rather startling (to him) report from a highly credible source that war between China and the Soviet Union was probable.[11] To him this was novel indeed. He had known of a conflict, but had not realized that things had reached such a crucial stage. To a historian, however, such a war may have seemed almost inevitable because of conflicts of interest and long-standing antipathy between the Chinese and Russian peoples.[12]

Consequence. An event's importance clearly depends largely on just how much impact it has on people. This notion really centers on the amount of *impact per person* (a snowstorm does more damage when it cripples a person than when it simply makes him late for dinner) as well as the *number of people* affected.

Of particular concern is the amount of impact on readers, listeners or viewers. Stories on taxes and the cost of living, for example, have high consequence because they relate directly to people's pocketbooks.

However, stories can have consequence in other, more subtle ways. Upon moving to Ohio in the late 1960s, the authors noticed several stories in the local press about the death sentence and its ramifications. Following is one such story.[13]

ROANOKE, Va. (AP)—Frank Jimmy Snider, Jr. wept when he said life in his cell seven feet from the electric chair has been a "living death." He has been on Virginia's death row for 13 years.

From his cell, he said Wednesday, he can "hear the hum of motors, the throwing of the switch and smell the burning flesh."

Snider, in Roanoke Hustings Court for a hearing on a petition for a new trial, contended his frequently scheduled executions and last-minute stays constitute cruel and unusual punishment prohibited by the constitution.

State Attorney Edward S. White, protesting Snider's testimony, said the former Gadsden, Ala., steelworker "is not qualified to testify that the death penalty is cruel, unusual punishment as he has not undergone it."

Snider was sentenced to death in 1956 on a charge of raping a 9-year-old child. In an exchange between White and Snider, the prosecutor said the convict's 13 years on death row have been his own doing, because of legal tactics, and "the commonwealth of Virginia has not kept him there."

Explaining the numerous appeals that have kept him alive, Snider said, "I am not an animal. I want to live."

The convict told the court he had lost 50 pounds since being placed on death row at the state prison in Richmond, but has gained two after being returned to Roanoke for the hearing. He said he has developed numerous illnesses, such as arthritis, asthma, rheumatism and sinus trouble.

The only exercise he gets is a weekly 14-foot walk to a shower and pacing up and down in his cell, he said.

Snider's plea for a new trial is hinged to a new U.S. Supreme Court ruling that prohibits the removal of prospective jurors opposed to capital punishment.

Judge William M. Sweeney said that he would not consider the testimony given by Snider in ruling on the petition.

At first, the authors felt that Ohio papers were merely being sensational in running stories of this type. Before long, however, we learned that capital punishment was then a major issue in Ohio. Then, in our eyes, such stories appeared to have a certain amount of impact or relevance apart from their emotional wallop. Citizens in a state that's debating an issue certainly have a right to be informed about related events all over the country.

Of course, the Roanoke, Va., story has a great deal of human interest or "soft news" value. In fact, the reporter saw to that when he relegated what may be the main issue (removal of jurors opposed to the death penalty) to a few words at the story's end. Our real point, however, is that a newsman must know the issues and the people in his area to properly assess a story's consequence.

Conflict. In a period of unrest and social change, many stories have impact partly because they mirror physical conflict as well as clashes among values and priorities. Student protests on college campuses, and at the 1968 Democratic National Convention in Chicago, have fascinated readers partly because of violence and destruction. But there is more to it than that. The protestors' language, dress and general behavior suggest to many people that our entire society is going to the dogs, that hallowed beliefs about right and wrong no longer have meaning.

It's important to note that customs and values change. As a result, events which conflict strongly with values at one time may not later. The authors can remember when use of marijuana by the young seemed shocking and almost unbearable. By 1970, however, a story of marijuana had very little shock value to readers who have become accustomed to hearing about LSD and "speed." The moral: *know your audience* and its ever-changing interests.

Sensationalism. A number of newspapers still regard blood, sex and gore as their major bread and butter (recall that in the days of "yellow journalism" many did). No newspaper can avoid reporting violence and crime. However, one can avoid sensational treatment by discussing causes and implications—and by avoiding overemphasis of such news.

This news element relates closely to conflict. Both tend to involve flaunting of basic ideas about what's important and right or wrong. For example, most editors would regard a story about incest as highly sensational because it touches one of society's most deeply held values.

To a large extent, of course, sensationalism results from the reporter's treatment. In covering a murder, one could emphasize blood and gore while ignoring such important issues as the possibility of publicity prejudicing a jury.

Human Interest. It's been said that a reporter has a good thing going when he finds a story about boys, dogs or Abraham Lincoln. One observer commented facetiously that a story about Abe Lincoln's son's pet dog would indeed be a circulation builder!

In the 1940s, growing numbers of editors began checking readership of particular stories systematically. Apparently forgetting the lessons of Dana, Pulitzer and Bennett, many were startled when human interest stories carried away top honors with amazing consistency. Even a very important story with a multi-column head on page 1 would often be lucky to gain 20-30 per cent readership. But run a picture of a local girl winning a beauty contest, spice it with some cheesecake, and you could almost count on 50-75 per cent readership.[14]

Chapter 10, dealing with feature writing, contains a more complete discussion of what human interest really is.

Prominence. It's gotten so the President of the United States can scarcely sneeze without getting front-page attention. Featuring prominent names may seem frivolous, catering to vanity and hero worship. Yet even staid, scholarly papers seem to regard prominence as an element of "hard news." The New York Times once gave 10 column inches to an attempted suicide—and an unsuccessful one at that—by the son-in-law of former Ambassador and New York Gov. Averell Harriman.

Many Americans show studied disdain for royalty and big shots. However, this is a land of celebrities like Willie Mays and Liz Taylor. Small wonder, then, that big names have a big following.

Even the most mundane act by a highly prominent person sometimes qualifies as news. During President John F. Kennedy's administration, a wire service story reported that Mrs. Jacqueline Kennedy went water skiing and fell twice!

Suspense. A mystery story is fun to read largely because we are uncertain of the outcome until the very end. Sporting events also keep us in suspense.

Recognizing this appeal, the television networks have more or less turned recent national elections into sporting events. Obviously, few people have a clear stake in election results. (In fact, cynics insist that America's major parties and candidates are generally so close together that the outcome really makes little difference to anyone except the candidates.) Sheer suspense must help explain why tens of millions of people stay up until early (or even late) morning to see a winner declared. (Of course elections do have a great deal of consequence for most people.)

Clarity and Certainty. Many journalism scholars do not regard clarity as a new element, apparently because it centers on what reporters know about an event, not on the nature of the event.

As a practical matter, however, this factor seems very important. It is interesting to watch a press association wire in the hours following a plane or train wreck. Initial reports are very sketchy, giving tentative casualty figures and often warning that even the available information is little more than unconfirmed rumor.

Because of deadlines, some editors have to run such sketchy reports (with appropriate disclaimers, of course). However, they would prefer to wait until detail and confirmation become available. Other things being equal, a more clear, complete, well confirmed news story merits more space than a sketchy, tentative one.

Some Additional News Judgment Concepts

We've noted that the news elements are not entirely separate from each other. For example, a story with lots of conflict or shock value is almost bound to be quite sensational. Also, timely stories are valued partly because they tend to have high consequence—they relate to things that affect us now.

In light of this, several authors have looked for concepts which may really make up the essence of news elements. It's suggested that a hurried newsman may think in terms of a very few such underlying concepts rather than 10 or 12 separate elements.

Westley, for example, suggests that the news elements more or less boil down to a matter of *identification*. That is, they focus on the extent to which a reader feels persons, places and events relate to him personally. Westley notes that millions of people devour weather news because it touches them personally. Psychological distance really boils down to a question of identification. And conflict, when analyzed closely, may amount to putting oneself in the shoes of a contestant and mentally "choosing up sides."[15]

In another widely quoted analysis, Schramm distinguishes between *immediate reward* and *delayed reward* stories. He suggests that we read human interest and sports stories because we get an immediate kick out of them. At the other extreme, we wade through long, technical stories so we can vote more intelligently in the distant future.[16]

People differ in their needs for immediate reward from the mass media. However, even serious-minded folk read the comics.

That which gives immediate reward to one person may not to someone else. Stock market news seems rather stodgy and "hard" to most people, yet an investor may get a very immediate reward as he notes that his own stock has gone up. Also, crime news which seems quite "soft" and sensational to most people may be a very serious matter to a criminologist when he analyzes it in light of his own theories.

The immediate vs. delayed reward distinction is often known by another name—*hard vs. soft news*. Several studies show that such a distinction is meaningful to editors and readers. In this research, people seem to choose or read stories in patterned ways. A person who reads one political story is pretty apt to read other political stories, and so on. Human interest stories have sometimes clustered together in this sense, as have civic affairs stories.[17]

It's important here to note that two schools of thought exist with regard to the meaning of hard vs. soft news.

1. Many newspaper editors equate hard news with timeliness. In their view, even a story of high consequence might be termed soft news if it's basically a feature item or a background piece. Only a story that goes to press within hours (or in some cases, perhaps, minutes) after the reported event qualifies as hard news.

2. Some editors and many scholars and critics of the press equate soft news with appeals to humor and emotion, as well as the bizarre, novel and unexpected. By this definition, a serious but not timely story would qualify as hard news.

In the discussion that follows, we'll adopt the second of these definitions. Our concern here will be with news value as seen by readers, and research shows this definition to be meaningful in their eyes. We would add that many stories (for example, a sensational murder) have both hard and soft news value by our second definition. The line between them is not hard and fast.

In a study of college students, consequence, proximity, timeliness, and sometimes conflict clustered together, apparently as hard news elements. That is, a story rating high on one of these elements was also likely to rate high on the others. Similarly, novelty, human interest and sensationalism tended to cluster together as soft news elements.[18]

The distinction between hard and soft news brings us to an age-old philosophical question. Should the editor give people what they want all the time? Or should he devote substantial space to what he thinks they need?

Many hard-bitten old-timers would argue that a paper must provide mostly what readers want or the publisher will go bankrupt. Few newsmen disagree with that entirely. However, some deplore any tendency to overdo soft news. Entertainment is really the domain of television, radio and magazines, their argument suggests. The newspaper is basically a medium of timely information.

Some soft-news advocates underestimate public interest in serious content. It's claimed that more Americans attend art galleries than football games.[19] And one study tentatively suggests that the average American adult, if there is such a person, spends a very substantial four hours per month watching, reading and listening to fairly sophisticated Culture with a capital C.[20]

Those who argue for very high emphasis on soft news also seem to ignore the growth of specialized departments like business, society and youth. Departments make it possible to aim with a rifle rather than a shotgun. That's probably healthy from a readership standpoint because most people get more excited about their special interests than about run-of-the-paper news. Many such departments (automotive and business, for example) are not generally regarded as soft news.

Discussion of specialized departments brings us to another concept often mentioned by newsmen—*balance*. It's widely assumed that the reader wants a balance between world and local news, between serious and light news, and so forth.

It's not clear just how many newsmen consciously strive for balance. A midwestern wire editor, nicknamed "Mr. Gates," has been studied in depth as he went about his work. Mr. Gates has insisted that he tries to judge each story on its own merit, without worrying about the balance on any given day.[21] However, the cheesecake pictures and brighteners appearing on front pages all over the country suggest much striving for variety and balance.

The so-called "play" theory of mass communication, also seems to suggest that a variety of stories will enhance reader interest. This theory implies reading a newspaper is fun partly because it gives us a wide choice. We can concentrate on the New York Times or the Daily News, sports or finance, Dr. Rex Morgan or Pogo. Such freedom provides welcome relief in lives that are highly regimented because of busy work schedules, nagging wives and so on.[22]

Another trend in contemporary thinking about news judgment is the increasing realization that newsmen must know their audiences. We've noted earlier that many stories which seemed shocking (high in conflict) in 1950 would look tame 20 or 30 years later.

As usually presented, the "news elements" are assumed to be universal. Every reader, it's suggested, is attracted by human interest, consequence and the like. While perhaps generally valid, such an approach glosses over differences from town to town, region to region, and time to time. In fact, proper application of the elements themselves demands knowledge of local problems and readers. A national Baptist convention is likely to have high consequence when reported in a community with lots of Baptists.

A few papers such as the Minneapolis Star-Tribune systematically study reader interests and news consumption habits. This would seem to be a wide-open field for the future.

MacLean and Kao have developed a device called the "editorial game" which can help the newsman test and improve his own judging skill. These researchers first asked a sample of audience members to sort pictures in order of preference. Editors then tried to predict audience preferences.

The $64 question: what kind of information about the audience would most help editors? General information about things like church membership and time spent watching television helped some. However, editors made much better use of knowledge about picture preferences as reflected in previous sorts.[23] The best way to predict news consumption, it's implied, is to study people's past consumption habits.

No discussion of news judgment would be complete without noting that it depends very largely on mechanical factors such as size of newshole, editorial staff size, morning vs. afternoon paper and number of news services subscribed to. Such variables often limit an editor's care and leeway in judging news.

One might expect emphasis on family planning in communities with crowded housing, much poverty and low educational attainment. Families tend to be larger under such conditions. However, one study found no more newspaper coverage of family planning issues where a city had much crowded housing and poverty than where it had little. Size of newshole was a much better predictor of play given to family planning.[24] Many other studies have also shown in various ways the importance of "mechanical" factors.[25]

Thus far we have talked of news value as defined by readers and listeners (B's in the Westley-MacLean Model). We now turn to the relationship between reporter (C) and news source (A).

The News Source—A Factor in Judgment?

There is evidence that, while journalists may like to believe otherwise, sources do exert subtle but important influences on news judgment. Several studies and a great deal of on-the-job experience suggest the need to look closely at a number of related processes. We now turn to these.

1. *"Built-in" conflicts stemming from the reporter's and his source's job demands.* Such divisions showed up in a study of medical coverage in North Carolina. To begin with, doctors have a great deal of scientific training. This, strengthened by the demands of the American Medical Society, leads them to be cautious, to avoid talking about a new drug or vaccine until they are certain it's safe and will work. Reporters, on the other hand, are trained to keep readers informed—even about breaking somewhat tentative stories.

This scientist-reporter conflict seems particularly clear when one contrasts the scientist's style of writing with news story format. In their own journals, scientists leave the punch line until near the end, forcing readers to wade through all sorts of detail and become painfully aware of qualifications. Such writing differs greatly from the reporter's practice of getting right to the point in the lead.

Also, doctors avoid seeking publicity as individuals partly because their professional colleagues frown upon it. At the opposite extreme, school administrators often have lots to gain from publicity. Unlike doctors, they sometimes complain about too little rather than too much newspaper attention. [26]

An analysis of California city government and the press revealed several built-in conflicts. The mayor and his cohorts naturally wanted *consensus* and approval so they could get projects accepted and carried out. Reporters, on the other hand, often tended to play up *conflict*. [27]

Both reporters and officials tended to defend the city against real or potential attacks by outsiders. However, the two groups differed as to just what was being defended. To the reporter, the *people* were the key, while officials tended to feel they were fighting for *government and its programs*. [28]

Reston notes very deep-seated conflicts between diplomat and reporter. The diplomat naturally wants secrecy while negotiations are under way. Publicity, after all, could easily offend envoys from other countries and tip off adversaries. Reporters, on the other hand, feel the democratic process is short-circuited when officials present a policy or an agreement—signed, sealed and delivered—before public debate can begin. [29]

While it may sometimes color coverage and irk newsmen, such job conflict strikes many people as natural and proper. Rivers, among others, has argued that news people and officials are inherently *adversaries*. [30]

Sometimes coverage suffers when reporter and source quit being adversaries—a point to which we now turn.

2. *Co-opting of the reporter by regular sources.* James McCartney, a veteran Washington correspondent, has written of this with particular insight. He notes that one who covers a beat such as the Pentagon must work very closely with bureaucrats. Such day in, day out contact provides tips and leads which are absolutely essential for good reporting.

After a few years, McCartney believes, a typical reporter may be hard put to avoid accepting the viewpoint of his regular news sources. There is usually no bribery or outright dishonesty. Yet a newsman can lose much of his value if his opinions and priorities change so he becomes a sort of inadvertent press agent for a particular official or agency. [31]

News executives may help add balance to coverage, in McCartney's view, by assigning a given reporter to cover all sides of a dispute. Exposure to several viewpoints may encourage a detached view (though knowing a newsman has contact with "establishment" types may make news sources such as the Black Panther Party or the Irish Republican Army less than anxious to talk). [32]

"Co-opting" tends to occur where a reporter covers one beat and deals with one set of contacts for months and years on end. Even the reporter who is new at city hall or the statehouse, however, may run into personality barriers and conflicts—our next topic.

3. *Personality and prestige differences.* Reston notes that reporters have often had trouble providing real depth coverage of American presidents. Like most Americans, journalists want to respect their leaders. The situation may be especially difficult with a forceful personality like Franklin D. Roosevelt or Lyndon B. Johnson in the White House.

Through the years, presidents have differed greatly in their approach to the press. Franklin Roosevelt and John F. Kennedy were both very articulate and tended to enjoy informal socializing with correspondents. Dwight Eisenhower tended to remain aloof, leaving press relations to his subordinates. Lyndon Johnson was not above calling a newsman's boss on occasion to vent his spleen about a negative story. And many observers claim Richard Nixon's somewhat introverted personality—coupled with an apparently calculated campaign to bring newsmen into line—has riled reporters. [33]

It's not clear precisely how—on balance—such White House strategies have affected press relations. There's reason to believe they have had considerable impact. Yet ideally, it would seem, newsmen should judge the news on its own merits, ignoring "personality" and prestige factors insofar as possible.

Carter's study of medical coverage, mentioned earlier, revealed the related phenomenon of *role reversal.* Carter reasoned that in everyday life doctors are more apt to join the local country club and become community leaders than are reporters. However, in the news interview, the shoe of power goes on the other foot in that the reporter has the capability—in theory—to write a story which could harm the doctor's reputation. [34]

Perhaps we can understand role reversal clearly by thinking of two servicemen, a colonel and a sergeant, who return from war. In the military, the colonel has been the sergeant's superior. In later civilian life, however, the ex-sergeant suddenly becomes the ex-colonel's superior. Surely this must happen on occasion, and the probable strain on both men (perhaps particularly the ex-colonel) is apparent. It's a small wonder that news sources sometimes clam up in the face of a similar strain.

4. *Strategies and "game playing."* In the California city government study noted earlier, some reporters enjoyed giving advice to the city fathers. The latter soon found they could inflate reportorial egos and improve coverage (from their viewpoint, at least) by occasionally appearing to accept such advice. However, the journalists saw through this to a degree and were not above giving city officials advice designed to create newsworthy conflict! [35]

In a related vein, a study of State Department correspondents revealed considerable hostility between press and diplomats. Much of this stems from officials who try to use the press by planting stories and slanting the news. It would seem that such hostility should stay out of news judgment. No one really knows how often it does. [36]

To this point, we've seen several kinds of differences between journalist and news source. Rivers' idea that such varied thinking is healthy seems reasonable only if each party accurately perceives the differences and regards them as tolerable. This brings us to our fifth and last point.

5. *Understanding, with or without agreement.* Returning to Carter's North Carolina medical study, both newsmen and doctors ranked several news-judgment criteria alike in order of importance. On the surface, this seemed encouraging. However, further questioning showed that doctors charged reporters with overemphasizing timeliness and public appeal at the expense of accuracy and completeness.

The point here is that, despite basic agreement, the two groups did not work together very well because understanding was lacking. Doctors saw a difference and—valid or not—this apparently led them to sit on some stories. [37]

What can be done here? The reporter can learn as much as possible about sources and their views. He can judge news only when he realizes what lies behind the doctor's jargon, the diplomat's silence and the politician's extreme willingness to talk. He should know much more about the technical side of his assignments than he would ever write in a story.

If he's a good reporter, he knows much more than a diplomat or doctor about what people can and will read. Many scientists and other specialists who accuse him of oversimplifying aren't very realistic. Most folks will not read a lengthy tome, and the reporter must often convey a sense of "ifs" and "buts" without going into minute detail.

Finally, reporters should not let themselves be scared away by obstinate, secretive news sources. At the other extreme, they should not be motivated by a personal vendetta to overplay an otherwise routine story. If serving the public interest rules out protecting news sources, it also rules out going after them just to satisfy one's temper.

Summary and Conclusions

News judgments or pegs have become embedded in journalistic lore about news judgment. Among these elements are proximity, timeliness, novelty, consequence, conflict, sensationalism, human interest, prominence, suspense, and clarity-certainty. While helpful, elements are too cumbersome to figure clearly in many decisions made under deadline pressure. The distinction between informative (hard) and entertaining (soft) news seems more meaningful based on research results.

Departmentalization—on the upswing in many areas—permits the reporter to aim at a clearly defined, fairly uniform audience that is apt to be quite interested in what he has to say. Also, recent study suggests that balance between hard and soft news, as well as between local and national-international news, may help readership.

While one judges news basically with an eye to the consumer, the role of news sources merits attention. As he works with a news source, the reporter may find himself sharing the source's perspective. This may not make for good reporting.

Furthermore, a reporter must understand his source's *motives* and *technical specialty* to evaluate information and report it meaningfully. Such understanding requires much experience and study.

We close with perhaps the most important point one can make about news judgment. New elements, balance, editorial games and the Westley-MacLean Model help little unless *the newsman himself keeps abreast of the news*. There is simply no substitute for knowing the issues and their impact upon one's audience.

LIST OF REFERENCES

1. Lippmann, Walter, *Public Opinion* (New York: The Macmillan Company, 1947), p. 352.

2. Johnson, Stanley and Harriss, Julian, *The Complete Reporter* (New York: The Macmillan Company, 1942), p. 20.

3. Westley, Bruce H., *News Editing* (Cambridge, Mass.: The Houghton-Mifflin Company, 1953), p. 333.

4. Cited in Westley, *Ibid.*, p. 333.

5. *Report of the National Advisory Commission on Civil Disorders* (New York Times Company, 1968), p. 384.

6. Westley, Bruce H. and MacLean, Malcolm S., Jr., "A Conceptual Model for Communications Research," *Journalism Quarterly* 34(1):31-8, Winter 1957.

7. Schramm, Wilbur, "Newspapers of a State as a News Network," *Journalism Quarterly* 35(2):117-82, Spring 1958.

8. Carter, Roy E., Jr. and Mitofsky, Warren, "Actual and Perceived Distances in the News," *Journalism Quarterly* 38(2):223-5, Spring 1961.

9. Jones, Robert L.; Troldahl, Verling C. and Hvistendahl, J.K., "News Selection Patterns From a State TTS-Wire," *Journalism Quarterly* 38(3):303-12, Summer 1961.

10. Phillips, James G., "Chillum Citizen Fights City Hall," *The Washington Post*, June 19, 1969, p. F1.

11. Salisbury, Harrison, "U.S. Foreign Policy and the News," Edwin and Ruth Kennedy Lecture Series, Ohio University, Athens, July 1, 1969.

12. *Ibid.*

13. Associated Press story appearing in the Athens (Ohio) Messenger, March 13, 1969, p. 2.

14. Swanson, Charles E., "What They Read in 130 Daily Newspapers," *Journalism Quarterly* 32(3):411-21, Fall 1955.

15. Westley, Bruce H., *op. cit.*, p. 336.

16. Schramm, Wilbur, "The Nature of News," *Journalism Quarterly* 26(3):259-69, September 1949.

17. Studies contributing to this general conclusion include: Guido H. Stempel III, "An Empirical Exploration of the Nature of News," *Paul J. Deutschmann Memorial Papers in Mass Communication Research* (Cincinnati, Ohio: Scripps-Howard Research,

1963), pp. 19-23; Guido H. Stempel III, "A Factor Analytic Study of Reader Interest in News," *Journalism Quarterly* 44(2):326-30, Summer 1967; and Peter Clarke, "Does Teen News Attract Boys to Newspapers?" *Journalism Quarterly* 45(1):7-13, Spring 1968.

18. Culbertson, Hugh M. and Stempel, Guido H., III, "An Experimental Investigation of Criteria Used in Judging News," Paper presented to Theory and Methodology Division, Association for Education in Journalism, Lawrence, Kan., 1968.

19. Weissman, George, "Good Art is Good Business," *Public Relations Journal* 25(6):8-10, June 1969.

20. Berelson, Bernard, "In the Presence of Culture," *Public Opinion Quarterly* 28(1):1-12, Spring 1964.

21. Snider, Paul B., "Mr. Gates Revisited: A 1966 Version of the 1949 Case Study," *Journalism Quarterly* 44(3):419-27, Fall 1967.

22. Stephenson, William, *The Play Theory of Communication* (Chicago: The University of Chicago Press, 1967), pp. 45-65.

23. MacLean, Malcolm S., Jr. and Kao, Ann Li-an, "Picture Selection: An Editorial Game," *Journalism Quarterly* 40(2):230-2, Spring 1963.

24. Shaw, Donald L., "Surveillance vs. Constraint: Press Coverage of a Social Issue," *Journalism Quarterly* 46(4):707-12, Winter 1969.

25. See Guido H. Stempel III, "How Newspapers Use the Associated Press Afternoon A-Wire," *Journalism Quarterly* 41(2):380-4, Summer 1964; Lewis Donohew, "Newspaper Gatekeepers and Forces in the News Channel," *Public Opinion Quarterly* 31:61-8, Spring 1967; Lowell Brandner and Joan Sistrunk, "The Newspaper: Model or Mirror of Community Values?" *Journalism Quarterly* 43(3):497-504, Autumn 1966; and Wayne A. Danielson and John B. Adams, "Completeness of Press Coverage of the 1960 Campaign," *Journalism Quarterly* 38(3):441-52, Autumn 1961.

26. Carter, Roy E., Jr., "Newspaper 'Gatekeepers' and the Sources of News," *Public Opinion Quarterly* 22(2): 133-44, Summer 1958.

27. Gieber, Walter and Johnson, Walter, "The City Hall 'Beat': A Study of Reporter and Source Roles," *Journalism Quarterly* 38(2): 289-97, Summer 1961.

28. *Ibid.*

29. Reston, James, *The Artillery of the Press* (New York: Harper and Row, 1967), pp. 5-8.

30. Rivers, William L., *The Adversaries, Politics and the Press* (Boston: Beacon Press, 1970).

31. McCartney, James, "Vested Interest of the Reporter," in Louis Lyons (ed.), *Reporting the News* (Cambridge, Mass.: The Belknap Press, 1965), pp. 97-106.

32. McCartney, James, "Must the Media be 'Used'?" *Columbia Journalism Review* 8(4): 36-41, Winter 1969-70.

33. For a good overall summary of presidential press relations, see Elmer Cornwell, Jr., *Presidential Leadership of Public Opinion* (Bloomington: Indiana University Press, 1965).

34. Carter, *op. cit.*

35. Gieber and Johnson, *op. cit.*

36. Cohen, Bernard C., *The Press and Foreign Policy* (Princeton, N.J.: Princeton University Press, 1963), p. 155.

37. Carter, *op. cit.*

CHAPTER 2

Qualities of Effective Newswriting

The cliche that sticks and stones can break your bones but words can never hurt you may make a lot of sense to little boys playing cops and robbers. However, the statement's absurdity is clear to a newspaper whose careless, unclear reporting has ruined someone's reputation and led to a costly libel suit.

Words are really tools for making distinctions. Perhaps because we use them so much and so easily, we come to take them for granted. Resulting sloppiness has helped create some of man's worst problems. For example:

—Social scientists have suggested that the use of labels can help turn a person into a stutterer or a criminal. Call someone bad or stupid often enough and he's likely to see himself that way. He has little to go on except words uttered by others in defining himself and his proper role in life.*

—Race prejudice stems in large part from fallacies of labeling. As we shall see later, the mere use of a word like Nigger, Wop or Nip calls attention to similarities among vast groups of people. Actually, people of any ethnic, racial or religious group vary greatly, and careless use of labels obscures these differences. By so doing, it adds credence to beliefs like "all Negroes are lazy" and "all Jews are aloof." Such beliefs, in turn, provide fertile soil for hatred and prejudice.**

In this chapter, we will lay a foundation for two important rules of newswriting. The rules go hand in hand in the sense that when you obey one, you are very likely to obey the other. They are:

1. Write *factually,* leaving your own opinions out of copy.

2. Write *concretely,* avoiding undue abstractness.

---

*The school of thought which emphasizes this most strongly is symbolic interactionism. See Erving Goffman, *Asylums* (Garden City, New York: Doubleday and Co., 1961).
**For a useful account of basic psychology of language, see Roger Brown, *Words and Things* (Glencoe, Ill.: The Free Press, 1958).

If he obeys these rules to the utmost, the reporter will naturally tend to be both *accurate* and *complete* in his writing. It's possible but highly unlikely that one will be concrete and factual, yet inaccurate and incomplete. We'll develop these notions further at the end of this chapter.

At first glance, the meanings for *concrete* and *factual* seem fairly obvious. However, there is a great deal more to both words than meets the eye. This chapter analyzes each one carefully to help keep the reader on guard by driving home the fact that *one can never be completely factual or concrete,* but he must keep trying (within certain limits to be mentioned later) while remembering that he can never achieve his goal completely.

We now turn to the rather sticky question of what a fact is. After discussing that and looking at some ways in which one can insure the factual nature of his reporting, we will consider concreteness.

Three Types of Meaning

Ogden and Richards—two semanticists—have noted that *anyone who uses language is using symbols* (words, pictures, graphs or drawings) to refer to *something* (perhaps a physical object, an abstract ideal like Christian love or a characteristic like beauty). The following diagram, a simplified version of one presented by Ogden and Richards, shows how these three parts of the meaning process fit together.[1]

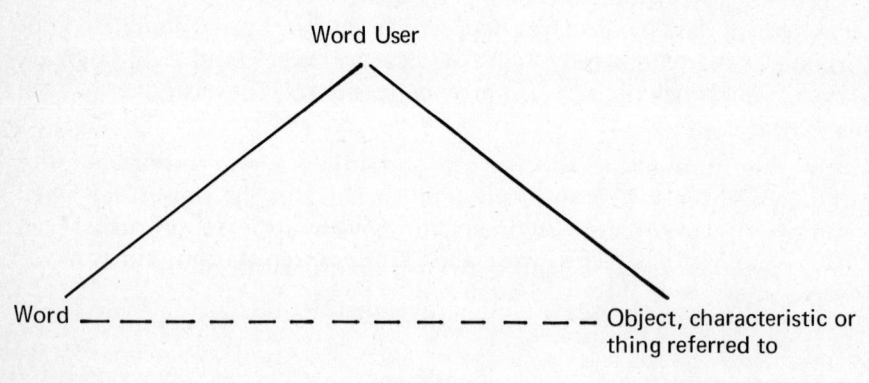

Word User

Word ⸺ ⸺ ⸺ ⸺ ⸺ ⸺ ⸺ ⸺ ⸺ Object, characteristic or thing referred to

Figure 2-A

The dashed line indicates that the connection between symbol and object is an arbitrary one chosen by the word user. Granted, on rare occasions, a word may physically resemble an object (for example, the word "whiz" seems appropriate partly because it sounds like the speeding objects it often refers to). However, this is rare. And even in such a case, the word user could talk about a "shreeming" object if he wished. There is no law of nature which makes him say "whizzing."

By now, the reader may have raised his eyebrows slightly. Sure, one could call a whizzing object a shreeming object, you might say. But what good would it do? It would simply confuse the readers and listeners, most of whom have not heard the word "shreeming" before and do not know what to make of it.

This point would be well taken. A writer and a reader would have the same meaning for "shreem" only if they have had similar experiences with that word. People get along and understand each other largely because they have had similar experiences with a great many words. Practically, then, you cannot use just any word you wish without losing your audience.

In a deeper sense, however, this analysis really supports the validity of the "dashed line" in the Ogden-Richards diagram. Meanings are in people, not in words.[2] Dictionaries are useful because they report common word spelling and usage within a society at a certain time. They do not reflect natural or God-given standards of proper usage.

The important thing is for the reporter to use words which will be understood. His job is to communicate with readers, not with himself. Whether a given word is understandable depends more on whether readers are familiar with it than on its length or complexity. To be sure, often-used words tend to be short and simple. However, some fairly complex words (for example, commentator, ecology and conservationism) are widely used and understood.

As an aside, it seems important to stress that we are *not* holding a brief for careless spelling, grammar and word choice. The argument that misspelled words are all right so long as they don't interfere with understanding (anyone would know that "alll right" really means "all right") has no place in journalism. A misspelled word tells your readers that you are careless and/or illiterate. No journalist can achieve genuine success with this kind of reputation, since newspapers do serve as educational instruments.

Following Ogden and Richards, word meaning really has three aspects—one centering on each element in the above diagram.[3]

First, *denotative* meaning centers on the *referent* or *object*. The statement that Joel Smith is 6-feet-10 tall gives us denotative information. Such a sentence may be true or false. In either case, it is highly denotative because it provides information about Joel which we can check. Generally accepted measurement procedures insure that we will agree on Joel's height, whether we chance to love or hate tall people.

Second, *connotative* meaning centers on the word user. The statement that the Taj Mahal is beautiful really tells us more about the observer than about the Taj Mahal. Most people feel it's beautiful, but some can stand only buildings with sharp turns and corners. Taj Mahal lovers really have no basis for arguing that deviants are in error. Beauty is in the eye of the beholder.

Third, *structural* meaning centers on the word itself as related to surrounding words. The sentence "Azlnx pounded Zlvbn" looks like nonsense. Yet the structure of the sentence tells us something about Azlnx and Zlvbn. It indicates they are both things. It also shows that Azlnx was capable of pounding Zlvbn, and that Zlvbn was capable of being pounded by Azlnx.[4]

Structural meaning often provides cues about denotative and connotative meanings. A note in an operatic piece has beauty partly because of surrounding notes (hence context provides *connotative* meaning). And the statement, "He hit a long _____ over the left field wall." gives us *denotative* information that he probably hit a round object called a ball (after all, few other things are hit over left field walls very often).

Getting back to the reporter, the demand that he stick to the facts seemingly requires that he stress denotative meaning. Semantic analysis makes it clear, however, that there is no such thing as pure denotative meaning—as perception without a perceiver.

A simple example should drive this last point home. Someone might be unable to make any use of his senses. To such a person, poor soul, the phrase 6-feet-10 would be meaningless. He cannot experience it in any way. Obviously, then, an object's height has no meaning without reference to the senses and skills of the observer.

How Can One Avoid Editorializing? Journalists have learned from other professional communicators' mistakes to avoid overusing highly connotative words. Perhaps the best-known abusers of such words, by the way, are diplomats. In a typical U.N. Security Council debate, charges against aggressors and imperialists abound. At best, such debate seldom leads to solutions (if they are to be found at all, solutions generally come in secret sessions where each side can talk specifics without using highly emotional words to impress the world). At worst, public debate may worsen a crisis by hurting diplomats' feelings.

Freedom of the press is a highly connotative expression that causes journalists many problems. Western editors often berate

QUALITIES OF EFFECTIVE NEWSWRITING

Pravda and other Communist news outlets for lacking freedom. Russian and Chinese observers also attack even prestigious western papers on the same grounds.

In the heat of such an argument, it's seldom pointed out that Communist and non-Communist editors really mean quite different things by freedom.

To the westerner, freedom of the press implies the right to criticize even top government officials. Only when fully informed about news of the day, including mistakes in high places, can citizens look out for their own interests at the polls, in town meetings and elsewhere.

Communists view things quite differently. As they see it, the Communist Party, as the controlling force in government, must help bring society through various political, military and economic steps toward a classless society as outlined by Marx and his more recent disciples. Freedom of the press really means primarily freedom to help the party retain public support. Criticism of the Kremlin is simply unthinkable to the editor of Pravda. To rule out such criticism would not limit freedom in his view.

To avoid such confusion, the young reporter must work hard to weed out the subtle editorializing that can creep into a story. Eventually, sticking to the facts will become second nature. In the meantime, however, one must remain on guard.

Perhaps the worst-offending words are loaded adjectives like *beautiful* and *good*. The reporter's job is to describe things like a person's physical characteristics (for example, blonde hair and dimensions such as 36-24-36) and accomplishments. That way he provides information needed to judge beauty and goodness. Yet he lets the reader do the judging.*

Adjectives such as *unique, strong, active* and *dynamic* carry more or less hidden implications of goodness or badness. Such words require special care because their meaning varies from usage to usage. For example, we expect politicians to be dynamic, but we may care very little whether druggists are or not. It follows that a dynamic politician may seem better than a dynamic druggist. Furthermore, if one uses "dynamic" in a story about politics, he should make it clear in what way a person is dynamic. Does he really get things done quickly and without hesitation? Or does he simply make lots of speeches and kiss hundreds of babies each year? Without such concrete elaboration, the word *dynamic* is dangerously vague.

---

*It's important to remember that one can objectively report a statement by another person that something is good or beautiful. Joan's beauty is a matter of opinion, but the fact that Robert said that she's beautiful is not.

Other "double meaning" words which lead to confusion are *runner* (sled vs. marathon) and *critical* (in very bad shape vs. making many comments implying a need for change). It's crucial that context make it clear which meaning is intended for such a word.

A reporter is often tempted to insert some commonly used, subtly loaded words and phrases because of habit. A *well-earned rest* is one example (to say that one is taking such a rest implies that he has worked hard and done a good job on something). Reporters generally have no business making such judgments.

In the same vein, many people often use the word *lady* in conversation out of deference to the fair sex. However, *woman* generally suits the reporter's needs better because it lacks certain connotative meanings (good manners, social respectability and high moral character to name a few) generally associated with *lady*. The reader should judge whether a given woman qualifies as a lady. He may decide instead that she is a crude, unladylike broad.

The phrase "passed on to his reward" is inappropriate in obituaries for at least two reasons. It sounds flowery. And it implies the deceased has shown good character and has gone to a pleasant life in the hereafter. A desire to honor the dead is understandable, but reporting specific accomplishments is the way to do it. Further, using a loaded phrase routinely in all obituaries—even for the worst of scoundrels—will eventually make the words seem meaningless. In much the same way, Hollywood has gradually drained adjectives like "outstanding" and "spectacular" of meaning.

Editorializing can also creep in with adjectives like *large, heavy* and *long*. At first glance, such words seem quite objective because they refer to dimensions (area, weight and height) which one can measure scientifically. However, heavy and long do not specify weight and height in measurable units. That which is heavy to a weakling may be very light to a champion weightlifter. Once again, each reader should be given clear data so he can decide.

Lest the reporter feel too restricted, he should realize that some subjective adjectives can be used where their application in a given story is clear. For example, one may safely call Miss America beautiful because she is chosen by a panel of authorities on beauty. Many people might argue, in fact, that the Miss America pageant helps determine the way in which Americans define beauty.

It's not accurate to equate objectivity with avoidance of connotative meaning. In fact, there's a growing belief that today's reporter must handle such meaning clearly and forcefully. President Johnson's Commission on Civil Disorders put the point as follows:

> By and large, news organizations have failed to communicate to both their black and white audiences a sense of the problem America faces... The media report and write from the standpoint of a white man's world. The ills of the ghetto, the difficulties of life there, the Negro's burning sense of grievance, are seldom conveyed.[5]

Ills, difficulties and senses of grievance are not easily measured. They center on the way people feel. The commission seems to be saying that the press cannot help people share meaning about complex problems in human relations without going beyond traditional, highly denotative reporting.

What can the journalist do to convey connotative meanings—as the Kerner Commission asks—without entering a semantic fog? For one thing, he may adopt the methods of the feature writer, who reports facts but does it in such a way as to make readers laugh, cry and feel anger. Good feature writers do not use loaded, unclear words. Second, the reporter can use modern social science techniques to measure opinions, feelings and frustrations with some objectivity. We will return to this in the concluding chapter.

By now the reader should have some feel for the great care required to be factual. We turn next to our second rule—good writing should, within limits, be concrete.

The Ladder of Abstraction

The continuum from abstract to concrete includes many shades of grey.

One of the authors has asked hundreds of students which word is more abstract, cow or animal. All agree on animal, but few can explain just why. To understand, we must remember the three parts of the meaning process—*symbol, symbol user* and *symbol referent*. Cow and animal differ in at least two ways with regard to these parts.

First, *animal* refers to a larger, more varied class of referent objects than does *cow*. Tiny insects qualify, as do whales and elephants.

Forgetting such variation can lead us astray. When we give something a label, we lump it and other things into a class designated by the label. In lumping, we tend to focus on similarities and forget differences among these objects.* In an oft-quoted example, people who know little about ancient Greece may assume that Socrates was masculine because he was a man. Actually, however, Socrates was effeminate in some ways.

---

*As used here, the word object is defined very broadly to refer to any entity. Entities can vary from physical objects like a table to concepts like freedom or concept systems like democracy.

Second, a concrete word like *cow* conveys lots of information. Tell one that you have a cow and he immediately knows your animal has four legs, four stomachs and probably eyes that look large and mournful.

Moving a few rungs up the ladder, the word *democracy* is more abstract than *animal*. However, the difference between *democracy* and *animal* does not closely parallel the difference between *animal* and *cow*.

For one thing, *democracy* has a great deal of emotional or connotative meaning for many people. Hundreds of thousands of American men have died to preserve democracy. The word's history has made it "loaded." Its mere mention stirs the adrenalin in many people—particularly political conservatives. *Animal*, by contrast, is a very bland word.

Secondly, people from several nations and backgrounds view *democracy* differently. They disagree about its denotative meaning (some people feel democracy refers to specific events like casting a secret ballot, but others would include civic freedom more broadly defined). And they differ on its connotative meaning (in the U.S.A. during the 1970s, many new leftists hate the thought of American democracy about as strongly as their parents love it).

It's interesting to note that, while *animal* is more abstract than *cow*, the two words differ little in connotative meaning. Both are quite bland. However, as we move further up the ladder of abstraction, a growing number of words tend to have lots of emotional loading. Even highly educated men let such meaning get out of hand. For example, "aggressor" has become a fighting word in the United Nations.

Concrete words can have emotional wallop, too. Take a sentence like, "Lying face down in the mud, Sam crawled inch by inch toward the edge of the battlefield." Fortunately, we can decide and agree on the denotative meaning of a concrete word—on its referent. This, in turn, helps us control and harness the connotative meaning to fit our needs. The moral to the newsman—be specific and don't write in broad general terms.

Dead-Level Abstracting. The general semanticists make one point that many of us overlook. Interesting writing tends toward the lower end of the ladder of abstraction, all right, but concreteness can be overdone.

One of the authors once attended a convention at a small college. Roommates were assigned more or less at random, and the author drew a talkative but seemingly harmless partner. Trouble was, this fellow had a great penchant for the little things. He went on endlessly about the blue wallpaper in our dormitory room, the soggy corn flakes in the cafeteria and so on. A few hours of such ultraconcrete minutae can make the poor listener or reader scream.

To be sure, extremely abstract writing can be just as boring. One sociology book contains 470 pages of statements like the following:

> It is true that seen from the logico-experimental point of view the theories involved in ritual prescriptions involve either error or unverifiable statements or both. The former element is by no means negligible. But in a positivistic context the tendency is to jump directly from proof of the existence of error to the conclusion that it is explained by a nonnormative, nonsubjective drive, or something of the sort.[6]

Concreteness depends on the *content* of a passage and the *choice of words* describing specific events which we can all easily imagine. The above sociological passage is bound to be quite abstract because of its content. However, the author could have added some concreteness by choosing words that clearly describe certain specific ritual prescriptions and errors in their interpretation.

General semanticists have coined the phrase *dead-level abstracting* to denote remaining steadfastly at one level—any level—on the ladder of abstraction. It is generally wise to stay on the lower rungs in the news business. Yet one needs to stand back occasionally and say something about how reported facts relate to what is past and what's apt to come later. This involves at least a dash of abstractness.

It's possible, for example, to write a brief story which does nothing more than quote a Black Panther leader as he calls for militant action—for a black nation quite separate from white America.

The story takes on greater interest, however, when the reporter stops to contrast the leader's rhetoric with the emphasis on integration which dominated the civil rights movement 10 to 20 years earlier. Such analysis revolves around a fairly abstract issue—separation vs. integration as a primary goal of black people. Without moving a step or two up the ladder of abstraction, the story would be incomplete, unclear and perhaps boring.

At the opposite extreme, young reporters doubtless tend to plant their feet near the top of the ladder of abstraction at least as often as near the bottom.

One way to avoid being too abstract is to define terms by analogy with some object or process familiar to the reader. One of the authors has frequently done this in reporting on agricultural science. Here are two examples from his files:

—*Elasticity of demand* puzzles people. However, the meaning becomes quite clear when one remembers that an elastic rubber band or garter stretches. By analogy, people almost quit buying a product with highly elastic demand when the market price goes up. In other words, they make a little bit of such a product stretch or go further. Thus defined, demand elasticity becomes clear to a newspaper audience.

—The *root system of alfalfa* seems rather unexciting at first glance. Yet one can add punch to a story about alfalfa roots by likening them to a food cellar. Mow or pasture alfalfa in September and you empty the cellar by forcing plants to spend the fall living off material stored in roots. As a result, alfalfa might starve during the long winter that follows.

A second approach to insuring against too much abstractness is to clearly define long, unfamiliar words or leave them out entirely. Treatment of a phrase like *broadcast seeding* requires special care. If he were to use it in a metropolitan Philadelphia paper, a reporter would need to define it in parentheses (scattering seed on top of the ground). However, someone writing for a farm page in a Fargo, N.D., paper probably need not define the term. He's writing for grain farmers, and *broadcast seeding* would be very clear to them.

Where it's clearly and easily defined, a term like broadcast seeding is appropriate as it shows readers you aren't talking down to them by using only third-grade language.

A third way of moving down the ladder of abstraction is to describe *how* an event happens and not just the *end results* of that event. A science writer once tackled what seemed to be a drab story on a rat poison called dieldrin. The result of dieldrin use—a bunch of dead rats—seemed less than appetizing. However, a little reading revealed that dieldrin is applied as a kind of dust. Rats get it on their fur, then eat it inadvertently while using their tongues to clean themselves. The picture of a rat being hoodwinked into licking himself to death seemed rather touching (perhaps humorous to some), and this formed the basis of the story lead.

Another story discussed a survey on those who skied during 1959 in the state of Michigan. Statistics such as gross annual income for ski resorts looked dry until the author hit on the idea of using them to portray an average skier and how he spends his ski weekends. Some arithmetic revealed that the typical skier spent $58.40 per weekend trip and traveled 580 miles per round trip to and from a ski area. Such figures painted a picture that readers could relate to themselves.

QUALITIES OF EFFECTIVE NEWSWRITING

After all, it's rather enjoyable to compare oneself with another person—even a hypothetical one.

Such attempts to be concrete, specific and factual tend to help the reporter realize perhaps his two most vital goals—*accuracy* and *completeness.* It's impossible to overemphasize these qualities. The public's dependence on the mass media for information needed to be effective citizens, places an awesome responsibility on the reporter's shoulders. He must *know* he is right; he cannot afford to guess or make any assumptions. If he makes a mistake, its effects can multiply and lead to serious consequences for himself, his paper or even his community.

We now pause to consider some experiences by newsmen which drive home the need for accuracy and completeness.

Accuracy

Joseph Pulitzer, one of the most respected—and damned—of all American newspaper editors, emphasized to his staff at the St. Louis Post-Dispatch the importance of accuracy in the slogan: "Accuracy, Accuracy, Accuracy." To Pulitzer and to all good newspapermen, accuracy in content is an obligation of all reporters as well as a practical matter and a question of pride and craftsmanship.

One of the most famous inaccuracies in American journalism crossed the Atlantic on Nov. 7, 1918. Roy Howard, then president of United Press, cabled from France that World War I was over. The UP cable desk in New York flashed the news across the country. Hundreds of papers ran it under banner headlines, triggering many wild celebrations.

Unfortunately for Howard, the armistice wasn't actually signed until Nov. 11. Howard had gotten his information in a conversation with Adm. Henry B. Wilson, commander of all U.S. Naval forces in France. The UP chief filed his story and went to grab some dinner. While waiting for his drink, he received a frantic message from Wilson that the dispatch was "unconfirmable." Howard's follow-up dispatch, designed to correct the error, did not reach New York until almost noon on Nov. 8.

Howard claimed, and Wilson admitted, that United Press really acted in good faith. In fact, one author later suggested that an armistice of some sort may have been signed on Nov. 7 with Kaiser Wilhelm's government, only to lose its official status when the Kaiser abdicated his office.[7]

Guilty of poor reporting or not, Howard came in for great abuse from fellow journalists. The Burlington, Vt., News cancelled its UP service, and other papers threatened to do so. The moral: *Even good intentions and reasonable care may not relieve the sting of an inaccurate story.*

Accuracy strongly emphasizes factual correctness, but it includes more than care with facts. There are many responsibilities of the reporter throughout the newsgathering process which contribute to the total accuracy and reader understanding in the final presentation of a story.

The reporter must have an accurate outlook on the subject he is covering. If it is complex, does he understand it? He must take accurate notes, for he will rely on them when he writes his story; if his notes are inaccurate, his story is likely to be, too.

He must be accurate in grammar, spelling and English usage—and these cannot be learned overnight. He should be accurate in his typing, and, if he has some shortcomings in this regard, he should be accurate in spotting and correcting his typing errors before he hands in his story.

Despite the extenuating circumstances of deadline pressure, there really is no excuse for inaccuracy in a newspaper. It happens, but it should never be shrugged off and taken for granted. If a man spells his name Smyth rather than Smith, that is his privilege, and the reporter has no right to spell it incorrectly. If Smyth's age is 70, saying he is 69 is not close enough. If he has been arrested and lives at 245 South St., listing his residence as 246 South St. will not make the people who *do* live there very happy.

Completeness

The New York Times slogan, "All the News That's Fit to Print," stresses a second virtue of good reporting—completeness. The Times, one of the world's most prestigious papers, is the only American paper that routinely runs presidential speeches and press conferences word for word, supplemented, of course, by accompanying stories.

At times, the temptation to tell only part of a story is very strong. Partly because of a concern for national security, the American press said very little about preparations for the ill-fated Bay of Pigs invasion against Fidel Castro's Cuba. New York Times staffers argued among themselves long and loud on just how much should be told.

In the end, President John F. Kennedy publicly scolded the Times for printing too much. Privately, however, the President reportedly told Times managing editor Turner Catledge, "If you had printed more about the operation, you would have saved us from a colossal mistake."[8]

The moral: *A reporter should never be satisfied with half a story.* There may be times when full reporting would jeopardize personal interests (as when a very young first offender commits a crime) and national interests (as with troop movements during wartime). However, these cases are rare. In any event, holding back information is always an editor's decision. The reporter himself should never feel comfortable with gaps in his stories.

One area in which the reporter must be on constant guard for inaccuracies and lack of completeness is when he must depend on other people for information. He seldom witnesses the events about which he is writing; but he knows that witnesses are notoriously inconsistent in their descriptions. In situations in which a murder has been staged in front of a group, for example, the variations are always extreme. Some of the witnesses almost always say the intruder was 6-foot-5, while others insist he was 5-foot-10. Some swear he had a 38-caliber pistol while others report a 22-caliber. Even supposed expert observers can disagree (a staged murder at a scientists' convention once sent a group of psychologists into utter confusion).

But what is the reporter to do if he did not witness an event and thus must accept information from witnesses? It's simply stated but difficult to do: *He must develop a sixth sense about which facts to check and which to accept.*

At first glance, all this may seem to imply that a good reporter would never trust anyone and would be cynical about everything he hears. Carried to extremes, it suggests that a sports reporter should not even take a coach's word that his star center is 6-foot-10.

Any experienced reporter will say this is absurd. In the first place, even should he wish to do so, he will seldom have the time to check every fact. Secondly, through his dealings with sources, the reporter soon learns whom he can trust. Thus, courthouse reporters generally will accept a policeman's word for a suspect's place of birth and age rather than taking the time to dig out the suspect's birth certificate. The reporter knows which politicians can be trusted for straight information, which businessmen can be depended upon, which teacher will not seek to hide problem areas.

In spite of this, further checking sometimes may clearly be called for. If he is to decide intelligently when he must dig deeper, a reporter needs at least three things:

1. *A thorough knowledge of the area he's covering.* The reporter must be an expert. He must understand his subject matter so well that subtle inaccuracies do not get past him. And only a reporter who has been around a while and knows his community will be likely to get tips or hear rumors which may lead to good stories.

2. *A dash of suspicion and a good deal of care in evaluating sources of information.* A reporter may often take the word of an honest, competent policeman who seemingly has nothing to hide. He must, however, know whom he can trust. And he must do as much as he can to help the reader make up his own mind about news sources.

3. *Alertness and skill in spotting inconsistencies.* The statement that an accident occurred at Palmer and Vine streets may look fine to a casual observer. But it should send the reporter to a city map if he suspects that Palmer and Vine run parallel to each other. Likewise the reporter will want to check further if two people disagree on some information.

Using such intangibles as these, James Reston of The New York Times acted very much like Perry Mason in breaking a major story about a 1951 Korean War armistice plan.

Reston got onto the story largely because he felt disturbed about several events suggesting a hardening American line at a time when peace talks loomed on the horizon. Secretary of State Dean Acheson referred to the Chinese as "sub-barbarians" in a Paris speech. A Pentagon leak indicated that an immediate truce would be a mixed blessing, since it would release Chinese armies for operation throughout Southeast Asia. These and other events—unrelated at first glance—added up to something in Reston's mind.

Curious, he began calling on Washington embassies of countries with United Nations troops in Korea. These calls revealed that the apparent hard-line approach actually was a strategic part of an overall peace initiative—precisely the opposite of what it sounded like on the surface. Thus alerted, Reston received confirmation from the U.S. government, earning a one-day beat on other less ingenious reporters.[9]

Speed

Accuracy and completeness are easier if one has all the time he would like—and if he uses the dictionary, atlas, city directory and telephone as he should—but the good reporter seldom has all the time he would like. This does not mean he dashes his stories out at breakneck speed without using adequate care and sufficient thought. It does mean that he is quick in getting himself to the scene of the story or is fast in getting the necessary information by telephone. It means he is fast as well as accurate in note-taking, fast in thinking of what he needs for his story, fast in organizing his thoughts, fast in writing the story, fast in typing and fast in editing his copy.

No one need be so naive as to believe that reporters spend all their time working at a mind-numbing pace. In newsgathering, there are slow periods and hectic ones, often during the same day, sometimes in the same hour. The reporter may find himself able to relax during half his working hours, spending more time than he actually needs to write his stories. And then, suddenly, he may be buried by several fast-breaking stories at the same time.

Speed is a quality which most reporters have to develop gradually. It may require weeks or months on the job before a reporter learns to remain calm under pressure. An experienced reporter rarely is pushed to the point of being uncomfortable—his ability to work at full speed has become *normal*. Understandably, not everyone can become acclimated to the pressure of daily newspaper deadlines; some beginning journalists may be happier in certain other media—such as magazines—with fewer and more distantly spaced deadlines.

The point is this: The reporter must be able to work under great pressure and still maintain accuracy throughout. Accuracy is necessary at all times; speed is necessary some of the time. The good reporter has both.

Summary and Conclusions

While it's often taken for granted, language can become unclear and even dangerous unless it's used with care. Such care requires that we be aware of *types of meaning* and *levels of abstraction*.

Semanticists have suggested three basic types of meaning. Connotative meanings reside in emotions like love and hate which occur in the word user. Denotative meaning provides information that most if not all people can check, and the emphasis here is on the entity referred to. Structural meaning stems from other symbols (for example, a musical note has beauty partly because of notes surrounding it).

In general, it's wise to write concretely. However, too much concreteness can make a news story just as boring as too little. The good writer moves up and down on the lower rungs of the ladder of abstraction. He doesn't stay in one place.

The distinction between abstract and concrete words is fairly complex. Abstractness involves:

1. Using a symbol to designate a large, varied class of entities (for

example, *animals*). Such symbols give the reader or listener little information. Further, they can lead to confusion. That's because, when we label a group of things, we tend to emphasize their similarities rather than their differences.

2. Using symbols like *democracy* for which different people have very different connotative and denotative meanings. This, too, can lead to breakdowns in understanding.

3. Using loaded words such as *freedom* with potent connotative meanings. These meanings are also evoked by concrete words skillfully used. Furthermore, concreteness helps people be precise about what they mean, thereby avoiding misunderstanding.

The notions of abstractness and meaning get little attention in many journalism courses. Yet they seem as crucial as grammar, spelling, and transition or "flow" in clear, interesting writing.

LIST OF REFERENCES

1. Ogden, C.K., and Richards, I.A., *The Meaning of Meaning* (New York: Harcourt, Brace & Co., 1923), p. 11.

2. Berlo, David K., *The Process of Communication* (New York: Holt, Rinehart & Winston, 1960), p. 184.

3. *Ibid.*, pp. 190-215.

4. *Ibid.*, p. 200.

5. *Report of the National Advisory Commission on Civil Disorders* (New York Times Co., 1968), p. 366.

6. Parsons, Talcott, *The Structure of Social Action* (New York: The Free Press, 1968), p. 210.

7. Morris, Joe Alex, *Deadline Every Minute: The Story of the United Press* (Garden City, New York: Doubleday & Company, Inc., 1957), pp. 94-101.

8. Bernstein, Victor, and Gordon, Jesse, "The Press and the Bay of Pigs," *The Columbia University Forum*, Fall 1967.

9. "The Troubled Press," *Fortune* 45(2): 124-6, 164, 166, 169, 176, February 1952.

CHAPTER 3

The Language of News

Don't believe it if you are told that newspaper writing is accomplished according to a rigid formula. There are rules of journalistic writing which the reporter follows as he prepares his copy, of course, but these rules assist the reporter by providing guidelines rather than restricting him. Those who insist that newspaper writing is stereotyped and rigid are confusing the existence of a newspaper formula with the fact that it sometimes is poorly used. In the hands of an imaginative, conscientious newswriting craftsman, the formula is elastic enough to result in interesting, informative and well-written copy. This is possible only when the reporter recognizes that quality writing of all types requires hard work. The individual who feels that good writing is easy and fun and who is not willing to struggle for perfection would never be pleased with anything that presumed to provide operating boundaries.

The beginning reporter, however, needs to pretend that the formula is rigid. He must follow its guidelines religiously until he has mastered the fundamentals of newspaper writing. Through constant practice, he must get to the point at which he can readily arrange any set of facts in an interesting, concise and precise manner. It helps if he has the benefit of criticism from a professional, either his teacher or a practicing newsman. But, even more important, he must be his own most severe critic, avoiding the luxury of falling in love with his own prose and constantly striving for quality. Only after he has internalized the basics can he begin to take liberties with the formula.

The first rule of newswriting is that it will be formally correct. Newspapers serve a utilitarian function—to convey the news from the person who knows about it to the person who wants to know about it. But they do so in a literary context which to be most effective must be solidly grounded in the standard principles of grammar, spelling, punctuation and semantics. Additionally, newspapers cannot avoid the fact that they are educational instruments and, therefore, must provide a proper example of language use.

The reporter must also remember that once he decides to work for a newspaper, he is writing for someone else. He can no longer write exclusively for his own enjoyment. He need not write on a third-grade level to reach everyone, but he must consider the individuals in his audience and structure his writing to facilitate communication with them.

Such considerations have provided the soil from which the style and structure of the newspaper story have grown. The ways in which readers use their newspapers provide the reasons why newspaper stories tend to have certain characteristics. This chapter seeks to explain what these characteristics are, how the newspaper story differs from other types of writing and some of the criteria by which a good newspaper story is judged. It will do so by dividing the "language of news" into its most essential ingredients and discussing them one at a time in the hope that the beginning reporter can gain a basis on which to launch his journalistic future.

Grammar

The news reporter is not excused from knowing the rules of grammar. Quite the contrary, he should be a grammatical fundamentalist, insisting that the language be used properly even when such use seems to conflict with the spoken word or "sounds funny." Most people may say, "The basketball team won their game last night" with no thought about improper grammar, but a reporter's copy must be more proper: "The basketball team won *its* game last night."

Lack of sufficient knowledge of or interest in grammar can appear in newspaper columns in two ways. The first, of course, would be in the actual use of poor grammar, but this is not common. A reporter who consistently uses incorrect grammar will have to learn and practice the rules or move to another occupation.

Even the good reporter, however, will have some areas of grammatical difficulty to which he must pay very careful attention. His first responsibility is to become aware of his problems, his second, to do something about them. In this sense, it is very helpful to have available resources which can answer grammatical questions. A partial listing of some of the most common grammatical problems is provided here, but two books which provide much more comprehensive listings are *The Careful Writer* by Theodore M. Bernstein (Atheneum) and *The Elements of Style* by William Strunk Jr. and E.B. White (The Macmillan Co.).

Among the most common grammatical problems are the following:

Accept-except: *Accept* means to take or receive, *except* as a verb means to exclude, and *except* as a preposition means with the exception of. Thus, "Virginia *accepted* the gift for her mother." "If you *except* the third point, the compromise will be ratified." "All made statements *except* the mayor."

Affect-effect: As verbs, *affect* means to influence and *effect* means to cause to come about. Thus, it should be "The negotiator *effected* a change in the attitudes of those in the room" and "That action will *affect* almost everyone." As nouns, *effect* is almost always the proper word, as in "He had an *effect* upon the makeup of the committee." *Affect* is roughly synonymous with emotion in psychology, and it's seldom used in the popular press.

Agree to-agree with: You may *agree to* a proposal and *agree with* another person.

All right-alright: It should be *all right,* two words. *Alright* is not generally accepted.

Compare to-compare with: *Compare to* should be used only to suggest likenesses between two objects, *compare with* to suggest likenesses and differences. Thus, "The typical 10-year-old boy is often *compared to* a howling hyena." "In *comparing* the book *with* the original manuscript, she found several variations."

Consensus: It's redundant to say *consensus of opinion.* The word *consensus* means general agreement, and automatically contains the idea of opinion. Thus, "The *consensus* was that White's argument was the correct one."

Council-counsel: *Council* means assembly, official group; *counsel* means advice or adviser. *Counsel* is also a verb, meaning to give advice. Thus, "The city *council* will meet tonight." "The lawyer gave me good *counsel.*" "He *counseled* me to be cautious."

Dangling modifer: This results from carelessness in clarifying the object of a modifier and usually leads to confusion of meaning. For example, "Absentmindedly stepping from the sidewalk, an automobile hit me" actually means the automobile stepped from the sidewalk and hit me. To correct, it is generally best to supply the proper subject in the dangling clause, as in: "When I absentmindedly stepped from the sidewalk, an automobile hit me."

Different from-different than: It almost always is *different from,* especially when followed by a noun, as in: "Apples are *different from* oranges." However, when followed by a clause, use of *from* can produce awkward construction unless the phrase "that which" is added. For example, the sentence which would properly be written "His thoughts at the end of the year were *different from* those which he held at the beginning of the year" would be less clumsy as "His thoughts at the end of the year were *different than* at the beginning of the year."

Either-neither: Always requiring singular verbs, both *either* and *neither* are properly used to designate one of two things. Thus, "*Neither* John nor George is home."

Farther-further: It is best to use *farther* for specific distances and *further* for depth or quantity. Thus, "He threw the ball *farther* than John." "Let's pursue that subject *further*."

Faulty parallelism: Parallelism makes clear the relationship among parts of a sentence; without it, sentences are almost always confusing and incongruous. In general, one should express in the same grammatical form parts of sentences that are parallel in thought and function. Thus, avoid: "She was given in marriage by her father, wearing her mother's wedding gown" in favor of "She was given in marriage by her father, and she was wearing her mother's wedding gown."

Its-it's: Although one of the few absolutes, usage of *its* and *it's* goes contrary to expectations. Even though the possessive usually is formed through use of an apostrophe, the possessive in this case is *its*. The only use for *it's* is as a contraction for *it is*.

Less-fewer: The general rule is that *less* refers to quantity ("He has *less* common sense than Harry" or "His donations were *less* than mine") and *fewer* refers to number ("They had *fewer* players in yesterday's concert").

Like-as: *Like* refers to nouns and pronouns ("His story is *like* mine"), *as* is used before phrases and clauses ("He left *as* he had arrived—alone").

Noun-pronoun agreement as to number (singular or plural), particularly with regard to nouns which encompass a group: It is correct to say, "The American Legion will begin *its* membership drive next week" and "Everyone cheered for *his* own team."

Verb number: Where a prepositional phrase modifies a singular noun which serves as the subject of a sentence, the verb of that sentence should be singular even though the object of the preposition is plural. Thus, "One of the boys *shoots* (not *shoot*) very well."

People-persons: Regardless of the choice made, usage here will always produce arguments, but, in general, it is best to avoid *people* with words of number. A dash of common sense always helps, but a general rule is that *people* relates to large or unspecific groups, *persons* is proper for an exact or small number.

Principal-principle: *Principal* (adjective or noun) means that which is chief in rank or importance; *principle* (noun) designates a general truth or belief. Thus, "He was not influenced by the minister's *principles*" and "The *principal* officer of this city is the mayor."

Toward-towards: *Toward* should always be used.

Unique: *Unique* implies only one of a kind. Something is *unique* or it isn't, and there are no degrees of uniqueness.

Word Choice

A reporter needs a full, rich vocabulary from which he can select the proper word at the proper time. In addition to adding variety, such a knowledge insures that readers will grasp his intended meaning.

For example, the words "thief," "burglar," "robber" and "bandit" frequently are used almost interchangeably, but, in spite of certain similarities, they have differences in meaning of which the reporter must be aware: a "thief" steals, especially secretly or without open force; a "burglar" breaks and enters the home or property of another with the intent of committing a felony; a "robber" takes the property of another from his person or in his immediate presence, against his will, by violence or intimidation; and a "bandit" is an armed robber. The good reporter would know those differences so he could pick the right word at the right time. Likewise, if a word has more than one meaning or if there is the slightest chance for confusion, the reporter either changes the word or provides the necessary definition or context to insure understanding. Every word in a news story should contribute directly to language accuracy and clarity.

Word choice also involves careful consideration of the types of people represented in the audience. The readers of The New York Times have different backgrounds and interests from the readers of a small Midwestern weekly, and the reporter will tailor his language accordingly. The reporter also recognizes the different levels of education in his audience and strives for communication with as many levels as possible. This is not necessarily a least-common-denominator approach, but use of a naturally clear style which will be understood by those with average word knowledge and which will not offend the better educated.

As he works for simplicity and clarity, the reporter knows which types of words he should use and which to avoid. As fully discussed in Chapter 2, it's generally best to use specific, concrete words, words which emphasize action and words which generally are understood by the majority of readers.

On the negative side, three of the types of expressions which the reporter avoids are (1) foreign words unless they have been accepted into the English language, (2) highly technical or jargonistic language and (3) cliches and trite expressions.

The first two types should be avoided for the obvious reason. Most readers are not familiar with them. If, for example, the court reporter says in a story that a defendant's plea was "nolo contendere," an explanation must be provided. In fact, many newspapers simply use "no contest" instead of the Latin. On the other hand, some foreign words and expressions have become so accepted that the reporter can assume most readers will know their meanings. Examples are the French "coup d'etat" and "faux pas," although caution is necessary even in these cases.

Science has become big news today and the reporter often finds himself interviewing persons who use unfamiliar scientific language which he must translate into lay language. This can require using more common terminology, using familiar analogies or defining terms which could not be avoided.

For example, suppose you are covering the illness of a distinguished statesman, politician or other person. In such a situation, the hospital may issue a formal statement or bulletin, often dictated by the physician in charge of the case. That statement may sound something like this:

> Senator Fudd was admitted Thursday evening in extreme discomfort, characterized by substernal anginal pain. Onset was acute though his medical history is asymptomatic. Subsequently, an electrocardiogram indicated the presence of a myocardial infarction. However, serum enzymes and other serial measurements denote minimal cardiac dysfunction. An uneventful clinical course is anticipated. He is resting comfortably.

From this, the reporter might write:

> U.S. Sen. Elmer W. Fudd, D-Calif., was admitted to Cedars of Heaven Hospital Thursday night, suffering from an apparent heart attack.
> A medical spokesman said Friday that continuing tests indicate the ill effects on the senator's heart were slight. He is expected to recover without complications.
> Fudd was rushed to the hospital when, without warning, he was stricken by severe chest pains. This morning, the spokesman said, he was "resting comfortably."

At the other extreme, some newsmen rely on expressions which may have been original and imaginative once but which have become so common they seem old and stale. This includes many figures of speech, including the following:

absence makes the heart grow fonder	age before beauty
acid test	back to the wall

THE LANGUAGE OF NEWS

better half
better late than never
burn the candle at both ends
chip off the old block
clear as a bell
cool as a cucumber
dead as a doornail
easier said than done
few and far between
fools rush in
green as grass
hard as a rock
hit the nail on the head
ignorance is bliss
last but not least
mad as a wet hen
never put off till tomorrow
nipped in the bud
picture of health
pretty as a picture
seething mass of humanity
sick as a dog
sleep of the just
slow as molasses
sly as a fox
sweat of his brow
tired as a dog
to the bitter end
toe the mark
two heads are better than one
wee small hours
wine, women and song

Sportswriters especially face the temptation to use cliches and trite expressions. It is very easy to adopt the "sports slanguage" approach and talk in terms of "cagemen," "diamondmen," "thinclads," the "gridiron," "hardcourt" and "keystone." Balls become "apples," "roundballs" and "spheroids." They are seldom hit, but frequently "socked," "whacked," "pounded," "punched," "ripped," "smashed," "clouted" or "belted." And players are always "coming through in the clutch" or "choking up."

Such expressions are used in sports or news to make stories conversational and colorful. Unfortunately, because they are used so frequently, they often detract from a piece of writing. And, most importantly, the reporter who makes frequent use of such expressions is taking the easy way out. He should try to create other phrases or expressions which aren't so overworked. These will be more effective and, at the same time, colorful.

One other type of word problem is redundancy. The reporter should know the meanings of words so well that he will not use modifying words which overlap in meaning with the noun to which they refer. For example, it is redundant to say an automobile was "completely demolished" in an accident. If a car was demolished, the definition of that term makes it complete. Likewise, it is redundant to say a person was strangled, drowned or electrocuted "to death." Death is part of the definitions of all three words. Such semantic repetition wastes the reporter's time, the reader's time and valuable space in addition to detracting from the preciseness of language usage.

Sentences

Just as with word choice, clarity is the key in constructing a good newspaper sentence. It has been well documented that sentences which are short, to the point and lacking in complexity stand the best chance of communicating effectively.

This means that the reporter generally restricts himself to simple, declarative sentences which contain only one major thought. Yet, structural variety is important, and it is added to a news story when compound and complex sentences are scattered throughout on a limited basis. Such variety varies the pace of the writing and helps hold reader interest. Thus, it's wise to lean toward simple sentence structure while occasionally including more than one thought in a sentence. When two or more thoughts are placed together, however, they must be clearly and closely related.

What is a short sentence from the newspaper point of view? In general, sentences should *average* no more than two typewritten lines (about 20 words). But notice that this should be the average. An occasional longer sentence (up to a maximum of about four typewritten lines) should be used to balance shorter ones.

Average sentence length also depends upon the effect sought. The story which emphasizes action, drama or excitement will have short sentences, perhaps some of only one or two words. If a more leisurely pace is desired, sentences should be longer and with greater flow. This is an important aspect of dramatic writing, a technique which will be discussed in greater detail in connection with feature writing in Chapter 10.

As an example of the way in which shorter length and reduced complexity can make sentences both more understandable and dramatic, compare the following two paragraphs:

> Jason R. Cabberet, president of the National Society for Real Education, speaking in Memorial Stadium, held up his hands as if pleading for response as he declared in a voice which carried to every person in the crowd of some 25,000, many of whom were shouting enthusiastically, "If our nation is to survive the educational crisis into which our leaders have thrown it, it is imperative that we band together to force establishment of a more realistic curriculum."

> Jason R. Cabberet, president of the National Society for Real Education, held up his hands as if pleading for response. The crowd of some 25,000 in Memorial Stadium responded enthusiastically. Many were shouting. But Cabberet's voice could be heard over the tumult when he declared, "If our nation is to survive the educational crisis into which our leaders have thrown it, it is imperative that we band together to force establishment of a more realistic curriculum."

The information in these paragraphs is the same, but the manner of presentation provides a very noticeable difference. The first paragraph is one long sentence. The second version contains four sentences, most of which are relatively short and simple, are more straightforward and do a better job of isolating facts. The greater impact and understandability of the second paragraph seems clear.

Variety among sentences also can be attained through careful attention to their beginnings. The reader may not specifically notice that most sentences of a story start in the same way, but he probably would have an uneasy feeling that the story is uninterestingly written. In some "personality" stories, sentence after sentence begins with the person's name or a pronoun. While many sentences should start this way, other types of beginnings would break the monotony. Such beginnings as "Since he had no particular occupational interest at the time, Miller joined the Army after high school..." or "A native of Boone County, Smith spent most of his life in New York City..." will provide helpful variety if not overdone. There are dozens of ways to start a sentence which will not complicate the meaning but will add variety to the writing.

Because the most important part of the sentence is its beginning, the newsman usually seeks to place first the information he wants to emphasize. Suppose a story concerns an automobile accident in which one person was killed and which occurred at a particularly dangerous intersection. If the reporter considered the individual death as the most important element, he would write a sentence somewhat like this:

> Mrs. Mary L. Swanson, 35, of 1414 S. Joneswood St. was killed yesterday when the car she was driving crashed into the side of the Acme Theater at the intersection of Broad Street and Fifth Avenue.

But if the reporter knew that several deaths had occurred at that intersection and he considered this the important element, he probably would emphasize that fact this way:

> The intersection of Broad Street and Fifth Avenue—for the fourth time this year—was the scene of a fatal accident yesterday when an automobile driven by Mrs. Mary L. Swanson, 35, of 1414 S. Joneswood St. crashed into the side of the Acme Theater.

There are many other ways in which this sentence could be structured, depending upon what the reporter considered the most necessary element for emphasis. But the important point is that whatever he chose to emphasize was placed first in the sentence.

Paragraphs

Various techniques have been developed to give newspapers an interesting and uncomplicated appearance. Among these is the use of paragraphs much shorter than in literary style. In literary style, all material relating to an idea should be kept in a single paragraph. Newspaper paragraphs, on the other hand, tend to be much shorter because they do not each develop an idea, but present "sub-ideas," each of which contribute a limited, but important, aspect of the whole. The reporter seeks to keep related material together, but in successive paragraphs rather than one.

There are a number of reasons for the shortness of the newspaper paragraph, all of which relate to simplicity and clarity in news copy. Behind them all is the fact that a typewritten line becomes two lines when converted into print of the width of the standard newspaper column. Thus, a 10-line paragraph on a typewritten page would be 20 lines in the newspaper. Long paragraphs are undesirable for at least three important reasons: (1) Short paragraphs are easier to read, (2) short paragraphs pound home effectively the main points because some readers will not read far into a long paragraph and (3) short paragraphs lend themselves to modern typography which values "white space" left by many sets of incomplete and indented lines at paragraph junctions.

For these reasons, the reporter generally forms a new paragraph when he has reached the limit of paragraph thickness. That limit is about six lines of typewritten copy (equal to about 12 lines in the newspaper). However, variety is important, so every paragraph should not be six lines long. Such uniformity would give the story a stiff and formal appearance. Six lines is the maximum, but a more realistic average would be about three or four typewritten lines. This means that longer paragraphs should be compensated by shorter ones, sometimes as short as one or two words.

Style

There are three things which the newsman calls "style." One—the topic of this chapter and the next—embodies those characteristics of the newspaper story which differentiate it from other types of writing. This type includes, among other things, the short sentence and paragraph, word usage and the usual newspaper story structure. The second is that quality or touch a person puts into his writing which makes it uniquely his. Such "personal style" is quite possible within the boundaries of the general newspaper formula but should never be used as an excuse for careless writing or stray too far from standard practice. Thirdly, "office style" is a statement of organizational preferences on a wide variety of matters.

At this point, we are most concerned with office style which provides a newspaper with uniformity and which relieves the reporter of the necessity of making some minor decisions. The need for office style grows out of the elasticity of the English language and the lack of agreement among scholars as to what is correct in some cases. Because they are arbitrary, rules may vary greatly from one publication to the next. The spelling section of the Associated Press Stylebook, for example, contains these preferences: adviser, cannot, employe, goodby, per cent and whisky. Other organizations might prefer: advisor, can not, employee, goodbye or good-bye, percent and whiskey. Also, some newspapers have expressed their preference for such shortened spellings as thru and tho.

But office style is more than spelling. It frequently will include statements of policy on such matters as identification of a juvenile or first offender, use of suicide stories or how to handle crank telephone calls or bomb threats.

The reporter seldom is expected to memorize the rules of his paper's office style. Usually, he will be aware of those which appear most frequently in his day-to-day activities and will keep a copy of the stylesheet handy for frequent reference on matters of which he is not as aware.

Identification

Names make the news. That has been said so frequently it is almost a cliche. But it does contain enough truth that the reporter tries to include as many in his stories as possible, particularly of well-known people. Few newspapers, of course, can go to the extreme of one small-town weekly editor whose goal was to include the name of each person in his community at least once a year.

To the reporter, this personal emphasis has several ramifications. First and foremost, he will use every means within his grasp to insure that the names he uses are proper, complete and spelled correctly. He usually will avoid nicknames. He will at least use the individual's middle initial if not his middle name. He will make frequent references to the telephone directory, city directory or any other available source to determine the full name and its spelling. When possible, he will ask the source to state and spell his full name and will make no assumptions that a standard spelling is correct. There are too many men named Jon for the reporter to take a chance on John, even though he usually will be correct. Usually is not good enough.

This is an aspect of news writing which demands perfection, a fact to which any reporter who has received a tongue-lashing from an irate person whose name has been misspelled will testify. There also are legal factors. Suppose, for example, the reporter writes about John J. Jones who was arrested for drunken driving when the individual's name actually was John G. Jones. There is a possibility of a lawsuit if John J. Jones suffers from the mistake.

Emphasis on names also means that the reporter will not depend upon his readers to know who Mrs. Susan R. Smith is. Some form of identification *always* is given. If the topic of the story or source is a person who holds an important office, that title is affixed to his name on first reference. Even the President of the United States, perhaps the best known individual in the world, is always identified by title.

For most average citizens, however, the reporter does not have a title to use as identification. Thus, he must find other means, the most standard of which is use of the person's name, age and address, if local, or home town if not local. If the individual is young, his parents' names and addresses usually are given.

Proper identification depends partly on the situation. A reporter probably would identify an individual as president of the local PTA in a story concerning that organization, but he would refer to the same person by address in a story having no connection with the PTA. Persons who hold public office, however, usually are referred to by their title in all situations because the public has a right to know of the conduct and activities of its officials.

Attribution

In most cases, the reporter is the middle man in the process of communication, whose function is to transmit information from a source to the newspaper readers. And, since he gained his information from some individual or group, the reporter always is careful to spell out that source in his story. This process—known as attribution—is an essential ingredient of almost every news story.

The guideline for the reporter is that attribution should be used in cases in which he obtains information from a source. Certainly, a "Jones said," "he said" or other form of attribution should be affixed to every direct quotation and most indirect quotations.

It is possible, however, to present too much attribution, and the reporter must use his judgment to determine the point which distinguishes proper credit for information obtained from so much attribution that it interferes with the flow of the story. It is reasonable to

THE LANGUAGE OF NEWS

expect that a story which makes relatively extensive use of quoted material will contain attribution about once in each paragraph. This is particularly true of speech and interview stories, as we will discuss in Chapter 6.

Verbal variety in the use of attribution can be gained in two major ways: (1) by shifting the location of the attribution relative to the statement and (2) by using different attribution words.

Obviously, attribution of a statement can be placed in any one of three places—the end, the middle and the beginning. Attribution at the end of a statement usually is preferred because the reporter will have emphasized the source early in the story and will not want to continue the strong emphasis throughout. Attribution at the end also tends to interfere very little with the flow of the statement.

Attribution in the middle of the statement often is appropriate because, once again, the source is not given primary emphasis. However, it's important to attribute at a logical breaking point within the sentence. In the following sentence, poorly placed attribution breaks the thought pattern: "I think the mayor," Jones said, "is making a very serious mistake in the program he presented to city council last night." Even worse would be: "I think the mayor is making a very serious," Jones said, "mistake in the program he presented to city council last night." On the other hand, there are at least two logical breaking points in the statement in which attribution could properly be inserted. These are indicated by asterisks in the following: "I think * the mayor is making a very serious mistake * in the program he presented to city council last night."

Generally, the least desirable, though sometimes proper, location is at the beginning. The speaker seldom is more important than the statement, especially when he has been adequately named and identified earlier in the story. The one major situation in which attribution at the beginning is very helpful is when it is needed for transition. Take, for example, the following quotations:

> "I feel the mayor is making a very serious mistake in the program he presented to city council last night," Jones said.
> "The mayor's program, without a doubt, provides the path which this city must follow if it hopes to get out of the current crisis," Smith said.

The problem is that the reader, after correctly crediting the first statement to Jones, will assume until the very end that the second also should be attributed to Jones. He will be surprised at the quick change in speakers. This is momentary confusion, of course, but even that is intolerable. The solution is rather obvious. If attribution had been placed at the beginning of the second quotation, the reader would immediately have known that the speaker had changed and would suffer no confusion:

> "I feel the mayor is making a very serious mistake in the program he presented to city council last night," Jones said.
>
> Smith, however, disagreed, saying, "The mayor's program, without a doubt, provides the path which this city must follow if it hopes to get out of the current crisis."

In a story of average length, then, attribution likely will be in all three locations. We should find it most often at the ends of statements, sometimes in the middle, and at the beginning only for special reasons.

The second way in which the reporter can gain variety in his use of attribution is by utilizing different attribution words. There are many which appear frequently in newspapers: "said," "stated," "pointed out," "noted," "urged," "suggested," "warned." The list could go on and on, and the reporter should select carefully from it to avoid overuse of any single word. Here are a few possibilities:

according to	counseled	related
added	cried	remarked
advised	declared	repeated
affirmed	demanded	reported
agreed	disclosed	responded
alleged	implied	retorted
announced	inquired	said
answered	insinuated	screamed
argued	insisted	shouted
asked	maintained	stammered
asserted	muttered	stated
blurted	noted	stuttered
cautioned	objected	suggested
claimed	ordered	testified
charged	pointed out	taunted
commented	proclaimed	urged
complained	protested	warned
contended	quipped	whispered

THE LANGUAGE OF NEWS

Three specific warnings must be heeded by the reporter in this regard:

1. Although the list of possible attribution words is long, the words have slightly different meanings, and the reporter must make certain he uses the proper word in the proper circumstances. Any standard dictionary can provide the meanings, but the reporter should become aware of the specialized meanings of those he prefers.

2. Too much attribution variety can cause problems. Particularly, it results in stories in which attribution is too obvious and too obtrusive because some readers notice such variety and because many of the usages are not appropriate. The reporter can trust the word "said" in a majority (perhaps up to 75 per cent) of the cases in which attribution is called for, selecting carefully from the other possibilities to meet specific needs.

3. Some words which may appear to be adequate for attribution are very poor choices. This is especially true for words like "smiled," "sighed" and "chuckled." While acceptable when used to describe an individual, they are not acceptable for attribution purposes. People do not "smile" sentences which contain information. They "smile" only smiles. Therefore, avoid such statements as: "That movie was the best I've ever seen," he chuckled. Or: "I just can't believe he would be that way," she sighed. If you think chuckles, smiles or sighs are important, use the terms descriptively, as in "he said with a chuckle." But be prudent, for it's seldom necessary to use such expressions.

One minor point: Journalists disagree over whether "Jones said" or "said Jones" is the preferable form. This really boils down to individual preference or whether a specific newspaper has a rule which applies. It is safe to say, however, that most newspaper copy uses the "Jones said" form more frequently.

Since attribution represents the insertion of an external element into a statement, it is necessary that the reporter punctuate so that it is clearly separated from the statement itself. For most declarative statements, this simply requires the use of a comma, such as:

> "We think the fire was the result of arson, and we will conduct an investigation," Chief Griffin said.
>
> "We think the fire was the result of arson," Chief Griffin said, "and we will conduct an investigation."
>
> Chief Griffin said, "We think the fire was the result of arson, and we will conduct an investigation."

In some cases, especially if the quotation is a particularly long one, a colon may be used after attribution which comes at the beginning of a statement:

> Chief Griffin said: "We think the fire was the result of arson, and we will conduct an investigation. . . ."

If the quotation is not a declarative statement, but a question or exclamation, the reporter simply uses the appropriate mark instead of the comma.

> "To whom should we turn when confronted with this type of situation?" Mahoney asked.
>
> "I will never agree to such a ridiculous statement!" he shouted.

The same general principles apply to the paragraph. Since reporters will seldom place more than one attribution element in any given paragraph, it may be placed at the beginning, the middle or the end and, in any case, will apply to all sentences of quoted material within the paragraph. For example:

> Conant said, "We, the private citizens, should let ourselves be heard. This could be accomplished through writing letters of praise when something pleases us or of complaint when we are not satisfied. If, however, media operators and the people fail in their duties, then the government must be called in to help."
>
> "We, the private citizens, should let ourselves be heard," Conant said. "This could be accomplished through writing letters of praise when something pleases us or of complaint when we are not satisfied. If, however, media operators and the people fail in their duties, then the government must be called in to help."
>
> "We, the private citizens, should let ourselves be heard. This could be accomplished through writing letters of praise when something pleases us or of complaint when we are not satisfied. If, however, media operators and the people fail in their duties, then the government must be called in to help," Conant said.

The standard punctuation for multiple-paragraph quotations is to use a quotation mark at the beginning of each paragraph of the quote and at the end of only the final paragraph, as in the following:

> "We, the private citizens, should let ourselves be heard," Conant said. "This could be accomplished through writing letters of praise when something pleases us or of complaint when we are not satisfied.
>
> "If, however, media operators and the people fail in their duties, then the government must be called in to help."

Transition

The most subtle criterion of quality in any type of writing, but an especially important one in newspapers, is the way in which the writing flows from beginning to end. Even an amateur will recognize a disconnected list of statements with no unified pattern of thought. The reporter's skill with transition must carry the reader from subject to subject, from fact to fact, from time to time, from place to place and from person to person within a story. Transition is the glue which holds a piece of writing together.

As he is writing, the reporter needs to be aware of the two basic types of transition, and he must use the one most appropriate to each case.

The first type, organizational transition, is very closely related to factual arrangement within a story. A story with good organizational transition is presented so that every fact follows logically from that which precedes it, and every fact leads logically into that which follows. The good reporter will lead his reader through a sequence of events or statements so that understanding will be almost automatic. Related information will fit together so that the reader will get the complete picture without jumping all over the story to fit the pieces together like a jigsaw puzzle. It helps to define unavoidable obscure terms immediately and to elaborate on one point before moving on to the next. If the story quotes a source as saying, "There are some disadvantages to following that course of action," the reporter must provide immediate examples of those disadvantages.

The second type of transition, functional transition, involves the use of words, phrases, sentences or occasionally even complete paragraphs to link thoughts or statements. Frequently, these are conjunctions such as "and," "or" or "but." They also can be words like "however," "moreover," "nevertheless," "meanwhile" and "also." They may be pronouns such as "this," "that," "those" or "these." Or they may be attribution words such as "continued" and "added." Note the function of such transition words in the following paragraph:

> If he wanted to keep his job, Custer could not publicly show his disagreement with the mayor. *But* he could work behind the scenes. *And this* he did. *Such* unpublicized efforts, *moreover*, were among the reasons for the mayor's defeat. *For example*, Custer was among the group of men who convinced the vice mayor to enter the election. . . .

The italicized words serve to link the various thoughts in the paragraph together. Without them, it would read too much like a list of statements whose connection would not always be clear to the reader.

Functional transition also will at times involve repeating a thought or some phrase in an effort to show the connection between story elements. For example:

> Although Ashburn was born in Arkansas, he spent most of his journalistic career as a reporter for the San Francisco Chronicle. It was *while serving as a Chronicle reporter* that he won the Pulitzer Prize. . . .

The repetition here provides smooth transition between thoughts. The same function could have been served if the reporter had elected to start his second sentence with "It was during *this time* . . ." In this case, the "this time" refers to the years with the Chronicle, providing a type of secondary repetition for transition purposes.

Complete sentences or even paragraphs also can serve as functional transition although they shouldn't be used often because they add little substance which is not available elsewhere in the story. Also, such sentences or paragraphs interrupt the flow of the story if overused.

One type of transitional paragraph which is used frequently may be called the organizational paragraph. It provides the reader with a list of the topics to be discussed:

> The board also approved three items of business which may have important meaning to the school system in the next few months. These items involved participation in a new federal program for disadvantaged children, efforts to hire a specialist in child psychology and the releasing of $150,000 to be used to broaden the school system's remedial reading program.

This paragraph does include some important content, but its main purpose is to tie three points together and inform the reader that these are the items which the reporter will discuss next in his story. When using such an organizational paragraph, the reporter is obligated to discuss the items listed immediately and in the same order.

The good reporter will be aware of both types of transition while writing any story. He will remember that the clue to poor organizational transition is an information gap in which some topic is mentioned but not adequately elaborated. The clue to poor functional transition is a very abrupt change in discussion topic. The reporter knows that something needs to be done when he sees a pair of paragraphs like this:

> Councilman Cook urged that action be taken on his proposal immediately so that the program could be implemented before federal authorities stepped in.
>
> A crowd had gathered outside city hall to voice its approval of the program. . . .

THE LANGUAGE OF NEWS

While there is a definite connection between these two events, the story, as written, does not make that connection as clear as it needs to be. So the reporter inserts some functional transition to provide the needed link:

> Councilman Cook urged that action be taken on his proposal immediately so that the program could be implemented before federal authorities stepped in.
> *Meanwhile, outside city hall and even as Cook was speaking,* a crowd had gathered to voice its approval of *his* program. . . .

Editing

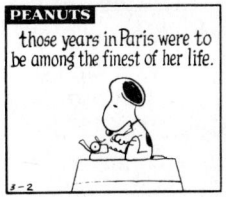

Used with permission of the United Feature Syndicate.

The editing pencil is just as important to a reporter as his typewriter. Few writers can sit down and produce a polished, completely acceptable story without at least some revisions—major or minor—being needed. The reporter generally is cautious about his first draft, but time seldom permits the writing of a second draft. Therefore, he uses the editing process as a backstop which permits him to make sure his story is complete and the writing polished. While editing, he can strive for closer compliance with the requirements of a good news story. If he has used the wrong word, he can change it. If his punctuation is incorrect, he can insert the proper mark and delete where necessary. If his sentences or paragraphs are too long or too short, he can make the needed changes.

In brief, good editing corrects mistakes made in the original writing and permits the reporter to change his mind at the last moment. Sometimes, it serves as a quick substitute for rewriting. If the reporter is dissatisfied with his first effort but does not have time to revise, he may cut the story into segments and paste these segments together in a different order. Then, with his editing pencil, he provides new transition to give unity to the second version.

If the veteran experiences difficulty on first writing and feels the need for editing, the beginner should especially feel that need. The rules of writing are not as firmly lodged in his mind and have not become as automatic. Through editing, however, he has a second chance for improvement. It is true that editing is a function of the desk man, but this does not relieve any reporter of the responsibility of making his copy as accurate and complete as possible before handing it in. A good copy editor can do much to improve a story, but he should never be put in the position of compensating for a reporter's carelessness—either in mechanics or content. The chances for error are increased measurably if the reporter fails to check his copy thoroughly.

Summary

This chapter has concentrated on some of those characteristics which distinguish news writing from other types of writing. The discussion has centered on a number of guidelines which assist the reporter in his efforts to effectively communicate the news to his readers. These guidelines, as outlined below, must be accepted as usual operating practices and not as rules which always are rigid. The situation must indicate to the reporter the degree to which any rule applies, and he must value his judgment in determining such applicability.

With that qualification emphasized, let us review some of the most important guidelines of the language of news.

1. A news story will be grammatically perfect.

2. Selection of words will be based on their simplicity and clarity. The reporter will value words which are specific in meaning, which emphasize action and which are generally understood. He will avoid highly scientific, technical or jargonistic words, foreign words, and cliches and trite expressions.

3. Most sentences will be short (averaging about two typewritten lines with a maximum length of about four lines) and will contain one major thought.

4. The most important element should be placed at the beginning of a sentence for emphasis.

5. Paragraphs will be short (containing a maximum of about six typewritten lines and averaging three or four lines).

6. Variety of word choice, sentence length and structure, and paragraph length will be sought.

7. A reporter's copy should conform to his newspaper's office style.

8. Each individual in a story will be properly and adequately identified by name and title or address. All names will be proper, complete and spelled correctly.

9. Material obtained from a source will be appropriately attributed to that source, especially when presented in the form of direct quotations.

10. Since a news story should represent a complete series of thoughts, statements or events, the appropriate transition will be used to provide connection for such thoughts, statements or events.

11. All stories will be adequately and carefully edited.

CHAPTER 4

Structuring the News Story

Story structure distinguishes newswriting from other types of writing probably more than the characteristics we have called the language of news. Structure is concerned with the way in which facts are organized. It is the blueprint, and the items discussed in the previous chapter are the building materials. Structure is not as easily defined as, say, sentence length because it always depends upon the facts available and the reporter's judgments about those facts.

Nevertheless, there are some guidelines which the reporter can use. Those guidelines, for most stories, are summarized in what has come to be known as the "inverted pyramid" construction of a news story, which gets its name from the shape of the following diagram:

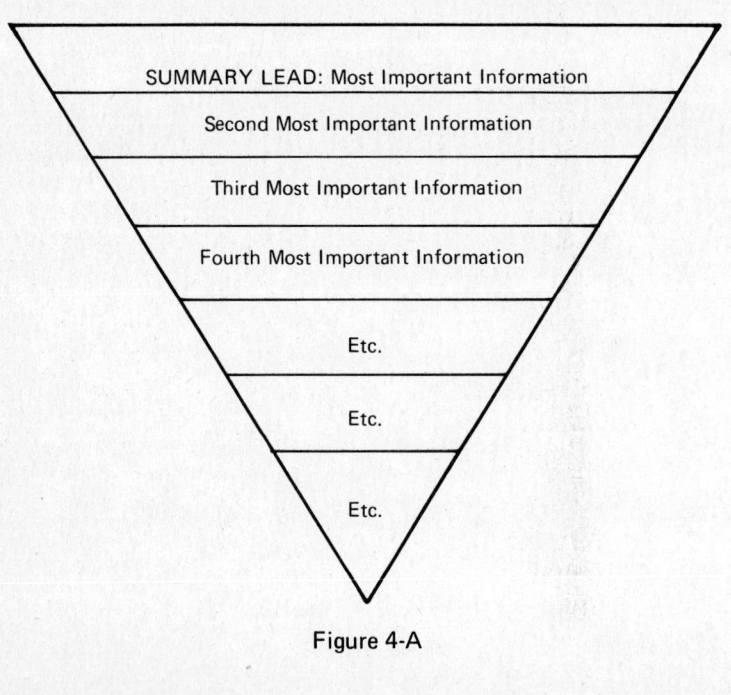

```
SUMMARY LEAD: Most Important Information
Second Most Important Information
Third Most Important Information
Fourth Most Important Information
Etc.
Etc.
Etc.
```

Figure 4-A

STRUCTURING THE NEWS STORY

The broad top of the pyramid represents the "lead" in which the reporter seeks to summarize the most essential information in the story. In using this type of structure, the reporter first presents that fact or group of facts which he considers most important, then organizes the remainder of the information according to its decreasing importance. In this way, at least in theory, each succeeding paragraph contains information which is less important than that which preceded it. Following the lead will be the second most important fact or explanatory material; then comes the third most important, and so on to the end of the story. In theory, although not always in practice, if the story has to be cut, one should be able to automatically omit the final paragraph as the least important.

The purpose of this type of structure is to present the news quickly, clearly and readably to help the reader easily understand the content. Its basic logic grows out of the different ways in which readers approach a news story. Some will be so interested in the subject they will read every word the reporter writes, regardless of how it is written; others read only a few paragraphs; many will read only the headline and lead. To provide all of these readers with maximum benefit, the reporter seeks to stack the deck from the top down. He does not deliberately waste the latter portions of his stories. This would be a waste of time and unfair to those readers who do want complete information. He presents the complete story, but in such a way as to accommodate all types of readers.

It is impossible to write many stories in the perfect inverted pyramid fashion. This type of story structure works only in certain situations and has definite limitations. It is never cut and dried or simple as this brief discussion of its basic pattern might indicate. For one thing, it is sometimes necessary to include rather lengthy passages of background material even though they don't deserve high play when viewed in isolation. They are placed in a story to aid understanding of other points which are important.

In some cases, particularly in interpretive stories, as we will see in Chapter 12, organization strays considerably from the pure inverted pyramid. When seeking to provide complete discussion of some issue, reporters would find it very difficult to arrange such complex material in descending order of importance. However, they usually are still guided by the principles and very seldom go as far as to adopt an "upright pyramid" style of the scientific journal in which the reader must wade through many qualifications and details before he gets to the real point of the story.

There also is the matter of individual judgment which must play a very important role in utilization of the inverted pyramid. There can be no way to assure that two reporters would assign the same priorities to a set of facts; thus, even though the facts may be the same, stories written by different reporters may have entirely different slants. Take, for example, the following stories which appeared on the same day, both in morning newspapers:

WILLIAMSBURG, Mich. (AP)—The well suspected of causing natural gas eruptions in this tiny, half-evacuated community has been capped, Amoco Production Co. officials said yesterday.

It would probably be at least three days until the danger is passed, state officials said, and precautions were still being taken to prevent an explosion.

Amoco, a subsidiary of Standard Oil of Indiana, dumped more than 1,300 barrels of heavy mud-water into the 6,200-foot well shaft Tuesday in unsuccessful efforts to block the gas flow. Still heavier mud was used yesterday.

Amoco has denied its well is the source of the gas, but state officials say they believe the well is responsible.

A series of natural blow-holes that began bubbling up in the area a week ago has forced evacuation of about 250 residents. State officials said the eruptions started three days after Amoco drillers lost control of the nearby well.

"If the gas pressure starts going down, then we know the matter is solved, and we know the Amoco well caused it," an official said.

WILLIAMSBURG, Mich. (UPI)—Highly flammable natural gas shot out of old craters with new intensity Wednesday as geologists worked to plug an oil well blamed for the geyserlike eruptions bursting from the earth in this resort village for a week.

The danger of fire increased because there was less water and silt mixed into the gas, officials said.

"Some of the first craters are blowing practically pure gas at this point," William Mullendore, a spokesman for the Michigan Department of Natural Resources, said. "It is increasing the fire hazard."

At the same time, the fact that the "older" gas craters had been cleared of water and silt meant there was better venting of the gas from the earth and thus less chance of the craters spreading beyond the four square-mile area to which they have been confined.

About 60 families had already been moved out of the immediate danger zone. Another family, although outside that area, was evacuated because the gas was so thick and the weather held it so close to the ground.

A spokesman for Amoco Production Co., a subsidiary of Standard Oil of Indiana, said the company sealed an oil well four miles south of the town that state geologists have blamed for the craters.

STRUCTURING THE NEWS STORY 67

The Associated Press writer led with the well's capping, a fact which the UPI writer delegated to his final paragraph. Which is correct? That's really a matter of judgment. The facts in the two stories are the same, but the reporters simply evaluated them differently.

On the other hand, there are circumstances where differences in story versions involve facts rather than judgment. These situations are intolerable. Although the factual difference in the following leads is minor, there is little question that at least one reporter was guessing:

> NEWPORT, Ky. (AP)—A jury found Newport Night Police Chief Donald Faulkner innocent yesterday of accepting bribes.
>
> The circuit court jury needed *less than 30 minutes* to reach a decision after closing arguments in the court of Judge Paul Stapleton.

> NEWPORT, Ky. (UPI)—A jury in Campbell County Circuit Court needed *only 45 minutes* Wednesday to return an innocent verdict in the bribery trial of Newport night police Chief Donald Faulkner.

Such factual differentiations, however, tend to be the exceptions, rather than the rule, among newspaper writers. Differences in judgment are more common. The necessity of such judgment explains why some people say objectivity is impossible in newswriting. The personal effect of the reporter on his copy is reduced, however, by the fact that, with experience, newsmen begin to think in rather standardized ways about relatively straightforward types of stories. These patterns, in general, are the principles of the inverted pyramid and the criteria for judgment of news discussed in Chapter 1.

To show more explicitly how the inverted pyramid influences arrangement of facts within a story, let us pause now to look at an example. Consider this sequence of events:

> Harry R. Jones had been to a party last night at the home of Mr. and Mrs. Roscoe G. Ferguson of 6832 S. Adamstone St. He left the Fergusons' home at about midnight to drive to his home on the other side of town, 2001 E. Cherrytree Drive.
>
> As he was driving through town, another car ran a red light and hit Jones' car on the driver's side. This occurred at the intersection of 23rd Street and Washington Boulevard. The other car was driven by George R. Torrey, who is 49 years old and who lives at 32 N. Congress Ave.
>
> The two automobiles were locked together by the impact, and Jones was trapped for two hours before the police rescue squad arrived on the scene and managed to get him out of the car by using

torches. An ambulance arrived at about 2:30 a.m. and took Jones to Memorial Hospital.

Torrey told police that he had fallen asleep while driving and had not seen the red light or Jones' car. He admitted that he was at fault for the accident and said he hoped Jones would be OK. Torrey was cited by police for negligence. Torrey was not hurt in the accident.

When the ambulance arrived at the hospital, Jones was taken to the emergency room where a doctor examined him, discovering that his back was broken and his skull fractured. The doctor said that, as a result of these injuries, Jones had died at the scene of the accident.

In this material, the most important information is not emphasized early; in fact, it is presented as the final sentence. The reporter would analyze all the facts presented for information which could be considered most important in the telling of the story. He may determine that the points he would want to emphasize were: (1) Harry R. Jones was killed in an automobile accident; (2) George R. Torrey, driver of the other car, was not hurt; (3) Torrey was cited by police for negligence. Having made this determination, the reporter would then write his story, filling in the gaps with explanatory material and omitting information he felt was not needed. The story probably would look something like this:

Harry R. Jones, 32, of 2001 E. Cherrytree Drive was killed in an automobile collision at the intersection of 23rd Street and Washington Boulevard at about 12:15 a.m. today.

A Memorial Hospital doctor said Jones had died at the scene of the accident of a broken back and fractured skull. Jones was pinned in the wreckage for two hours before the police rescue squad used torches to extract his body.

The driver of the other car, George R. Torrey, 49, of 32 N. Congress Ave. was not injured.

Torrey told police he had fallen asleep while driving and had not seen Jones' car approaching the intersection. He was cited for negligence.

Jones had been returning to his home from a party when the accident occurred. He was alone.

Consider the reader when comparing these two forms of information arrangement. If the reader did not read all the chronological material, he would not know that Jones had been killed; in fact, he would not learn until the second paragraph that Jones had even been in an automobile accident. He may have regarded the story as a social note about a party. On the other hand, if the reader gets through only the first paragraph of the inverted pyramid version, he knows about Jones' death in the accident, and that is the central point of

STRUCTURING THE NEWS STORY

the story. Then, if he is interested in more detail, he can read on, receiving a little more in each succeeding paragraph.

In addition to the advantage for the reader, the inverted pyramid has other advantages for the writer. Probably the most important of these in view of the speed with which many stories have to be written is that, because of the rather standard format, it makes the story easier to write and edit. Additionally, it is a format which can easily be expanded or shortened if the practical necessities of newspaper publication call for either.

The beginning reporter should be very familiar with the guidelines provided by the inverted pyramid and should seek to apply them to most stories he writes. It is not the only story structure, as we shall see, but it is the one used in newspapers for the presentation of the majority of news stories.

The Lead

The most notable characteristic of the inverted pyramid structure and the one which should be mastered first by the beginning reporter is the "lead" or beginning of the news story. There are several types of leads, but the one most often used with the inverted pyramid is known as the "summary lead" because it seeks to summarize the story in a few lines. Because it transmits the essence of the news at the beginning of the story, the summary lead is not an introduction like that learned in English composition classes. It is a brief bulletin, summary, climax of the news story, all in one concise package.

One important point needs to be emphasized at this time. While it is common to refer to the lead of a story as the first paragraph, this is not always the case. The lead is most appropriately defined as the presentation of the essential ingredients of the story, and that may be accomplished in one paragraph, but it frequently may take two or more.

Usually, in most relatively simple stories, the lead wraps the story into a small, neat bundle by attempting to answer all or most of these very familiar questions concerning the facts: Who? What? Where? When? Why? How? Take, for example, the following lead:

> Three young Northville residents were killed last night when their car skidded on rain-slick U.S. 101 near Centerville and plunged over a 40-foot embankment.
>
> Police identified the victims as...

This summary lead gives the bulk of the information so completely that it could almost stand alone. It tells: Who? "Three young

Northville residents"; What? "were killed"; Where? "on U.S. 101 near Centerville"; When? "last night"; Why? "their car skidded on wet pavement"; How? "plunged over a 40-foot embankment." The lead is a complete summary of the story.

Of course, these six ingredients do not always apply in every story, and they don't fit into every first paragraph. The Who? question, for example, might not exist in some types of stories, such as one about a landslide in which there were no property damages, personal injuries or deaths. The reporter, again, evaluates the available information to determine if one of the standard ingredients does not apply. This must be done cautiously, however, for every story should at least answer the questions What? Where? and When?. If there are no answers to these, there seems to be little basis for writing a story.

Since the trend today is to make opening paragraphs as brief and to the point as possible, the reporter frequently will find himself evaluating the "five W's and H" to determine which to place in the first paragraph and which can be saved for later, usually the second paragraph. For example, in the lead above, the writer chose to identify the accident victims first as "three young Northville residents," saving the specific identifications for later. In this type of situation, a lead will consist of at least two paragraphs. Any of the basic elements can be reserved for later use in this manner.

But the principles of the summary lead dictate that the reporter present the information as quickly as he can; thus, it is the exceptional story in which the lead information must be spread over more than two paragraphs. In situations in which going beyond two paragraphs is justified, it usually is the case that the writer has chosen to "featurize" the lead, that is, to write a first sentence or paragraph which is designed more to attract attention and create interest.

The summary lead actually can take two main forms, depending upon the amount of information the reporter decides to include in it. The first of these occurs when the reporter determines that there is one major point he would like to get across. He then hits that point immediately and directly in his opening statement. For example:

> The city of Centerville will build a new recreation complex—including a regulation-sized swimming pool—on the current site of the city parking lot, Mayor Elmer Rawdon announced at the city council meeting last night.

This lead emphasized the one main element of the story, including the answers to most of the "W's and H" questions, and also provides additional specific information on the swimming pool. But if city council had taken several equally important actions at the meeting

STRUCTURING THE NEWS STORY 71

instead of one, the lead probably would have been of the second type which seeks to summarize several major points:

> City income taxes will be raised by 1 per cent next year so that the city can build a new recreation complex, make necessary improvements on the water treatment plant and pave all streets in the Edgewood Section.
> City Council made these decisions last night. . . .

Note that this lead actually mentions four major decisons, admittedly a more productive meeting than most, but nevertheless an example of how it is possible, and desirable, to pull a number of items together into one relatively brief summary lead. Of course, the reporter does have the alternative of writing several separate stories, but doing so depends on factors which are not always under his control.

Because there are innumerable ways in which a specific set of facts can be organized, there can be no formula appropriate for every summary lead. But most reporters make rather extensive use of the principles of emphasis which were discussed earlier in connection with sentences. In this way, the reporter highlights certain pieces of information by putting them first in his lead. Thus, again using the "five W's and H," it is possible to speak of "who" leads, "what" leads, "where" leads, "when" leads, "why" leads and "how" leads, depending upon which the reporter chose to emphasize.

Note, for example, the following leads:

Emphasis on "Who"
   Officials from the Ohio Office of Security will open an investigation within the next week into the financial activities of the three organizations responsible for purchasing state highway equipment.

Emphasis on "What"
   An investigation into the financial activities of the three organizations responsible for purchasing state highway equipment will be opened by the Ohio Office of Security within the next week.

Emphasis on "Where"
   The three Ohio organizations responsible for purchasing state highway equipment will be the subjects of an Office of Security investigation, beginning within the next week.

Emphasis on "When"
   Within the next week, officials from the Ohio Office of Security will open an investigation into the financial activities of the three organizations responsible for purchasing state highway equipment.

Emphasis on "Why"

Charges of financial irregularities by the three organizations responsible for purchasing state highway equipment have prompted officials from the Ohio Office of Security to set up an investigation, to begin within the next week.

Emphasis on "How"

A three-man committee will be named within the next week to conduct an investigation into the financial activities of the three organizations responsible for purchasing state highway equipment.

All six of these provide the same information in different forms, the only real difference being in the emphasis. And that emphasis is rooted in the reporter's determination of which element is the most important and his mechanically placing that element in the opening portion of the paragraph. The remainder of the information is placed in what seems a logical arrangement. Note, too, that all the leads satisfy the general requirements of a summary lead.

Such variations in emphasis provide only one way in which variety is gained in the construction of summary leads. There are many others. Obviously, a lead can be started with almost any type of grammatical construction, provided that the information given first merits such treatment. For instance, a question, followed by the answer, may be used. In speech and interview stories, a lead can be a direct quotation, an indirect quotation or a complete paraphrase of a speaker's statement.

On the other hand, there are some general guidelines as to what is generally avoided by reporters in their leads. For example, "who" is stressed only under special circumstances because the statement or action usually is the important fact of a story, not who does it. Some newsmen never start a lead with a name.

Another element which seldom deserves emphasis is "when." In fact, the "when" example above would not be accepted by most reporters and editors. Not only is it vague, but the time element of the investigation cannot rank as more important than the investigation itself. Many reporters would say this applies not only to leads, but to all sentences, and they would avoid starting sentences with the time element.

The practice of putting nonessential information in the place of emphasis in a lead is known as "backing into the lead" or "burying the lead." It is rejected by newsmen because it does not present the important information first. The beginning reporter should try hard to hit the main point clearly and immediately. Note, for example, how the following leads present secondary information first and get to the point only later:

STRUCTURING THE NEWS STORY

In a man-on-the-street survey conducted by the Midtown Chronicle at the intersection of Court and Rainey streets yesterday morning, it was discovered that *Midtown residents solidly support the women's rights ordinance presented last week by city council.*

A speech was delivered to the annual meeting of the American Association of General Practitioners in Memorial Auditorium last night by Harry S. Stone, special adviser to the Department of Health, Education and Welfare, in which he said that *socialized medicine is inevitable in the United States.*

Harry S. Stone, special adviser to the Department of Health, Education and Welfare, told the American Association of General Practitioners in Memorial Auditorium last night that *socialized medicine is inevitable in the United States.*

In each of these examples, it should be obvious that the most important element is the italicized section at the end of the lead. The information presented first is necessary, but not so important that it merits the most significant location available. The good reporter would have written leads which looked more like the following:

Midtown residents solidly support the women's rights ordinance presented last week by city council, according to a man-on-the-street survey conducted yesterday by the Midtown Chronicle.

Socialized medicine is inevitable in the United States, a Department of Health, Education and Welfare adviser told members of the American Association of General Practitioners in Memorial Auditorium.
The speaker, Harry S. Stone, added that. . . .

Skill in writing leads may be attained only through much practice and through very careful analysis of one's own writing and the writing found in newspapers. Beginning reporters should read their newspapers very carefully, making a regular study of leads a part of their daily reading. In making such analyses, the reporter should be very aware of the requirements of emphasis and completeness. Additionally, he can ask the following questions: Might the lead stand alone, if necessary? Is the lead conclusive? Is a good headline suggested by the lead content? If the answer to any of these questions is in the negative, the reporter knows he should check his lead more closely to make certain it is satisfactory.

The discussion to this point has been concerned exclusively with summary leads. There are other types, as we shall see later, but mastery of the summary lead is the first task of the beginning reporter. If he can work himself to the point at which he can construct a smooth-flowing lead which contains complete information, he will have made a good beginning toward journalistic proficiency.

Perhaps it would be helpful at this point to look at some additional examples of how the reporter would take a set of facts and construct a lead. All of the following spot news leads would result naturally from the process we have discussed here:

Facts	Leads
—New organization will be formed on Ohio University campus —Will be known as Students, Inc. —Purpose will be to represent students on matters pertaining to them —Will work with university administrators, faculty, the city, etc. —Organizational meeting Friday at 7 p.m. in 227 Student Union —Information comes from John Smith, a senior in history and one of the founders	An organizational meeting will be held at 7 p.m. Friday for a new group, Students, Inc., which will seek to represent students in disputes.
—Fire in Middletown —Pleasant Valley Nursing Home —Modern, brick, one-story —Cause of fire unknown —21 elderly residents killed —27 others injured —50 people known in building at time of fire	Twenty-one elderly persons were killed and 27 injured as fire swept through the Pleasant Valley Nursing Home in Middletown yesterday. Two residents are still missing.
—YMCA Board of Directors —Will meet Friday at Middletown Hotel —Noon luncheon meeting —Two major items on agenda —One is passage of next year's operating budget —Other is a capital repair fund drive	Next year's operating budget and a capital repair fund will be discussed by the YMCA Board of Directors at its noon luncheon meeting Friday at the Middletown Hotel.

STRUCTURING THE NEWS STORY 75

—Man killed in auto accident
—Donald Lee Albers of Middletown
—He was 26 years old
—Pronounced dead at Middletown Hospital
—1:15 a.m. today
—Car he was driving plunged over a 40-foot embankment on U.S. 50, three miles west of Middletown
—Hospital officials said he died of broken neck

A 26-year-old Middletown man was dead on arrival at Middletown Hospital at 1:15 a.m. today after the car he was driving plunged over a 40-foot embankment on U.S. 50, three miles west of town.

The Lead-to-Body Connection

The lead-to-body connection may be only a word or two or it may be several paragraphs, but its importance to the unity of a newspaper story cannot be overstated. A common fault in newspaper writing is failure to adequately connect the summary lead with the running commentary in the body of the story. This makes it appear as if the lead is little more than a headline and the story actually begins upon its completion. Notice the lack of such transition in this example:

> A proposal for the establishment of a city racial relations commission was presented last night by one of the candidates for mayor in the November election.
> "The situation of racial minorities in this city has become worse than at any time in history," Republican Samuel R. Peabody said.

The information presented here is good and probably captures the essence of Peabody's speech quite well. But the presentation is seriously lacking in flow and uniformity for two reasons. In the first place, although the relationship between the two paragraphs is logical, the statements are not tied together in any functional way. From a literary standpoint, therefore, the paragraphs are disconnected. Secondly, the reader may have grown to expect certain information quickly because he's become accustomed to the "five W's and H" which constitute the summary lead. The most obvious missing element is "where." Such omissions leave gaps over which the reader, at least subconsciously, must stumble in his efforts to grasp the full meaning of the lead.

Now note this revised version:

> A proposal for the establishment of a city racial relations commis-

sion was presented last night by one of the candidates for mayor in the November election.

Speaking to members of the City Republican Coordinating Committee, Samuel R. Peabody urged such a commission because "The situation of racial minorities in this city has become worse than at any time in history."

These paragraphs utilize transitional elements to satisfy the two major requirements of the lead-to-body connection: that it provide information which has been withheld from the lead itself, and that it direct the reader's thought smoothly from the summary lead to the details in the body of the story. In this case, it does so by adding the expected information, thus removing stumbling blocks to understanding, and through the use of repetition which provides functional transition.

Filling in identifications which are too detailed for the lead is a common practice in the lead-to-body link. For example:

> Three young Northville residents were killed last night when their car skidded on rain-slick U.S. 101 near Centerville and plunged over a 40-foot embankment.
>
> Police identified the victims as Harry R. Kinney, 18, of 1314 S. Main St.; Ruth R. Golding, 17, of 32 Roosevelt Drive; and Peter S. Wazkowski, 18, of 805 Cherry Blossom Lane.
>
> The accident occurred when. . . .

Provision of identification in the lead-to-body connection usually is restricted to situations in which the list is somewhat limited. If the story had been about an airplane crash in which 43 persons were killed or about a group of 72 high school students who had been honored for academic excellence, the reporter would not have provided the list immediately. He would either have saved the list for the latter portion of his story or he would have made the list into a separate sidebar which would have been used in conjunction with the main story.

Reporters also will often provide some elaboration or clarification of a lead statement in the lead-to-body connection:

> The local chapter of Theater Arts, Inc., has issued a call for persons to try out for parts in "Oklahoma!" which will be presented in Memorial Auditorium in July.
>
> Persons interested in trying out for the roles for five women and six men remaining to be cast may report at 7 p.m. Thursday to the Theater Workshop, 657 S. Virginia St.

And, notice how the reporter, in writing the following lead, omitted all but the "what" element from his opening paragraph, placing the remainder in the lead-to-body connection:

STRUCTURING THE NEWS STORY

> "If the railroad tracks are not moved from their present location adjacent to the city park, I predict that sooner or later we are going to have an accident which will shock the whole city."
>
> With this warning, Tracy T. Townsend, president of the Centerville PTA, urged last night in a speech to the Lions Club in the Gibson Hotel that the community unite in an effort to have the tracks moved.

These are but a few of the ways in which reporters seek to make their lead-to-body connection effective both with regard to providing transition from the lead to the body and with regard to providing the reader with more needed information.

Variations of the Inverted Pyramid

While the principles of the inverted pyramid apply to most news stories, the way in which it is used depends upon several factors, but chiefly upon the complexity of the story. The simplest form of the inverted pyramid, shown in Figure 4-A, is effectively applicable only to stories which are very simple or in which only one major aspect is to be presented. Although there are exceptions, a short story of one or two pages (or "takes" in journalese) probably will feature only one major incident and thus will require the simple form which has been the subject of this chapter to this point.

But, as stories become more complicated, the organization becomes more complicated, involving more shifting from topic to topic within the story. Since the basis of the inverted pyramid is that the essence of the story should be presented first, it may be said that the reporter should avoid introducing any new important material after the half-way point of the story. If he provided considerable discussion of one or two major points before introducing another, the chances are good that he would be beyond the mid-point of the story. Thus, it is necessary to introduce all the major material very early in the story, then return to each point one by one later for details and explanation.

Let us now return, by way of an example, to the city council meeting mentioned earlier in which there were four major items of interest: (1) that income taxes will be raised by 1 per cent, (2) that a new recreation complex will be constructed, (3) that improvements will be made on the city water treatment plant and (4) that all streets in the Edgewood Section of the city will be paved.

At least three types of story organization are suggested for this multiple-incident story.

The first, shown in Figure 4-B, is the simplest type of multiple-item organization. It would not utilize the same type of summary lead presented earlier for this story, but would take each of the items individually in a multiple-paragraph lead, returning to each later in the story for elaboration. Of course, use of this form of organization depends upon the reporter's determination that it is possible to place the items in priority, that is, possible to say that one item is more important than the others. If he could not make such a determination, he would have to use another variation of the inverted pyramid.

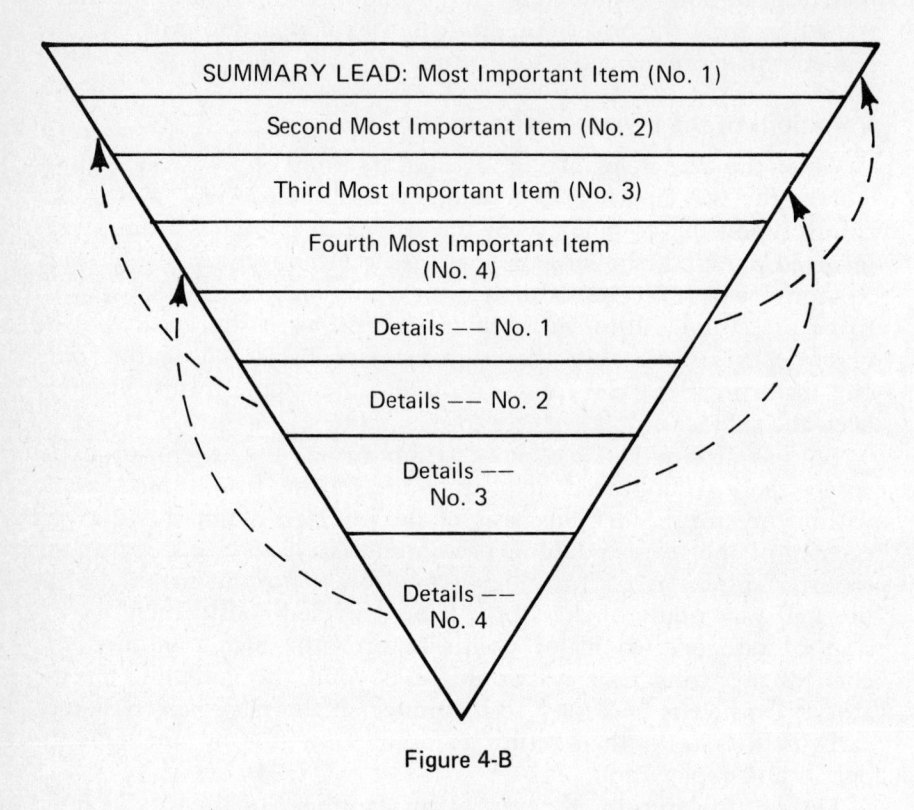

```
SUMMARY LEAD: Most Important Item (No. 1)
Second Most Important Item (No. 2)
Third Most Important Item (No. 3)
Fourth Most Important Item (No. 4)
Details -- No. 1
Details -- No. 2
Details -- No. 3
Details -- No. 4
```

Figure 4-B

Use of such organization would produce this type of story:

> City residents will find their paychecks reduced by an additional 1 per cent next year after a city council action last night which effected an increase in the city income tax.
> The additional income—estimated by City Treasurer Albert Williams at about $5 million—will be divided among three major projects, the most visible of which will be a $3.5 million recreation complex to be constructed on the site of the city parking lot.
> Also receiving a portion of the money will be improvements on

STRUCTURING THE NEWS STORY

the water treatment plant and the paving of all streets in the city's Edgewood Section.

The tax increase will be the first for the city since. . . .

Note the difference between this three-paragraph lead and the one-paragraph summary lead presented earlier. They contain the same announcement of the important aspects of the story, but the three-paragraph lead provides more specific information which the writer of the first lead had saved for later use. The important point is that they provide the reader with essentially the same information.

After the three-paragraph lead, the remainder of the story would consist of individual discussions of each of the four major items, with all details being provided for each in one section. Of course, the items are so interrelated that it would be impossible to separate them completely, but the reporter would seek to discuss them as separately as possible.

A slight variation of the inverted pyramid shown in Figure 4-B is that of Figure 4-C. The only major distinction between the two is

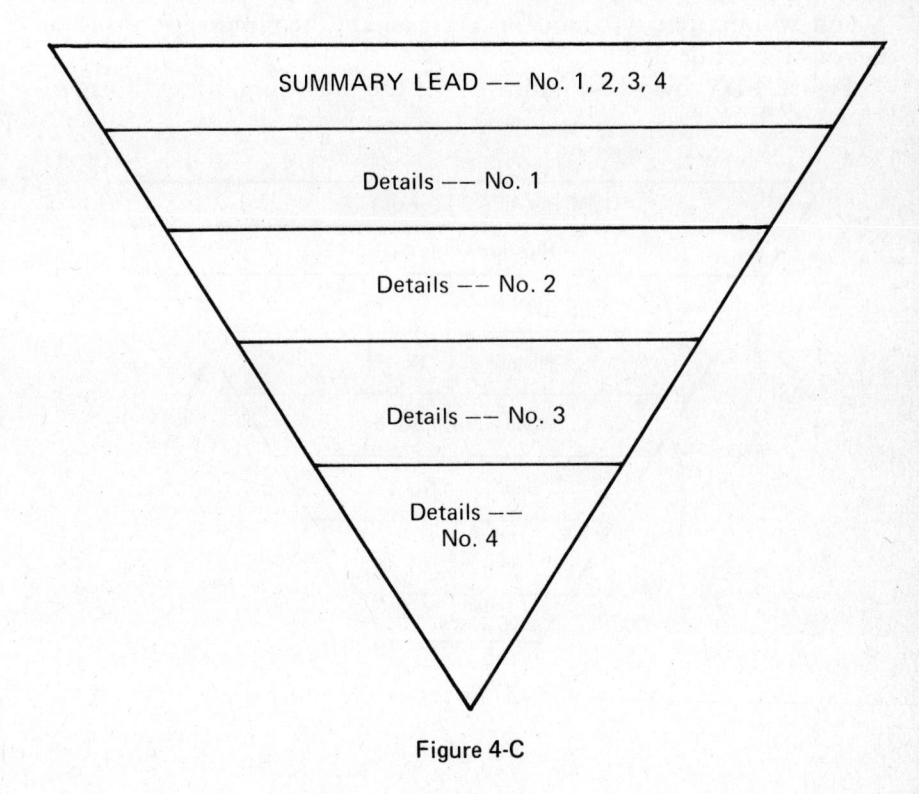

Figure 4-C

that, as Figure 4-C shows, the latter form would utilize the one-paragraph, limited-detail summary lead shown earlier. This form would follow the summary lead with a transition paragraph, then launch into an explanation of the four items one at a time. For example:

> City income taxes will be raised by 1 per cent next year so that the city can build a new recreation complex, make necessary improvements on the water treatment plant and pave all streets in the Edgewood Section.
>
> City council made these decisions last night in what officials termed the "most productive" meeting of council within the past decade.
>
> The income tax boost—the first for the city since 1965—will raise an estimated $5 million, City Treasurer Albert Williams told councilmen at the meeting. He and Mayor Bert Jamieson labeled this amount as the minimum requirement for necessary city progress.

From this point, the story would continue with its explanation of the tax raise, then pursue the other three items individually with as much detail as available. It would look both at the discussion and action within the city council meeting and at the ramifications of the actions for residents.

Figure 4-D provides an indication of the most complicated form of

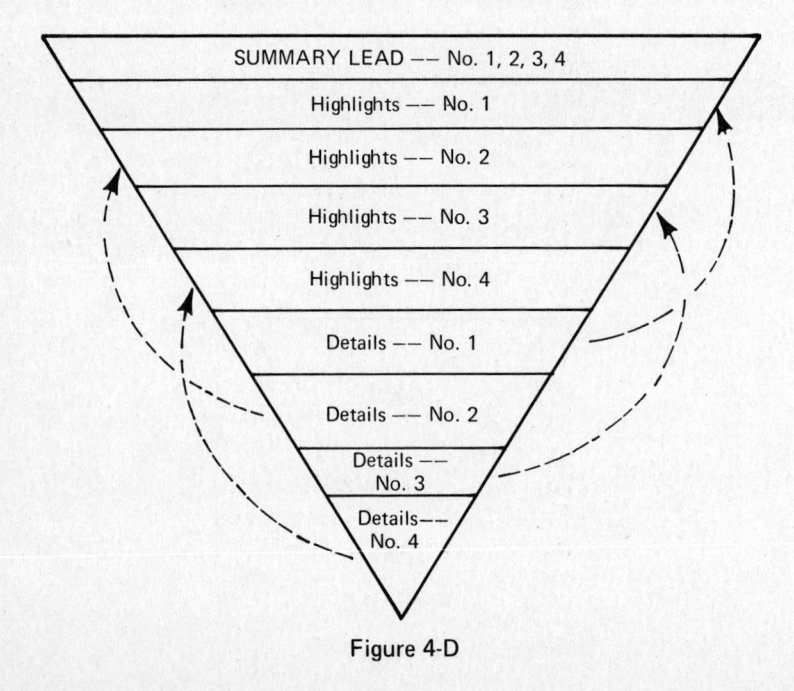

Figure 4-D

the inverted pyramid. It involves a rather drastic splitting of the information into various segments, necessitating very careful attention to transition. This form usually would use the one-paragraph summary lead and transition paragraph as before. Then it would differ from the other forms, dividing each set of facts into highlights on the one hand and details on the other. After the summary lead, the most important information about each item would be presented, but not fully explained. After this brief discussion of each item, the story would return once again to each, presenting the remainder of details.

While this variation of the inverted pyramid is used frequently in newspaper writing, it should be utilized only in situations in which the information is quite complex and with many details. In such a case, it would be impossible to handle each item separately because that would place the later items too low in the story.

The major problem with this variation is the need to spell out very carefully the transition from one item to the next. The reader must know precisely at all times which of the news items is being discussed and which set of details relates to the previous presentation of highlights.

The general principles of the inverted pyramid are such that they can be applied in almost any number of ways; the four discussed here are presented only as examples of the most common forms. As always, the best organization depends upon the reporter's assessment of the particular situation. He may use one of the variations described here or create his own, in general accordance with the basic principles.

Other Types of Structure and Leads

While it is true that most newspaper stories use some form of the summary lead and inverted pyramid structure, the regular newspaper reader will no doubt notice other types appearing with some frequency. Usually, these are special situations about which the reporter has judged that the inverted pyramid would not be the most effective form of organization. Most frequently, these represent one or another version of the feature story, to be discussed later, or an effort by the reporter to "featurize" a news story.

The two major types of leads which appear in addition to the summary lead are the narrative lead and the feature lead. The narrative lead simply involves starting at the beginning, in storytelling fashion. It makes no early effort to present the gist, or summary, of the story, but is a general introduction which, in a sense, sets the stage for what follows. Here are some examples:

Once upon a time, there was a little girl who had blonde hair.

Sam Camdon is an ordinary type of guy, but he has one unusual feature.

It all started when the distinguished senator from North Carolina decided he would push for passage of a bill to make jaywalking a federal offense.

The feature lead, on the other hand, can take practically any form. Its major characteristic is that it reverses the two functions of the summary lead, placing most attention on attracting attention and only secondarily telling what the story is about. The feature lead will be discussed in greater detail in Chapter 10.

The two major types of story structure in addition to the inverted pyramid are the suspended interest and narrative organizations. In the former, the reporter uses a narrative or feature lead, deliberately avoids giving too much information early in the story and leads the reader through the details to a climax or surprise ending. Usually, this type of story is quite short and of the feature variety. The narrative story may use a summary, narrative or feature lead, then proceed chronologically (or, at least, sequentially) through the event being described. These, and other, forms of organization appear in newspapers only when they are considered superior to the inverted pyramid.

Concluding the Story

Unlike academic theses and English class papers, the newspaper story seldom provides its readers with a conclusion as a separate entity. Ending the newspaper story usually is very simple: When you have said everything you want to say, quit writing. The inverted pyramid construction is based on the philosophy that the last paragraph will be the least important in the story. If the structure has been handled properly, everything worth saying will already have been said by the time the end of the story is reached.

Young reporters frequently want to do one of two things to the end of a story: provide the reader with a summary statement (If one is important enough for use, it probably should be the lead) or provide the reader with their own personal opinion about the story (Avoid, as much as possible, the insertion of opinion into a story). In short, no form of concluding statement is desirable for most news stories.

As we shall see later, feature stories may be different, for they often provide the reader some conclusion, perhaps a statement of the climax or a comment from the reporter, usually humorous, about the incident which has been described.

Structuring the News Story

In his day-to-day writing, the experienced reporter seldom will consciously consider each of the principles of story structure which have been discussed here. His years of practice have made their application automatic. The beginning reporter, on the other hand, must be very deliberate in his evaluation of available information and in determination of how to write the story. He must be acutely aware of every step in the process.

Using a set of familiar facts contained in the story of Red Riding Hood, let us now seek to provide an example of how this process should work.

First, does the story of Red Riding Hood have news value? According to the criteria of news worthiness discussed in Chapter 1, it does. What happened to her might happen to any little girl delivering goodies to her grandmother's house in the woods. A mother might say, "That could have been my daughter instead of Red Riding Hood." The facts have human interest because they concern a little girl, a hero and a villain. They also involve a dramatic rescue and considerable excitement. It might also be said that the story could serve a social good by warning other parents to be careful of allowing their daughters to walk alone in the woods. It is, therefore, safe to say that a reporter would write a story if confronted with the facts of this incident.

He would start, of course, with the lead. Remembering that the lead should present the climax of the story in summary form by answering the questions posed by the "five W's and H," he probably would determine that his lead should concentrate on the following: Who? "sportsman"; What? "saved Red Riding Hood's life"; Where? "at her grandmother's house"; When? "a long time ago" (but for current purposes, let us assume that the story will be in a newspaper of that time; thus, we can say "yesterday"); Why? "the wolf was about to eat her"; How? "he shot the wolf." Of course, the reporter could have taken a different Who? approach, concentrating on Red Riding Hood instead of the sportsman. To do this, however, his lead would have to use passive voice ("Red Riding Hood *was saved*..."), and he knows that newspapers prefer active voice ("sportsman *saved* Red Riding Hood"). In spite of such a preference, either approach is a valid one for the reporter would seek in either case to include both elements in his lead.

Stringing these elements together, the reporter could write the following lead:

>A sportsman saved the life of Red Riding Hood at her grand-

mother's house in the woods yesterday when he shot a wolf which was about to eat her.

This summary lead satisfies all of the requirements and thus is acceptable in content. But it is somewhat dry and lifeless in its presentation. The good reporter would add life to the writing by emphasizing the action, by adding to the human interest and by filling in the fate of the grandmother. When doing this, however, he knows that he must remain within the length limitations of the newspaper lead. He can add only so much, and he may decide to withhold some of the elements for later use. Given these considerations, the reporter could revise his lead in this manner:

> Quick action by an unidentified sportsman saved the life of a 10-year-old girl yesterday when he shot and killed a wolf which had eaten her grandmother and was about to eat her.

The information omitted from this lead would be placed in the second paragraph. For example, the Where? element should be mentioned quickly. Red should be identified by a listing of her parents' names and home address. The grandmother should be fully identified. And more specific information about the activities of the wolf should be provided. If the information were available, the sportsman certainly should be identified. But let us assume in this instance that he remained anonymous. Seeking to provide this information as well as smooth transition from the lead to the body of the story, the reporter could continue:

> The young lady, Red Riding Hood, daughter of Mr. and Mrs. James Hood of 1313 Forest Lane, said she was delivering some cakes and butter to her sick grandmother when the wolf, disguised as the elderly lady, declared he was going to eat her.
> The grandmother, Mrs. Robert Hood, 79, of 32 Elm Lane apparently had been eaten before little Red arrived, police said.

After leading the reader smoothly through the first three paragraphs, the reporter would seek to provide the details of the incident in as concise—yet interesting—a way as possible. His major effort in the body of the story would be to arrange the facts according to inverse importance. He would try to get across all the new material within the first half of the story; in the second half, he would provide secondary, but needed, information. The logic of his factual organization would be dictated by the type of inverted pyramid structure he chooses to follow and what he determines as his specific purpose in using certain facts.

In writing, the reporter would seek to use techniques which would highlight the mood of the story, thus supplementing the content.

STRUCTURING THE NEWS STORY

This means he would vary sentence and paragraph length, would use dialogue when possible and would omit superfluous details. At all times, he will not neglect the principles of grammar, semantics, word choice, sentences, paragraphs and style.

His final product could look something like this:

Hunter Kills Wolf, Saves Life of 10-Year-Old Girl

SUMMARY LEAD: Statement of the essence of the story

Quick action by an unidentified sportsman saved the life of a 10-year-old girl yesterday when he shot and killed a wolf which had eaten her grandmother and was about to eat her at her grandmother's house in the woods.

ORGANIZATION is single-item inverted pyramid

SECOND PARAGRAPH provides full identification for secondary ID in lead; transition between lead and details in body of story.

The young lady, Red Riding Hood, daughter of Mr. and Mrs. James Hood of 1313 Forest Lane, said she was delivering some cakes and butter to her sick grandmother when the wolf, disguised as the elderly lady, declared he was going to eat her.

The grandmother, Mrs. Robert Hood, 79, of 32 Elm Lane, apparently had been eaten by the wolf before little Red arrived, according to police.

BODY: Quoting police and central figure, present details of incident according to inverse importance.

Red told police she had met the wolf previously in the woods as she was walking from her home to her grandmother's house. She said he had been very polite at that time and had told her to give his "love" to her grandmother.

Apparently, the wolf had determined her destination in that conversation, police said, and then taken a shortcut, getting there before the girl, eating her grandmother and taking the grandmother's place in bed.

The young lady said she had lingered during the walk, playing in the woods, so the wolf could easily have arrived ahead of her.

	When she arrived at the house, the wolf apparently mimicked the grandmother's voice, telling her to come in. Once inside, she told police, she noticed that something was wrong. She said she asked the wolf about his long arms.
	"The better to hug you, my child," the wolf told her.
	Then she asked about the wolf's very large ears and was told:
	"The better to hear you."
FINAL DETAIL is return to lead statement	Red told police she then noticed the wolf's large teeth and, knowing her grandmother did not have such teeth and becoming more frightened, asked about them.
	"The better to eat you up now," the wolf is reported to have cried as he grabbed the young lady.
LAST TWO PARAGRAPHS provide transition to next day's stories	At that instant, a shot rang out and the wolf fell dead. The sportsman checked on the condition of the child, and, finding she was not injured, immediately left. Police arrived moments later, having been called by a passer-by.
	Police are attempting to identify the hunter.
NO FORMAL CONCLUSION	The funeral for the grandmother, Mrs. Hood, is pending.

Summary

The structure of most newspaper stories is according to the principles of the inverted pyramid, which basically say that the most important information should be presented first in the story and followed by the remainder of the information according to inverse importance. The usual way in which the most important facts are presented first is through use of the summary lead which may be either a statement of the most important fact or a combination of the several most important. While there are other types of structures and leads, they are reserved for special situations in which the reporter determines that the summary lead and inverted pyramid are not the most appropriate.

Other important aspects of the inverted pyramid are the lead-to-body connection (which essentially seeks to provide smooth transition from the story's lead into the presentation of the details in the body) and the conclusion (which, in newspaper writing, involves quitting when everything has been reported).

There are, of course, different forms which the inverted pyramid may take, and use of any of these generally depends upon the complexity of the information being presented. And there are other types of organization (for example, suspended interest and narrative) and leads (for example, the narrative and feature), but the bulk of newspaper writing is according to the inverted pyramid. This is the starting point for the beginning reporter. If he masters the inverted pyramid, it will be easy to move into other forms when they are appropriate.

CHAPTER 5

Spot News: Immediate Description

Spot news is the newspaper's primary reason for existence, at least as far as most readers are concerned. Consequently, most reporters devote much of their time to covering this kind of story.

The reader expects to be informed by his newspaper, and spot news stories are almost wholly informational. The reader may also expect to be entertained, educated and made aware of opinions—and some spot news stories contain bits of these elements. But they are informational stories first and foremost.

A spot news story may cover almost any subject. It may be an obituary. It may be a report of a minor fender-bender traffic accident or of an airline disaster which kills scores of people. It may describe the theft of a lawn chair or a spectacular bank holdup. It may be an account of a fire, an election, a snowstorm, a city council meeting or a speech by a nationally prominent visitor.

But one element distinguishes spot news stories from most other material in the newspaper, and that element is *immediacy*.

The spot news story must be used *now*. Its timeliness will be slipping away tomorrow. Next week it will be getting considerably musty around the edges. And next month, unless the story is of such importance that it demands follow-up attention, the news will be stale, valueless, forgotten and, therefore, no longer news.

Most of the news one receives from radio and television is spot news. Newspapers, however, offer both spot news (usually in more detail than the electronic media can provide) and features, in-depth reports and interpretation to supplement it.

Interpretive "think pieces" obviously are not spot news. Feature stories which do not lose their interest value overnight—and which are not bound by rigid timeliness—are not spot news. Background stories about continuing issues may not be spot news.

Spot news happens *now*, and the reader justifiably wants to be informed of it *now*.

We can conclude, then, that spot news is:

1. Timely and immediate.

2. Straight, factual and unembellished in most cases.

3. Extremely diverse in subject matter.

It might seem at first glance that spot news is covered primarily by general assignment reporters. The layman might think that beat reporting (discussed in Chapter 8) would always involve great depth, significant complexity and semi-scholarly digging into the issues.

Not so, at least in these terms. Many general assignment reporters, while producing the diverse stories which usually characterize their jobs, may be spending a great deal of time on feature stories and simple rewrites. And beat reporters, if they are covering their beats singlehandedly, are writing far more spot news stories than in-depth reports.

Beat reporting provides countless spot news stories. The police beat, by its very nature, with the exception of the in-depth stories written by experienced police reporters, produces a constant barrage of spot news stories. Reporters of city government, the courts, the schools—these and other beat specialists cannot afford to ignore the spot news happening in their realms every day.

A newspaper's size and scope can help determine what spot news it publishes. What is considered worthwhile spot news for one newspaper will be ignored by another.

For example, a 10,000-circulation paper serving a small city and surrounding rural area may well consider a minor traffic accident with no personal injuries worth a story four inches long. The metropolitan newspaper, however, with a premium on available news space in relation to the thousands of spot news stories it could use, may follow a policy of not using any accident stories which do not involve serious injuries.

The small newspaper may run an obituary for every death occurring in its circulation area, while the large paper probably will limit regular obituaries to "important" people.

It should be noted that a majority of the material received by newspapers from the wire services is spot news. Today's congressional actions, an earthquake in Peru, the death of a European statesman, a spectacular kidnaping-murder on the other side of the country—these are examples.

Because of the panoramic diversity of spot news, space limitations make it impossible for us to discuss every kind of spot news story the reporter will encounter. Bear in mind that most of the same principles of good newswriting can be applied to *any* spot news story, no matter what its subject.

The young reporter can expect to cover certain recurring types of spot news, however—obituaries, accidents and disasters, crime, the weather. These are considered in more detail below.

The beginner can also expect to spend some time covering what other people have to say, via speeches and interviews, and these stories are discussed in Chapter 6. Spot news tied to some of the beats is noted in Chapter 8.

Obituaries

The cub reporter often makes his debut by writing obituaries. He may not be happy about it, however. He may consider such a story beneath his talents.

Admittedly, a routine obituary is less challenging than most other kinds of news stories, but the beginning reporter is likely to find himself writing quite a few obits for two reasons.

First, obituaries have to be written—deaths are news—and rank has its privileges. In other words, why should a journeyman reporter have to bother with something so prosaic when a beginner has the time to do it? (There is some danger in this kind of thinking, if carried to extremes, because the need for professional quality is just as great in an obituary as in other stories.)

Second, the routine obit is a convenient vehicle by which an editor can evaluate a beginning reporter and judge him for a gradual transition into more difficult stories. It is also less "hazardous" to entrust an obituary to a beginner because of the relatively restricted, formula-type writing involved and because the facts for the story are usually quite accessible and easy to verify.

In short, obituaries must be written, and if the cub reporter cannot perform well at this level, why should the editor entrust more significant, interesting stories to him? The reporter must write many stories of many kinds—not merely the ones which interest him.

Most newspapers observe a fairly firm formula in obituaries. Unless the obit is about an exceptionally prominent person and is given general news play away from other obituaries, most of these little stories are alike; only the names and details are changed.

The lead of an obituary will generally contain the person's name, age and address, when and where he died, and—if appropriate—the cause of death:

   William T. Wilson, 72, of 245 Talbot St. died Thursday at his home after a long illness.

Note that this is one of the few cases where the first words of a

SPOT NEWS: IMMEDIATE DESCRIPTION

story are a person's name. Since it is obviously an obit, the reader knows *what* happened, and the principal item of interest is *who*. The reader wants to know *who died*.

When elderly people die natural deaths, "a long illness" is specific enough. There is no need for further description. But if a 40-year-old man dies as a result of a heart attack, that fact may well be included in the story.

A person can die unexpectedly, but everybody dies suddenly. It is redundant to write that a man "died suddenly after suffering a heart attack." The fact that he died "unexpectedly" is more meaningful.

Although background material about the person's life will follow the lead, news judgment may call for the placement of an important fact in the lead itself:

> William T. Wilson, 72, founder of the Roll Along Trucking Co., died Thursday at his home, 245 Talbot St., after a long illness.

Then, additional background:

> A native of Chicago, Mr. Wilson received a degree in business administration from the University of Illinois. He served in the U.S. Navy for 25 years, retiring in 1945 with the rank of captain.
>
> Mr. Wilson established his trucking business in 1946 and retired from the firm in 1965.
>
> He was a member of the Ohio Sportsmen's League, the Shrine Club, the American Legion and the First Presbyterian Church.

Many newspapers follow a policy of using "Mr." on subsequent references to a man in his obituary while dropping it in other news stories. A few papers use the title in all stories.

Background is generally followed by a listing of survivors, mentioned in reasonably logical order of relationship with the dead person:

> Survivors are his widow, Anne Davis Wilson; a daughter, Mrs. James (Marie) Snyder, Chicago; two sons, John and Steven Wilson, both of Indianapolis; five grandchildren; two sisters, Mrs. Stewart (Elizabeth) Johnson, Miltonville, Ohio, and Mrs. Marvin (Margaret) Edwards, Pittsburgh, and a brother, Thomas Wilson, Gudgeonville, Pa.

In listing survivors, as in other areas of newswriting, variations exist among individual newspapers. Some refer to "widow," while others use "wife." Many papers do not follow the name of a well-known city by its state. And often the grandchildren are not named specifically unless there are very few other survivors.

Finally, the funeral arrangements:

Friends may call at the Anderson Funeral Home from 2 to 5 and 7 to 9 p.m. Friday, Saturday and Sunday. The Rev. David F. Schwartz of the First Presbyterian Church will conduct the service at 2 p. m. Monday at the funeral home. Burial will be in Fairlawn Cemetery.

When both the subject's residence and the funeral home are in the same city as the newspaper, the name of the city need not be mentioned. If the city is small enough, the funeral home's address can be omitted.

Style and format may differ considerably from newspaper to newspaper. The amount of information included in an obituary will often vary according to a newspaper's size. It is up to the reporter to adjust to the requirements of his editor.

If the funeral home has done its job, writing an obituary usually requires no digging on the part of the reporter. He simply takes the information delivered to him or telephoned to him by the funeral director.

The funeral director, incidentally, should not be permitted to supervise or dictate the writing style of the obit. He has no such right unless he is paying for the item, and this is a rare practice. If he wishes to euphemize by stating that the person has "passed away," he may do so in the paid death notice section of the classified ads; the reporter is not concerned with these. The obituary, however, is a news story, and people do not "pass away" in good news stories. They "die"—it is a perfectly good word.

The dead man is not "the deceased." He is not survived by "his beloved wife." (Although you as a reporter may be sure she is his wife, do you really know she was beloved?) In newspaper writing, people are most often "buried" (unless they are cremated, which often is not stated in the story at all). Do not say a person was "interred" unless the body was placed in an above-ground tomb. And persons certainly do not "pass to their rewards."

Some funeral directors, in an effort to make their clients seem more important than those of other funeral directors, will pad the information provided the reporter. The background information you receive will vary in length. Most will be usable, but some insignificant material sometimes must be cut.

For example, if the information declares the subject was "a member of a pioneer Akron family," it behooves the reporter to make sure it is true before he uses it. If it is said that "Mr. Underhill was fond of gardening," eliminate such commonplace material about a hobby unless you know he won a number of prizes for his roses—and then say *that*.

As in all kinds of copy, typographical errors can cause consternation in obituaries. If a man has led an unspectacular life, his obit may be the first and last time his name has ever appeared in a newspaper. His family will expect the story to be correct in every detail. (Sometimes the reporter can do little about typographical gremlins, unfortunately.)

One newspaper decided to avoid referring to "a long illness," because sloppy proofreading occasionally resulted in attributing death to "a lung illness" when such was not the case. The paper decided to switch to "an extended illness," the thinking being that nothing much could happen to that. There was considerable upset, then, when an old gentleman who had led a very quiet life was reported as having died after "an exciting illness." The current effort at that newspaper involves using "a lengthy illness."

Accidents and Disasters

Most people, if asked to define a spot news story, probably would make some reference to accident stories in their definition. Despite the great number of accidents occurring every day, they are still the exception rather than the rule. They are unexpected—at least as far as the victims are concerned. Consequently, they are news.

Drawing a distinct line between accidents and disasters is virtually impossible. The distinction made by the dispassionate observer is based on the scope of the event, but the line may be drawn differently by someone directly involved. An earthquake which swallows up thousands of people is an obvious disaster to most readers. The sinking of a cabin cruiser with a loss of 12 lives may be a disaster only to the families and friends of the victims. And a single-car crash which kills one man is not a disaster to the general public, but it may be the most directly felt disaster of the widow's entire life.

Thus, accidents and disasters, wherever the twain meet, must be considered together. It is up to the newspaper to determine how extensively the story is treated, in light of its impact on the readers.

Not all accidents are fatal, of course. Some do not even involve injury to human beings. The treatment of the story again depends on the size of the paper.

The cub reporter can expect to handle a variety of accident stories. The police beat reporter may write most of them, but there will be an overflow, with the experienced man writing the most significant ones and the rest going to general assignment reporters.

The possibilities for accidents—and stories about them—are almost endless:

1. Home and industry: falls, electrical shock, burns, cuts, poisoning.

2. Automobile: from the wrinkling of fenders when one car bumps another to the multiple-car freeway crash killing a dozen people.

3. Airplanes: from the light plane skidding off the runway and jostling the passengers to the mid-air explosion or mountain-top crash which kills all aboard.

4. Other vehicles: from the tipped-over golf cart that causes a broken leg to a fatal train derailment.

5. Fires: from the one-paragraph story about firemen dousing a smoldering beef roast to the conflagration which levels an entire city block.

6. Drownings: from the water skiing accident to the sinking of an ocean liner.

7. Man versus nature: from a tumble on an icy sidewalk to a devastating hurricane which claims hundreds of lives and causes millions of dollars worth of property damage.

There are other accidents and disasters, of course, beyond this categorization. Mankind is prone to many methods of experiencing death, injury and property damage.

Most accident stories can be written in much the same way—with a lead describing what happened, followed by gradual use of details via the inverted pyramid style of newswriting.

In major accident and disaster stories, additional stories of a less rigid nature—personalized sidebars and color stories—may supplement the straight news accounts of the events.

For example, the straight news story of a major accident might start like this:

> Four teenagers drowned Tuesday when their overloaded canoe capsized in the Black River rapids north of Gorgeville.
> Volunteers recovered the bodies of . . .

Accompanying the main story could be a sidebar:

> Foaming water and sheltered inlets, summer breezes and a sunny sky—the perfect setting for a picnic outing.
> But it turned into tragedy Tuesday when rough water sent four young persons to their deaths.
> "Never saw such a happy group of kids," said Lester Frost, who watched in dismay as the canoe was swept into the rapids . . .

SPOT NEWS: IMMEDIATE DESCRIPTION

The reporter must keep his perspective in writing the story. For example, if a driver is killed while testing a $75,000 racing car, the most important fact is the death of the driver, not the demolition of the expensive vehicle. Probably both facts will be worked into the first sentence, but in almost all cases death takes precedence over property damage:

> Champion race driver Marlon Smith was killed Saturday when his car spun out of control and crashed into a retaining wall at Brooks Speedway.
> The $75,000 custom-made Simonetti racer was demolished when it crashed and burned. Smith was trapped in the wreckage . . .

Here are some of the elements to be considered in covering an accident or disaster. Not all of these elements will be applicable or necessary in every story, but they must be included if appropriate:

1. Casualties (dead and injured): names, ages, addresses, further identification, nature of injuries, how injuries were received, disposition of deaths and injuries.

2. Property damage: estimates, description, how damage was sustained, insurance and recovery, other property threatened. (Unless property damage is very high, many newspapers merely describe it and ignore dollar estimates.)

3. Causes: discovery, alarm, negligence, precautions.

4. Time and place.

5. Rescue, relief, heroism: names, ages, addresses, description of action, equipment, handicaps.

6. Other features: eye-witness accounts, unusual elements, investigation (such as in cases of arson or hit and run), legal action, similar accidents and disasters.

All of the information used should be authenticated—that is, it should be obtained from official, reliable sources.

Consider the following hypothetical example of how a reporter might cover a fatal traffic accident. We'll assume you are a reporter for a newspaper in a medium-size city (100,000-200,000 population).

Through the police radio in the newsroom or through a phone call from a friendly police officer, you learn that two cars have crashed and that there are serious injuries.

Considering the size of the city, and consequently of its newspaper, chances are that a photographer will be sent to the scene while the reporter remains in the office and gets the story information by telephone.

Your first information from police (your primary source in this kind of story) probably will be the location of the accident and some general impressions of the scene: It happened at 9:45 a.m. at the intersection of Broad Street and Taylor Avenue, near the city limits. A light rain had been falling, and streets were a bit slippery.

Police tell you both cars, one a convertible and one a sedan, are overturned in the intersection. Two ambulances are at the scene. Each car had two occupants, and all four persons are injured. Bystanders have told police the convertible failed to obey the traffic signal.

Hopefully it is not long before police can provide identification of the injured: Driver of the convertible was James F. Johnson, 24, of 489 Dover St. His passenger was Irene A. Curtis, 20, of 723 Harper Rd. The sedan was driven by Morton R. Ferguson, 53, of 4506 Washington St., and he was accompanied by his wife, Agnes, 52.

Police add that Johnson was traveling west on Broad, which has a 50-mile-per-hour speed limit, when he went through the red light. Ferguson was driving south on Taylor. All four persons were taken to Canterbury Hills Hospital.

(At this point the good reporter would make some mental notes for later use: Is the 50-mile-per-hour limit on Broad too high for traffic conditions there? Hasn't this intersection been plagued with a number of accidents recently? Are there warning signs to alert drivers about the traffic signal? The situation may call for an in-depth story within the next few days.)

You call the hospital and get the following information: Ferguson died on the way to the hospital; he had a fractured skull and broken neck; the body has been taken to the Matthews Funeral Home. His wife is in serious condition with internal injuries, a broken arm and severe facial lacerations. Johnson is being treated for a broken leg and nose; his condition is good. Miss Curtis (you determine she is single) is in fair condition with extensive lacerations and a concussion.

The next call will be to the funeral home. You learn that Ferguson was vice president of Tradewinds Manufacturing Co. Funeral arrangements have not yet been determined, but the funeral home will try to obtain a picture of Ferguson from his family and rush it to the newspaper.

Meanwhile, the newspaper's photographer has returned and is working on the pictures he took at the accident scene. One of them, showing the wrecked cars in the intersection, will probably accompany your story.

In later editions, you will have to update the conditions of the injured, include complete obituary information on Ferguson and keep in touch with police to determine whether charges are filed as a result of the investigation. But this story must be written now to meet the deadline of the current edition:

One driver was killed and three other persons were injured this morning in a two-car crash at Broad Street and Taylor Avenue.

Dead is Morton R. Ferguson, 53, of 4506 Washington St. He was vice president of Tradewinds Manufacturing Co.

The injured are Ferguson's widow, Agnes, 52, in serious condition at Canterbury Hills Hospital; the driver of the other car, James F. Johnson, 24, of 489 Dover St., and his passenger, Irene A. Curtis, 20, of 723 Harper Rd.

Police said Johnson was traveling west on Broad Street when, according to witnesses, he failed to stop for a red light at the intersection. Ferguson was driving south on Taylor Avenue.

The crash caused both cars— Johnson's convertible and Ferguson's sedan—to overturn in the intersection.

A light rain had been falling during the morning, and streets were somewhat slippery, police said.

Ferguson, who had a fractured skull and broken neck, died in the ambulance on the way to the hospital. The Matthews Funeral Home, 283 Hanover St., is in charge of arrangements.

Mrs. Ferguson is being treated for internal injuries, a broken arm and severe facial lacerations.

Johnson is listed in good condition at Canterbury Hills with a broken leg and nose. Miss Curtis, who has a concussion and extensive lacerations, is in fair condition.

Police are continuing their investigation of the accident.

Crime

Although most crime news is handled by the police reporter, chances are that the young general assignment reporter will have to write a great many relatively minor crime stories for which the beat man simply has insufficient time.

And occasionally the cub reporter will have the opportunity to cover a major crime story because the police reporter is already occupied with one or more big stories of his own.

Once again, it depends on the size and scope of the newspaper whether some of the small stories are covered and used. The metropolitan paper is not likely to include a story about a break-in if nothing valuable was stolen. The smaller newspaper probably would print at least a short account of the event.

The crime story, like most other spot news stories, is usually a straightforward account of *what happened*. In spectacular crime stories, as in major accidents, the primary news story may be accompanied by additional, more colorful sidebars.

The minor burglary is likely to be covered with a one- or two-paragraph story:

Household goods valued at $75 were stolen Friday night from the home of Mr. and Mrs. Willis M. Norris, 305 Greentree St.

Norris told police Saturday that a rear door had been broken open when no one was at home. Reported missing were an electric can opener, a blender and a radio.

Covering a bank robbery, kidnaping or murder, of course, is much more complicated. Many more details will be available, and readers will be sufficiently interested to want a complete account.

Furthermore, the story is likely to be a continuing one. After the initial reporting of a murder, for example, readers will want to know of progress—or lack of it—in the case. The sequence of coverage (not necessarily day by day without interruption) might go something like this:

1. A body is found in a wooded area. The victim had been shot. He is identified, and some background about him is obtained. Some material is included about the start of the police investigation, without interfering with the case.

2. The next day, even if no major developments arise, the reporter probably will keep the reader up to date by providing more background on the victim and further discussion of the investigation.

3. A suspect is picked up for questioning. The reporter will find as much information as he can about the suspect and will include some details to update the investigatory aspects of the case.

4. The suspect is charged. The story will report his arraignment, jailing and bail specifications and imminent court procedures.

5. The trial begins. At this point, the story probably will be dropped by the police reporter and taken over by the courthouse reporter.

6. The verdict, sentencing and wrap-up of the case.

Some of these items, of course, will involve continuing stories in their own right. The trial itself may last for many days, and a reporter will write a story about each day's testimony.

It is up to the reporter covering the story to get as many facts as he can for every story he writes. In a developing story, such as the murder case above, some facts that the reader (and the reporter) would like to know must necessarily be omitted—simply because the facts are not yet known. However, the editor is not likely to forgive the cub reporter if he does not mention the victim's age because he forgot to ask for the information.

Weather

Nobody has been able to do very much about the weather, but it remains a time-honored subject for discussion—sometimes in a light conversational sense, but often with a very real news connotation.

Newspapers publish the daily reports and forecasts of the United States Weather Bureau, and standard procedures are adopted by a paper to get these items. Often a cub reporter has the daily responsibility of telephoning the bureau's local office for the next day's local forecast, to supplement the national weather information arriving on the wire.

Spot news? Certainly. What could be more current, more immediate, than the weather?

And there are occasions when the weather—not forecasts of future weather, but what the weather has just done or is doing now—provides major news stories in its own right.

Some newsmen look with distaste on writing a weather wrap-up story after a snowstorm which seems only a bit heavier than usual. "All the reader has to do is look out his window, and he'll know it snowed last night," they lament.

But the reader may want to know more than that. He probably is interested in how many inches of snow fell, what roads are closed by drifts, what the city and state are doing to open the highways and eliminate slippery conditions, what the official low temperature was during the night and whether any personal injuries or property damage were attributable to the snowfall.

People are indeed interested in the weather and its perversity—and some reporters do enjoy writing about it. In fact there is a legend about the reporter who became so accustomed to his job of newswriting, including many weather stories, that he began to *talk* in lead form; he might enter the newsroom and declare to his colleagues, "Nine inches of snow blanketed the downtown area tonight, but all main streets are open."

Summary

Spot news, whether it is covered by the general assignment reporter or the beat man, is the bread-and-butter material of the newspaper. It provides the factual information desired by most readers.

In-depth coverage of issues, beyond the reporting of events, is also a duty of the newspaper and is discussed later in this book. But straight, factual reporting of spot news—timely, immediate stories about a myriad of happenings, large and small—remains of utmost importance.

Spot news is likely to occupy the beginning reporter's attention for some time when he starts his career. He is not apt to receive the opportunity to write in-depth material until he demonstrates an ability to cover spot news well.

CHAPTER 6

Reporting What Others Say

Browse through today's newspaper and see how many stories are based on what people have to say. You may be surprised.

Despite the wealth of spot news concerned with events—the hard facts about what happened—countless stories result from somebody saying something. The "something" can be important or interesting or, hopefully, both.

The President announces his views on congressional spending. A prominent naturalist visits your city to give a speech on ecology. Four college presidents take part in a panel discussion on campus unrest. A barnstorming senatorial candidate swoops into town to address a political fund-raising rally. The mayor holds his monthly press conference. You interview the new president of a local industry. You conduct a man-on-the-street interview with ordinary citizens. You get a spot news story by telephone.

All of these, even though the statements may be about concrete events as well as subjective viewpoints, are stories based on what people have to say. Taken together, instances of this kind of story comprise a tremendously significant and growing part of the news.

Covering Speeches

Covering a speech can be agonizing if the speaker is not interesting, but even a dull speech can be newsworthy in content. Not everyone who has something important to say is an exciting or even a competent public speaker.

For example, although television has made physical appearance and platform smoothness almost a must in national politics, a surprising number of successful state and local politicians are dreadful speakers.

Although the general assignment reporter usually will cover a speech on an isolated topic, the beat reporter may often cover speeches pertinent to his own area. If he covers the courthouse and a prominent jurist gives a speech, it is logical and helpful for the courthouse reporter to cover the story.

If the speech is about a subject quite unfamiliar to the reporter, he should take the time to brief himself before he covers it. He must, of course, understand what the speaker says in order to write a meaningful story for his readers.

Often it is sufficient to cover the speech itself. But when the speaker is more noteworthy than usual, and when he is willing and able to take the time, he should be interviewed by the reporter before or after the speech.

In speech coverage—and in other kinds of stories discussed here—note-taking ability is vital. The reporter must be able to take notes rapidly and accurately. Notes which are slowly and painstakingly recorded may be accurate, but they will not begin to catch all that will be needed for a complete, lucid story. The speaker will not back up and repeat for the slow reporter; he may not even know you are covering the speech.

Some techniques for effective note-taking are described in Chapter 7. However, several factors are worth emphasizing here.

The reporter must cultivate the ability to listen to and absorb one sentence while still writing what the speaker said in the previous sentence. It isn't easy, but experience generally provides this skill. Your own system of "shorthand" might appear as gibberish even to you a week later, but bear in mind that your notes in most cases will be used to write your story the same day.

Be selective in what you include in your notes. Not everything in a speech is important. A good reporter can spot a significant quote as it starts; he learns to recognize key points quickly.

However, many beginners will find that it behooves them to take more notes than they are likely to need early in a speech. Don't keep waiting for something better to come along; it may not. The speech may end and leave you holding the bag because you failed to take enough notes. (Some speeches *are* refreshingly short.)

It can be argued, of course, that the importance of the material in a speech should dictate how long a story is written about it. Thus, if you have taken few notes on the assumption that you are getting only the worthwhile points, won't your story be geared to the volume of your notes? Ideally, yes—but realistically, there will be times when your editor, edging close to deadline, has saved space for an 11-inch story about the speech; and he may insist that you write, indeed, an 11-inch story. Your notes should be equal to the task.

At the same time, the reporter will encounter occasions when he is reluctant to include a fairly minor point because its complexity would require too much space to express clearly. Importance is one

REPORTING WHAT OTHERS SAY

thing, amount of space needed for clear expression is another, and the two don't always correlate perfectly. It is better to omit a point than to state it unclearly.

Sometimes a reporter's job is made easier by the availability of prepared texts of a speech (or of a formal announcement for a press conference). This is fine, but a strong warning is in order: The good reporter still goes to the speech and listens.

It is helpful to receive an advance copy of a speech, because some of the writing can be done early. But some speakers deviate from prepared texts. New developments may compel them to comment in more detail on a topic or change what they had prepared earlier. If you simply write your story beforehand and ignore the actual delivery, you and your newspaper may appear to be foolish indeed—particularly if you include the story in an edition distributed during or before the speech itself.

One of the authors recalls an extreme instance of jumping the gun with a prepared text. The governor of his state was to deliver a luncheon speech. The text had arrived at news media offices the day before (with a specified release date for the time the speech actually was to be given). The author, working for a morning newspaper, was assigned to cover the event, as was his counterpart from the evening paper. But the other reporter had written the speech story earlier in the morning, and it was appearing in the mid-day edition of his newspaper as the audience sat down for lunch. After some delay, the local party chairman rose and announced that the governor's plane had been grounded at the other end of the state because of bad weather. The author chuckled as his competitor dashed to a phone to try to kill the story, but it was too late—thousands of copies of the paper were already on their way.

Writing Speech Stories

Beginners often find it difficult to write good leads for speech stories. If they are oriented toward covering stories involving hard, cold events, they are apt to write a lead like this:

> Bellingham R. Thornton, well-known inventor, spoke Friday in Milton Auditorium on the subject of "Patent Protection."

Leads like this *do* appear occasionally, but that does not make them any less terrible.

On the contrary, the lead should emphasize what the speaker *said*, not the fact that he spoke. Chances are, the reader already knew that he spoke—and if the fact that he spoke *is* the most important angle, it probably doesn't even merit a story.

(There are exceptions, of course. If the President of the United States appears briefly at the local railroad station and utters a few platitudes before going on his way, the important event is his appearance rather than what he said.)

Instead of the news-less lead above, this would be a possibility:

> Outmoded patent laws do not give American inventors adequate protection, inventor Bellingham R. Thornton said Friday in Milton Auditorium.

Note that the improved lead does not begin with the speaker's name. *What* he said is more newsworthy than the fact that *he* said it. Note also that the subjective "well-known" has been removed; let the reader decide for himself whether the speaker is famous.

The lead of a speech story can take a number of forms. It may be a summary of the main theme of the speech (but not a mere statement of the formal subject); the improvement above illustrates this.

It may be a key point from the speech:

> Fifty major inventions in the last decade have been "stolen" from their creators because of outmoded patent laws, inventor Bellingham R. Thornton declared Friday in Milton Auditorium.

Or, the lead may be a direct quotation which epitomizes the theme:

> "Necessity may be the mother of invention, but our outmoded patent laws are not helping in the delivery," inventor Bellingham R. Thornton said Friday in Milton Auditorium.

In choosing a lead for the story, it is up to the reporter to decide what will best tell the reader the main facts of the story.

He must also consider what will grasp the reader's interest and make him *want* to read the story. Thus, in the absence of any obvious, gripping hard news element, it's possible that a feature lead may be considered effective:

> Picture a group of lawmakers seated on a collapsible patio. Press the "collapse" button, and spray them with starling repellent as they are folded into the contrivance.
>
> The inventor of these items hinted Friday that such treatment might be poetic justice for the writers of the nation's outmoded patent laws.
>
> Bellingham R. Thornton, speaking in Milton Auditorium . . .

The reporter generally will not know what his lead will be until the speech is over; sometimes the most important point is in the speaker's conclusion. It may be in the question-and-answer period, if there is one, and a good reporter does not leave until the question period ends.

After the lead, in addition to the content of the speech, the reporter must include the occasion or sponsorship, if any; reaction of the audience (enthusiastic, hostile) if obvious and appropriate, and background of the speaker. This material can generally be worked into the copy in an unobtrusive way, and occasionally such information is significant enough to use as a separate sidebar story.

The story must contain the important things the speaker said. Do not simply give the speaker's statements in the order in which he presented them. He wrote a speech, but you are writing a news story.

Vary the construction. Don't start every paragraph with the speaker's name; that will amount to visual boredom for the reader.

Speech stories are written in past tense—Thornton "said" something, not Thornton "says." However, it is permissible to say the speaker "believes" something, since he presumably still believes it even though he is not still saying it. When quoting from a published source, it is customary to use present tense: "Freud says . . ."

Despite the fact that your entire story may be about the speech, the comments throughout must be attributed to the speaker. The statements cannot simply stand alone. You must make sure the reader knows the comments are the speaker's, not yours. Every direct quotation must be attributed, and there should be at least one attribution per paragraph of indirect quotations.

A good speech story does not consist entirely of direct quotes, nor should it have none. One rule of thumb is to use one direct quote for every two indirect quotes. Sometimes the reporter can get the speaker's point across in better, more understandable words than those used in the speech. Overuse of direct quotes is a form of laziness in which the reporter does nothing but give the exact words of the speaker, clear or not. At the same time, a complete absence of direct quotes may indicate a note-taking deficiency on the part of the reporter.

Direct quotation is valuable when the speaker expresses himself in an unusual, profound, attention-getting or humorous way. Also, a statement of opinion is often more effectively used as a direct quote, as opposed to a factual statement which is not entirely the speaker's. Judicious use of direct quotes can personalize a story and enhance its readability, by making it seem to the reader that he actually is listening to a person talk. Long, dry, pedantic quotes, however, would lose this advantage.

Not all direct quotes must be the complete sentences of the speaker. A useful technique is the inclusion of partial quotes, involving key phrases in the speaker's own words set within the paraphrased indirect quotes by the reporter. An example:

Thornton said government handling of patents amounts to "an abominable bureaucracy."

How direct should a direct quote be? Ideally, any comment with quote marks around it should be exact and literal. This is the goal. However, an experienced reporter generally has some leeway in omitting or adding a word or two within a direct quote, perhaps to improve clarity or conciseness, *if it in no way changes the meaning intended by the speaker.*

Continuing with the hypothetical Thornton speech about patents, here is how it might look as a finished story, assuming your editor called for a short one. Remember that most speech stories can be written several different ways, and this is not the only form the story could take:

Fifty major inventions in the last decade have been "stolen" from their creators because of outmoded patent laws, inventor Bellingham R. Thornton declared Friday in Milton Auditorium.

Speaking to 500 members of the Western Pennsylvania Association of Inventors, Thornton described government handling of patents as "an abominable bureaucracy."

The speaker charged that existing patent laws are geared for a bygone age and cannot protect inventors' rights quickly enough in an era of rapid transportation and communication.

"By the time a patent application has crept through the long trail of red tape," he said, "word of one's invention has made the rounds—and someone else suddenly 'invents' it." This happened most recently in the case of an improved, high-tension trouser hanger, he added.

Thornton suggested that tightened security within the patent office itself might help solve such problems.

Patent laws must be modernized to require streamlined procedures, he said. Most of the inventions "stolen" because of slow-moving patent processes, Thornton stated, have been automotive accessories and food packaging improvements.

Thornton, who operates a workshop in Tinkerville, Ohio, urged association members to launch a campaign to improve both legislative and administrative treatment of inventors.

"Necessity may be the mother of invention, but our outmoded patent laws are not helping in the delivery," he said.

Among Thornton's inventions are disposable window screens, a starling repellent and a collapsible patio. He is one of about 20 full-time independent inventors in the United States.

The above story, written to your editor's space specifications, presumes that there was no significant question-and-answer period and

REPORTING WHAT OTHERS SAY

that you did not interview the speaker. An alert reporter, in consultation with his editor, might well write an interview story on the speaker himself.

Man-on-the-Street Interviews

There is considerable difference between simply taking down what a speech-maker says and having to ask questions to draw information from people.

The beginning reporter may find that his first experience in interviewing—and usually his easiest—is a "man-on-the-street" story. He is sent outside, often with a photographer, to find the opinions of a half dozen or more people on a given question.

Usually these stories are not very significant, but they gain high reader interest. The reader can often "identify" with the "ordinary people" who are voicing a variety of opinions, often paralleling his own.

The reporter approaches people one by one—perhaps on the sidewalk, in a park or outside a business establishment—and asks his question. The responses are often undeveloped and not backed up with the reasoning which led to them, but if the question is a timely and interesting one, the answers will be of interest, too.

The reporter should try to approach a variety of people for this kind of story. Within the confines of the simplicity and lack of depth in such a story, he should avoid restricting himself to people of the same sex, age, occupation or apparent economic status. Furthermore, he should strive for a variety of content if at all possible.

Some people will decline to participate in the interview. Others will give heated, outspoken responses and then ask that their names not be used. The reporter must get full names (Mrs. Smith is not sufficient) and addresses to make the responses usable. Don't be discouraged if you have to approach a dozen people to get six usable responses.

Although this kind of story has little hard news value (because the size of the sample and the way it is taken do not permit generalizations or conclusions about the total population), accuracy is just as important in quoting the man on the street as it is in quoting a visiting dignitary.

One of the authors is embarrassed to admit a situation in which he misquoted a person on the street because he did not pay adequate attention to what the man said. The author was showing a picture of a controversial and rather strange work of art—consisting of wood, wire and other materials—and was asking for comments about it.

The misquotation consisted of only one misunderstood *letter,* but that one letter reversed the meaning of the statement. What the respondent actually said sarcastically was, "I suppose it's pretty good lumber." What was reported, however, was, "I suppose it's a pretty good number." Needless to say, there was a telephone call the next day from the man who had received considerable kidding from friends because of his supposed public support of this extremely controversial work of art.

There are two ways to organize a man-on-the-street story. First, it can be done as a group interview story, with responses blended throughout the copy. Or, more commonly, the story will consist of a lead followed by a paragraph or two from each respondent, quoted one by one.

Writing the lead is sometimes difficult, particularly if the responses show no unanimity or consistency. If six respondents agree that cities should take action to combat "noise pollution," the lead can easily say so, of course. If five out of six agree, the lead could say, "American cities should act to combat noise pollution, according to a majority of people questioned today at the corner of Market Street and Fleet Road." But if opinions are scattered all along the spectrum, you may have to lead with a reference to "mixed feelings" or "no agreement."

The Interview

It should be emphasized that the reporter can expect his questioning of other people to take many forms. The man-on-the-street interview is perhaps the simplest and shallowest. A common form of interview, of varying complexity, occurs when the reporter is sent to talk individually with an important person. And the beat reporter, even though he knows his sources well, is, in effect, interviewing them on an almost daily basis.

While the techniques of interviewing are discussed at length in the next chapter, some observations can be made here.

Beginning reporters often find themselves thrown rather quickly into the business of obtaining information from other people. Once the nervousness disappears, the reporter should find it a challenging and interesting experience. Not every interview source (or speaker) will be interesting, of course; some will be dull, some will be apparently "dense," and others will be downright hostile.

The reporter's first interview often breaks the ice sufficiently to permit him to be more at ease—and more skilled—in future encounters. The first interview conducted by one of the authors as a professional newsman was with a Scotland Yard inspector who had served as Sir Winston Churchill's personal bodyguard. The author still remembers his stage fright and his fear of asking a foolish question; fortunately, the visitor also delivered a speech, which permitted the reporter to turn in an appropriate amount of copy. Later interviews went more smoothly and brought gradually increasing confidence.

Backgrounding is even more important for the one-on-one interview than for covering a speech. Not only is it vital in many cases so that your story will be coherent, but it can avoid making you seem uninformed as you conduct the interview. Again, one of the authors recalls getting 15 minutes notice that he was to interview Wernher von Braun, the space rocket expert—and those 15 minutes had to be used to drive to the industry von Braun was visiting. Since the author's knowledge of science was minimal, he feared the possibility of a communication gap, particularly if the scientist answered questions with a brief "yes" or "no." Luckily, von Braun provided lengthy and fairly untechnical answers, and a story did result—but perhaps not a very good one.

Such instances are unfortunate and should be avoided whenever possible. A reporter with a knowledge of or interest in the subject should be assigned the interview. And he should have time to formulate pertinent questions to make the most of the subject.

Writing the interview story is quite similar, in most cases, to handling the speech story. However, there can be some differences.

For example, the interview is far less an event than a formally delivered speech is. Therefore, it is quite possible—and in many cases desirable—to treat the interview story in more featurized form. Since the interview can be more personalized, perhaps more direct quotes will be used than in a speech story.

Some publications, in fact, use direct quotes entirely, with a question-and-answer format. After the story lead, the account would continue:

> Q. What do you consider the city's most pressing need?
> A. Adequate street lighting, it seems to me, must be considered first. We have too many dark, dangerous streets.
> Q. How much would a suitable lighting program cost, and where would the money come from?
> A. I would guess we could get the job done for about $75,000, and the funds could be obtained in a couple of different ways—by a tax increase or by assessing the adjacent property owners...

At any rate, while a speech is an "occasion," chances are that the interview is not; just as the source is talking fairly informally with the reporter, the interview story may well give the reader an impression that the source is chatting with *him*.

Not all interview stories are featurized to a great extent, of course, and not all show an informality of tone; but the opportunity for these characteristics is present in many. The reporter soon learns to judge individual cases. Perhaps an interview with the governor about major state issues will be treated with a straightness accorded a speech story—but an interview with a champion hog caller would be wasted if it were not given some light, informal personality.

The Detroit News, for example, took a light approach in an interview story about a taxidermist:

By BEVERLY ECKMAN
News Staff Writer

Irwin Watts has a life-sized girl in his taxidermy workshop, but it's just a plaster mannequin modeling leather goods.

He doesn't stuff people. And he doesn't even recommend mounting pets.

"People just sit and look at them and grieve," he said. "They feel sad all over again.

"On purpose, I make it expensive to mount a pet—I tell people they are much better off to take the money and buy themselves a new pet."

But he loves his regular business, mounting trophy animals and museum specimens, everything from deer heads and pheasants to moose feet and fish.

And, according to Hank Augustyn, supervisor of the Belle Isle Zoo and Aquarium, Watts is "one of the best in the Detroit area," a "painstaking worker" who uses "museum techniques" in arranging "the most lifelike mounts in realistic action poses."

Watts has spent hours studying animals, birds and fish, their conformation and musculature, and their environment in his efforts to recapture their wildlife look and preserve them.

"I like animals and the outdoors and nature," Watts said. "You have to be outdoor-minded to appreciate the beauty of the animals and birds and fish."

He considers himself an ecology-sound preservationist because he is trying to preserve that beauty.

"I get 15 or 20 calls a year on mounting of protected species like hawks, owls and songbirds but I tell them absolutely not," Watts said . . .

Reprinted with permission from The Detroit News.

And the story continued (the complete story being about three times the above length) with a variety of informational and personalized material.

The important thing for the reporter to remember is to gauge the style to the source and the subject and, where possible, to inform and entertain the reader at the same time.

News Conferences

Many important people call a gathering of reporters before making a major announcement. In fact, the news conference in America has become a complex institution—particularly as developed by recent presidents.

At its worst, a news conference (or press conference, as it was called before the emergence of the broadcast media) can become a sinister tool to cover up information—to issue lengthy prepared statements that cut off reporters' questions and to sound slick and well-informed while actually saying very little.

Readers and listeners as well as reporters often have little trouble spotting the euphemistic gobbledygook which characterizes some news conferences. One can listen on occasion to a public official talk for 20 minutes and then ask one's self, "What did he say? Anything?" Words, as shown earlier, do not always provide significant meaning.

On the positive side, however, the news conference can insure that an overemphasis on "scooping the opposition" is minimized, thus permitting more opportunity for backgrounding and perspective.

This is more true on the national level, however, where a president simply does not have the time to see every reporter individually. On the local government level, a news conference is far less justified in the view of many reporters.

For example, if a reporter has been following developments in urban renewal for several months and then sees a major announcement on the subject given to all reporters at the same time, his sense of fairness can be insulted and his initiative impaired. It is really unfair to undercut him by handing an important story on a silver platter to other reporters who otherwise wouldn't have had the vaguest notion of what was going on.

Basically, a news conference is a group interview with one or more news sources answering questions fired by a number of reporters.

Once again, backgrounding is important. To ask intelligent questions, the reporter must have some knowledge of the news source's realm. In other words, don't ask questions when the answers are already common knowledge; this is showing your own lack of awareness and is wasting the time of the news source and of the other reporters who must fidget while the obvious answer is patiently (or impatiently in some cases) explained. This type of sloppiness results when the small newspaper or radio or television station expects one or two reporters to cover almost all facets of the news. In such understaffed situations, it is small wonder that they show up at news conferences underinformed.

Many officials pass out mimeographed sheets containing their own remarks and backgrounds. These can be helpful, and reporters should encourage the practice. However, it is wise not to depend too heavily on these handouts. As in speech stories, a source may depart from his prepared statement or fail to show up at all. Ideally, the reporter writes what he sees and hears, not what he reads, although that ideal is not always possible.

Writing the news conference story requires news judgment. Generally the news conference does not confine itself to one subject; reporters' questions will make the source flit from topic to topic. Some of the questions and answers may not be newsworthy. It is up to the reporter to determine the news value of each portion of the news conference in deciding what to include in the lead and what to include at all.

Because of the diversity of subjects in a single news conference, it is possible that the best lead will mention several different and unrelated items, unless one topic stands far above everything else in news value.

Here is a blanket lead:

> Plans for a presidential visit to France, a reorganization of the State Department and the expansion of five national parks were announced by President Richard M. Nixon at his press conference today.

Or, the single-item lead, followed by a second-paragraph blanket:

> All United States ambassadors to Latin American countries are being summoned to Washington for three days of strategy meetings, President Richard M. Nixon announced today.
>
> The President also stated at today's press conference that he will ask Congress to move more quickly on anti-pollution measures, that he will visit seven key states during the congressional election campaign, and that he believes the economy has been effectively stabilized.

In either case, all of the items in the lead would be discussed further in the same order. Once those portions of the story are completed, topics not mentioned in the lead would be used in descending order of importance.

The news conference is a valuable tool on the national and, perhaps, state levels. Many important stories can result from this tool. But on the local level, news conferences are open to question as to necessity and desirability; the local reporter will hopefully use his initiative, skill and persistence to get the story before it reaches the news conference stage.

Panel Discussions

In a day of controversial issues, the panel discussion seems to be gaining increased popularity. Rather than schedule a single speaker on a subject, it is often the practice to bring several viewpoints to the same event.

This kind of story can be covered in much the same way as a speech, but it is a bit more difficult. In a speech story, the reporter can usually settle back and listen to a fairly unified presentation by one man—and write a story on what is said. But the panel discussion may provide some conflict, not only in viewpoints but in the variations of speaking style and articulation.

The principal guideline here is that the reporter should make every effort to present a fair and balanced account of the discussion. Even if he believes one of the participants did a better job than the others, and even if one speaker verbosely hogged the platform, the reporter should attempt to give "equal time" or "equal space" to all of the viewpoints expressed. (If one or more of the participants seemed illogical or ultra-emotional, a well-written, fairly-presented story will certainly convey that impression to the reader.)

The reporter should consciously try to take notes on all of the various elements or viewpoints presented in a panel discussion, and then he should be sure to include them in his story. Unless there is a definite, significant news peg which clearly overshadows other viewpoints, the lead itself should aim for as much balance as possible.

Once the lead is written, the story can be organized either by topic or by speaker. The topical arrangement would bring the comments of all speakers into each facet of the discussion; the speaker categorization would handle all the comments of each participant one at a time.

Attribution

In "sparring" with news sources, reporters have come up with a baffling array of compromises—none very acceptable but all often better than getting no story. We now pause to consider some of these arrangements.

Figure 6A might be termed a "ladder of freedom." Other things being equal, the higher a reporter climbs on this ladder, the better his copy will be.

At the top, both direct and indirect quotations of named sources are permitted.

At the very bottom rung, a news source goes "off the record." If the reporter agrees to such an arrangement, his hands are tied completely as long as the blanket of secrecy remains intact.

Often, when a source asks to go off the record, a reporter will refuse to go along. He may even walk out of a meeting room, hoping to get the story later. If he were to stay and accept an off-the-record agreement, the reporter might feel obliged to sit on a story even if he should also get it from another source who seeks to impose no restrictions.

A reporter should generally think twice about sitting still for off-the-record comments when a great many people—reporters, non-journalists or both—are listening to what's said. Someone in any large group is almost bound to spill the beans. Then the story will be fair game for everyone. However, the reporter who violates the agreement is still apt to wind up scoring a beat at the expense of more "ethical" colleagues.

Despite these drawbacks, there may be times when a reporter can profit from an off-the-record session or backgrounder. While one can't publish the story right away, he can anticipate and prepare for later follow-up coverage of related events.

If the bottom rung of the ladder is perplexing, the rungs in between are often more so. Confusing, and sometimes conflicting, terminology abounds. However, there appear to be three basic arrangements which permit the newsman to say something but not all that's really needed.

Each step down the ladder involves all restrictions imposed at the step immediately above and more. We now look at the various "in between" rungs in some detail.

Rung 2—*Indirect Quotation Only*. Here the newsman can attribute fully by name, but he can't use quotation marks to indicate that a given quote is verbatim.

The next time you read the paper, you'll almost certainly find no direct quotes attributed to the President of the United States. Such an arrangement is rare with sources other than the President, the Pope and perhaps a few more "superpowerful" world leaders.

Some critics contend that even (and perhaps especially) the world's top leaders should be held responsible for what they say.

On the other side, however, such leaders recognize that their slips of the tongue can have grave consequences. Therefore, they may refuse to talk openly and completely unless they feel they can later disown their own mistakes.

Few reporters get terribly angry about the "indirect-quotation-only" arrangement, because it really doesn't limit news *content*.

REPORTING WHAT OTHERS SAY

Type of limitation on newsman		Name of arrangement
None.	(1)	Full attribution by name, direct and indirect quotes.
Writing style only restricted.	(2)	Full attribution by name, indirect quotes only.
Writing style restricted, clarity and completeness reduced.	(3)	Euphemistic-source attribution.
Writing style restricted, clarity and completeness lowered. Deceit becomes likely.	(4)	No attribution at all (the Lindley Rule).
Hands tied. Can say nothing about content or source of what is said	(5)	Off the record.

Figure 6-A.

To be sure, the rule does restrict style of writing. Many observers feel direct quotation *personalizes* copy and adds a dash of *variety*. And it may improve *authenticity*, since the reader knows he's getting precisely what is said rather than an observer's summary.

Rung 3—*Euphemistic-Source Attribution.* Here, instead of quoting by name, the reporter uses only euphemistic expressions such as "a usually reliable source," "a source close to the White House," or a "high-ranking Pentagon official."

In theory, euphemisms are supposed to serve as red flags of a sort. They implicitly tell the reader, "Look, this guy is associated with the Pentagon, and you ought to keep that in mind when you assess what he is saying."

There is considerable doubt, however, that a majority of readers, listeners and viewers interpret euphemisms as red flags. Many studies indicate that the typical American is not a very astute, critical news reader.

At best, euphemisms aren't clear, concrete words. It follows that such attribution ties the reporter's hands by forcing him to be *vague and incomplete.*

Rung 4—*The Lindley Rule.* Washington columnists often agree to this arrangement, reporting leaked information but saying absolutely nothing about the source.

Named after Newsweek editor Ernest K. Lindley, who is often credited with first openly proposing it as a means of source-reporter coexistence, this rule is really a court of last resort for prying the lid off a story. Surely the practice was used long before Lindley came along. However, it apparently was seldom discussed openly as a reasonable journalistic procedure.

The Lindley Rule forces the journalist to be vague and incomplete, but that's not all. It tends to breed *deceit* because complete lack of attribution tends to suggest one or both of two things which are almost never true:

1. That the reporter himself thought up the item with no outside help at all.
2. That information was obtained randomly or haphazardly, with no planning by the news source. In fact, veteran correspondents such as James Reston and Douglass Cater agree that news leaks almost never happen this way. Bureaucrats frequently arrange them for personal gain.

In conclusion, city hall reporters will sometimes run into declarations that a source is going off the record. On rare occasions, they may encounter demands for euphemistic attribution.

The Lindley Rule and the indirect-quotation-only provision almost never come up except in Washington. However, all newsmen need to be aware of these matters. Free expression is important to all serious journalists. Furthermore, as local officials become more shrewd in news management, "Washington" arrangements such as the Lindley Rule may spread to City Hall, the courthouse and the statehouse.

Summary

Covering what other people say is a major function of most reporters. It is a function which generally takes experience, and even the journeyman reporter should always be improving in his ability to gather this kind of material smoothly and accurately.

Once a reporter achieves some skill in this area, these stories are not generally considered difficult. A speech story, for example, is very easy—once one has handled a number of them. The one-on-one interview is perhaps the most difficult in this family of stories be-

REPORTING WHAT OTHERS SAY

cause the reporter must use his skill to draw the information from the source; no one else is doing the reporter's work for him, and he is as much on display to the news source as the source is to him. The reporter's personality, poise, awareness and ability—or the lack of them—cannot be hidden.

Two factors, beyond the mere writing of the story, must be emphasized for almost all "what others say" stories: backgrounding and note-taking ability.

The more the reporter knows beforehand about the person and his subject, the better the story will be. Covering such an event "cold" and uninformed can result at best in embarrassment over one's lack of knowledge and unintelligent questions—and at worst in an inaccurate or unclear story.

Note-taking is an art that must be developed. Whatever method or system the young reporter uses, it must produce one result—complete, accurate, usable notes which will permit him to write a complete, accurate, usable story.

CHAPTER 7

Tools for Gathering Information

As Chapter 12 points out, journalists are debating—often with considerable heat—how one should collect information and assess its validity.

While such debate is healthy, much of it may be unnecessary. Social scientists, historians and other scholars have developed and refined a great many tools for research. And all too often, journalists write superficially and with little basis because they fail to use these tools.

At the end of this chapter, we'll consider use of the library and some key periodicals. First, however, we will take a close look at the interview—the most common single means of collecting journalistic information.

Conducting the Interview

> Mr. Ambassador, don't you feel that America's underhanded, more or less treacherous effort to drive the Reds from the Dominican Republic could prove disastrous because it might alienate Latin Americans generally?

Questions phrased roughly like this one sometimes show up in press conferences. Reporters who ask such questions are hunting for headlines, and they are quite likely to find them. For one thing, the ambassador is apt to get his dander up at words like *underhanded* and *treacherous*. This in itself often leads to quotable statements. It's rather hard to answer an impassioned, loaded question in a calm, dispassionate way.

Quotable or not, however, is the ambassador likely to reflect his actual beliefs? Probably not. At least, there is lots of evidence that he would probably give a far different answer if the question were phrased more clearly and calmly. An improved version might go like this:

> Mr. Ambassador, do you feel that America's recent actions in the Dominican Republic might affect this country's relations with the Latin Americans generally? If so, how?

Reporters often pay little attention to such subtleties because they tend to take the interview for granted as a means of gathering information. This is understandable. Interviewing is really conversation, and we rely on conversation almost constantly in our daily lives. We are seldom led astray by our friends and co-workers (we may run into an occasional practical joke, but that's a rarity except in settings like a fraternity initiation).

Social scientists have found, however, that the interview is really a very fragile tool. Basically that's because conversation is a two-way process. Answers depend about as much on how the interviewer acts as on the person being interviewed. For example:

—In a 1940 poll about America's role in World War II, interviewers who personally favored America's helping England found about 1.5 supporters of U.S. aid to the British for every opponent. On the other hand, interviewers who opposed American aid allegedly discovered 1.5 opponents for every supporter.[1]

—In another study, Christian Americans were asked whether they thought the Jews had too much influence on American business. Half of those interviewed said yes when the interviewer was Christian, only 22 per cent when he was a Jew.[2]

—An analysis of 61 press conferences held by President Kennedy revealed that the length of his answers depended to a surprising degree on the length of the questions asked. Ask a long question, apparently, and you are apt to get a long answer.[3]

Such results seem rather discouraging to the person who makes his living interviewing. Presumably he is after the truth. But when he gets differing answers, depending upon the form of the question and the way it's asked, which answer is more truthful? There is often no clear way to tell.

In part, this kind of question reflects confusion about truth. A person may actually feel anti-Semitic when interviewed, then kindly toward Jews a few minutes later. It would be a distortion to call him pro or anti-Semitic *for all time.* Such labels can be very unfortunate.

Herbert Hyman, a survey researcher, traces many problems to *stereotyped* thinking by the interviewer. For one thing, he says, people make far-reaching judgments about each other based on personal appearance. Many of us naturally assume that a bearded, long-haired student has radical political beliefs. Such an assumption can subtly influence a reporter's facial expression and tone of voice so as to alter the course of an interview. An air of hostility may result, making honest, complete answers very unlikely.[4]

Try as he might, an interviewer often cannot become an objective blotter soaking up unalloyed truth. However, he can be aware of his own biases. And he can work hard to reduce their influence on his tone of voice, mannerisms, and question wording, as well as on recording and interpretation of answers.

Journalists have given little systematic study to these matters. Fortunately, they can learn a great deal from behavioral science research and experience. We now turn to some general principles that have proved useful to pollsters like George Gallup. We will amend these principles on occasion to fit the reporter's needs.

Getting and Keeping Cooperation

When you conduct an interview, you really ask a good bit from the person being interviewed. You seek valuable *time* without pay (publicity seekers, of course, see getting in print as a kind of pay). Further, you hope the interviewee will speak frankly and openly—a difficult task if he fears publication or sees your questions as prying and embarrassing.

Survey researchers are fond of saying that an interviewer should build *rapport* with those being interviewed. This is important, but it can be overdone. Webster's dictionary defines rapport as an intimate or harmonious relationship. While a high level of intimacy can be fun(!), it can also lead one to say things that seem apt to please the interviewer. Many studies have shown a tendency to give "socially desirable" responses. In one case, a third of those who said they'd contributed to a Community Chest campaign actually hadn't.[5]

A hypothetical example will show some steps toward gaining cooperation. Assume that Dr. William Zap, an expert on fluoridation, lectures at a college in your town. Fluoridation is a hot issue locally, so your editor assigns you to interview the expert while he is in the area. The lecture itself may provide some information, but the editor wants you to dig deeper. You don't know Zap from Adam, and he's apt to be in a hurry. Thus, landing an in-depth interview may be hard.

Your first step is to learn as much as possible about fluoridation and Zap's own viewpoint. Unfortunately, you may often lack the time to do good background research. However, if you can swing it, a trip to the library may pay off. A first step there would be to check the card catalogue and read everything you can find that Zap has written. Also, a few brief interviews with the college's dental school faculty may clarify what position the lecturer is apt to take and why. Later, when you interview the lecturer, you can gain his respect by showing that you aren't just an uninformed reporter assigned to the story on a moment's notice.

Your visit to the dental school may well pay a further dividend. Perhaps Zap was a graduate school friend of Prof. John Smathers at the school. Smathers tells you that he and his wife will be hosting the Zap family for two days. He suggests that you interview Dr. Zap sometime after the lecture in the quiet of the Smathers' living room.

Thus reinforced, you might call Dr. Zap long distance to arrange the interview well in advance. You politely introduce yourself. Then you explain that your town is soon to have a referendum on fluoridation. Thus it would be most helpful if you could interview him about some specific questions not likely to be covered in his lecture.

On the phone, you might mention that many local people have expressed concern about possible long-term effects of fluoridation—the major topic of Zap's address. Thus a story on his work would be very newsworthy in your area. Comments of this sort, along with some mention of Zap's research about fluorine's effect on swine, will convince the speaker that you have done your homework and mean business. This, in turn, should help you get a foot in the door.

Before hanging up, you might mention your contact with Smathers. Assure Zap that the interview will not take more than perhaps an hour of his time (if you specify a time limit, abide by it—your interview is apt to go sour if Zap begins looking at his watch and chafing at the bit). If possible, offer to meet Zap at any time and place that fits his schedule.

Zap agrees to meet, but he says he'd rather arrange for a specific time after he arrives in town. You say OK, thank him and hang up.

The Zap family arrives in town on a Thursday morning. Zap gives his hour-long lecture at 1 p.m. You show up a little early and introduce yourself to the speaker as students file into the dental school auditorium. He remembers you and wonders if you'd be willing to come to the Smathers home at 10 a.m. Friday for the interview. He'll be visiting with dental students on Thursday afternoon, and he'll need some rest Friday morning. You agree and take careful notes on the lecture (something that is fairly easy since you have read several Zap articles and books, and few of his present comments are really new to you).

On Friday morning, your hours of careful study have provided several questions which you resolve to ask. It's a good idea to write these questions out so you'll be sure to cover your essential points. However, be sure your prepared questions don't limit flexibility if Zap mentions important things that you hadn't anticipated but ought to probe further.

The lecture probably has brought you up to date on fluoridation nationwide, so your questions might deal rather specifically with your town. There may be many retired folks in the area, and perhaps there is some doubt that fluoridation really pays where teeth have already begun decaying and coming out. Also, you wonder how local dentists might respond to anti-fluoridationists who look at the issue in political rather than medical-scientific terms. Such questions might give you an all important local angle.

It's a good idea to start the interview on a light-hearted personal note. Perhaps Smathers has mentioned that he and Zap worked their way through school by waiting table summers at a Las Vegas casino. Mentioning this may help put Dr. Zap at ease. (Don't mention the incident, of course, if you feel that it could prove embarrassing.)

Before getting down to brass tacks, you might put Dr. Zap at ease by assuring him that you will check your story with him (or with Smathers if he lacks the time) before it goes to print. Reporters often shy away from checking stories with news sources, feeling that this would allow outside control or censorship. Such concern may often be warranted, but it's generally wise to check back where statements are highly technical and could be misinterpreted. In years of working with scientists, one of the authors has found them very willing to check a story's accuracy without trying to rewrite it or change its basic thrust.

Social scientists often build rapport early in an interview by assuring the interviewee that he will remain anonymous. Journalists, of course, can seldom insure anonymity—they must generally attribute fully. On occasion they find they must avoid naming names to protect the source and pry a story loose. However, such "covering up" should be avoided where possible.

Building rapport can be difficult when one interviews a person very different from himself. In an interesting study, one researcher found it very hard to establish "common ground" with male homosexuals. He finally solved the problem by asking them to help compile a list of terms used by homosexuals. Interviewees found this interesting and felt at ease from that point on.[6]

Here are some further tips for building and maintaining rapport.

1. Open the interview with a few relatively innocuous, general, unembarrassing questions. Then ask your most important questions. That way you will cover most of the key points even if you should happen to be interrupted before finishing.

2. If you have embarrassing, sensitive questions to ask, place them as late as possible in the interview. Then you will get most of your information before leading the interview onto thin ice.

3. In doing a poll, soften sensitive questions about things like income by explaining that you are seeking income data about the community as a whole, not about any one person. Incidentally, survey experience indicates that questions about respondent income aren't as embarrassing as one might think. It seems to help if one indicates his income in approximate terms (perhaps checking a bracket like $5,000-$6,000 or $10,000-$11,000) rather than naming a specific figure.

4. Be alert for signs of nervousness like frowns or hand wringing. If you sense something is wrong, steer the conversation to more routine matters for a time to rebuild rapport.

5. Dress and act something like the person you are interviewing, but don't strain to do so. Your tone of voice should be conversational, yet businesslike. Some interviewers in India have failed because—being from a prestigious caste—they insist on wearing fancy clothes while talking with peasants. At the other extreme, however, one need not wear a tattered shirt and socks with holes when he interviews derelicts on Skid Row. The derelicts would feel there is something wrong—after all, no one really expects or wants a middle class reporter to act like a bum.

Having established rapport, you can move to your real purpose—gathering information. Here you need to consider several issues.

Phrasing and Asking Questions

Open-ended versus Structured Questions. *Open-ended* questions give the person being interviewed great freedom in answering. Take the question, "How successful would you say the United Nations has been during its nearly 30 years of existence?" One person might answer by noting the organization's lack of *military* might which has prevented it from quickly ending or avoiding wars in Korea, Bangla Desh, the Congo, the Middle East, etc. A second respondent could focus on positive results in *economic* development through the UN's Food and Agriculture Organization (FAO). And still another answer would probably touch on the very limited *cultural* exchange to date through the United Nations Educational, Social and Cultural Council (UNESCO).

One definition problem causes a lot of confusion when people discuss open-ended questioning. Open-endedness really refers to freedom and "ad libbing" in *answering* questions, not in *asking* them. (The asker does sometimes ad lib questions called *probes*, and we will discuss them later.) An inexperienced reporter should give especially careful thought to how he will word most questions, even open-ended ones. Then, unless he feels he is being misunderstood, he should stick with the same wording whenever he asks a given question. (In some cases, of course, ordinary citizens may fail to grasp a question that is perfectly clear to someone like a physicist. Then a change in wording may be in order as you move from a "lay" interviewee to a specialist.)

To the beginning interviewer, open-ended questions seem very attractive. They often open up topic areas which the reporter hadn't considered previously. They permit a respondent to let off steam. Also, they help the interviewer avoid the feeling that he is putting words in someone's mouth.

When it comes time to write his story, however, one who has used only very open-ended questions may feel rather frustrated. There are at least three reasons for this.

First, responses tend to be *incomplete.* In the United Nations example, the interviewee who talked mainly about military weakness has neglected to tell how he feels about economic development, just how important he thinks it is, and so on. We would have a very sketchy story unless we use some rather specific, structured questions to pin him down.

Second, open-ended questions often force the *interviewer* to decide where a respondent really stands. Our critic of the U.N. military posture may have hinted he dislikes the organization on balance, but he hasn't come right out and said so. More structured questions (for example, "All things considered, would you say the United Nations has been more successful than, less successful than, or about equal in effectiveness to the old League of Nations?") place the burden on the *respondent.* And in most cases, the respondent probably knows himself better than the interviewer knows him.

Third, *answers to an open-ended question often aren't comparable* as you move from one interviewee to another. In our United Nations example, the three persons were really talking about different issues (minimizing armed conflict, economic development and cultural exchange). It's rather meaningless—if not downright deceptive—to lump them together by asserting that one-third of the three-person sample favors the United Nations and two-thirds oppose it. This last statement implies the three people were thinking about the same topic when they were not. Structured questions would force each respondent to assess U.N. performance in all three areas. At the same time, a question or two asking the respondent to rank issues from most important to least important in assessing a world organization would reveal the relative importance of each issue in painting a total

TOOLS FOR GATHERING INFORMATION 125

picture. Used in this way, structured items can yield rich, meaningful data.

Some topics require more structured questioning than others. Assume, for example, that you are trying to determine how people feel about a new type of lawn grass. You can assume in advance that grass is evaluated on the basis of how quickly it comes up, speed of growth, cost, drought-resistance, beauty and so on. You may feel pretty safe in simply asking respondents to rate the grass variety on each listed criterion. (Of course, even here you would probably ask one or two open-ended questions to insure that you have covered all bases and to avoid the impression that you are putting words in people's mouths.)

Other issues like disarmament are more complex. Here one might visit informally and open-endedly with a few people to see just what dimensions they feel the problem has. Then, in later interviewing, fairly structured questions can get at such dimensions (avoidance of war, maintenance of national honor, savings from an end to the arms race, and so on).

The questions you ask should also depend partly on the person you are interviewing. An ordinary "man on the street" may be quite comfortable giving brief answers to structured questions. A company president or senator, on the other hand, will feel he "outranks" most reporters. He may feel badgered unless he seems to have at least some control over the interview situation. This doesn't mean a reporter should simply bow and lose control. It does call for a liberal sprinkling of open-ended questions and patience in probing.

Most interviews require a combination of open-ended and structured questions. It's common to lead with open-ended items, letting the respondent reveal his deeper thoughts and explore the issue. Then more structured questions permit him to state specifically where he stands on the issue in question.

Pollsters have developed a series of five question types in sequence that yield clear, meaningful results. The five types are as follows:

1. *General knowledge* (open-ended): What does fluoridation really mean to you?

2. *General opinion* (open-ended): What course of action, if any, do you think the people of Pinderville should take on fluoridation?

3. *Specific opinion* (structured): If a referendum were held today here in Pinderville, would you vote for adding fluorine to the drinking water or would you vote against it?

4. *Why* (open-ended): Why would you take the position you have just indicated?

5. *Intensity* (structured): How strongly would you say you favor (or oppose if so indicated in response to question 3) adding fluorine to Pinderville's drinking water? Very strongly, strongly, not very strongly, or not strongly at all?

A reporter will probably seldom use the above sequence in full because of the time required to complete all five questions on each of many points. However, he might often approximate it.

It's generally a good idea to ask one or two open-ended questions during an interview. In particular, one at the end will permit the interviewee to let off steam. One of the authors once helped conduct a mail survey in which respondents felt very strongly about the topic. Many answered the structured questions rather carelessly, then wrote a page or more of vigorous, sometimes profane prose in response to a closing open-ended question. This prose really helped little in interpreting the data. Yet respondents would have been very unhappy had they not had such a safety valve.

Neutral Wording. One way of putting words in an interviewee's mouth is to ask him loaded questions. Take the following:

> In light of the fact that we seem powerless, with no real chance of avoiding war among the Red hordes, would you favor this country's remaining completely neutral in the event of armed conflict between the Soviet Union and Red China?

"Loading" here takes several forms. To begin with, several highly emotional words are used (Red hordes, war, and powerless, for example). Such words are likely to influence the answer. No one is apt to advocate starting something which he is powerless to finish. Also, a phrase such as "the two largest Communist nations" would be more straightforward and matter-of-fact than "Red hordes."

Second, the question states one *premise* (America is powerless) while ignoring others. Many would argue the premise is false, and most would agree that it is "slanted" in an anti direction. The interviewee should generally have the chance to provide his own premises. It may often be important to see how people feel about the validity and importance of a particular premise. However, it's seldom if ever wise to put only one or a few selected premises in an opinion question.

Third, the question itself provides only one answer (remaining neutral). Respondents will often agree simply because it's easy to do so, they haven't thought of alternative answers, and to disagree might seem impolite. It's important to spell out all possible answers clearly and with equal force. (For example, "Would you favor this country's supporting China, supporting Russia or remaining neutral?")

When you spell out possible answers, be sure they are:

1. **Mutually exclusive.** That is, be sure that one will not feel inclined to say yes to two or more of the alternatives. It would be most confusing to ask whether one favors (a) providing military aid to China, (b) providing economic aid to China, or (c) providing humanitarian aid in the form of hospital missions. One could easily agree with two or more of these responses.*

2. **Exhaustive.** Be sure your specified alternatives exhaust the possibilities. Asking for a choice between increased and decreased troop commitments fails to allow for the possibility of no change. Such an omission can make the questioner look rather silly.

Clarity. In addition to being loaded, our question about America's stance regarding Sino-Soviet relations was vague. What, precisely, does remaining neutral mean? Providing no armed forces? Severing relations completely with both countries? Or pursuing improved relations with both Russia and China so long as we treat both equally? And what constitutes armed conflict? A border skirmish? Or a nuclear war? *Unless he words the question so as to remove such vagueness, a reporter may assume one meaning and the source another with neither party spotting the difference. Confusion and distortion can result.*

Even experienced researchers often use words that seem clear to them but not to respondents. During World War II, a noted political scientist found that the word "loyal" means different things to different people. His study inquired as to how many Germans living in the U.S. were loyal to America. Probing showed that about one-third of the sample tied loyalty specifically to citizenship (to them the question was irrelevant, since a German citizen could not be loyal to a non-German country). Still another third defined loyalty as referring to sentimental factors like forgetting the old country. Only about 10 per cent perceived the intended meaning—supporting rather than sabotaging the U.S. in the war effort.[7]

The best way to weed out such unclear words is to try out or pre-test your questions on a few people. This should reveal problems in time for you to correct them before you start interviewing in earnest. Even if he is interviewing just one person, a reporter might try questions out in advance on one or two people.

---

*Some novice interviewers provide a list of possible responses and permit the respondent to check as many as he agrees with. This approach seldom works, partly because respondents differ greatly in number of items checked. One can never tell whether a person really disagrees with unchecked items, or whether he simply lacks the patience to bother with them.

It's crucial to pre-test on people like the ones you will study later on. Obviously a pre-test focusing on college students may fail to uncover words that would later prove unclear when you interview in an urban ghetto.

Questions are often unclear because they are *double-barreled*. That is, they really lump two items into one. Take the question, "Should the U.S. withdraw all troops from Europe and pursue a policy of peace in the world?" Here are really two items (withdrawing troops and pursuing peace) rolled into one.

Double-barreled items often crop up where a questioner equates the two parts in his own thinking. He should avoid assuming that all persons interviewed will equate them. A few may, but some will probably answer the question about withdrawal, others the question about a policy of peace. Still others may get confused and answer only in a careless, haphazard way.

Unfortunately, a double-barreled question does not permit one to identify those who interpret it in one way rather than another in a story involving multiple respondents.

Filter Questions. It often makes little sense to ask a question of someone who is not equipped to answer it. Let's say that your city editor decides in 1970 that he'd like an in-depth piece on the impact that recent nation-wide steps to increase grass roots participation have had on local Democratic party affairs. He assigns you the story. You decide to interview a number of party workers at several levels—precinct, city, county and state.

Chances are many workers at the lower levels will have little awareness of party workings generally, to say nothing of the "unit rule" debate at the 1968 National Democratic Convention. (Under the unit rule, local opponents of a measure that passes a county Democratic convention are denied a voice when that county's delegation votes on the measure at a state-wide event. The same principle has traditionally held up to the national level.)

You may try to assess what impact repeal of the unit rule might have on your area's Democratic Party in the years ahead. Obviously, it makes little sense to ask for such as assessment where the respondent has never heard of the unit rule.

In dealing with an ignorant respondent, you really have two choices.

First, you can explain what the unit rule is, let him consider it for a moment, and then ask for his assessment of probable implications. Unfortunately, he is apt to give a vague, rather meaningless answer. After all, he has only a few minutes to think about the matter. The more complex the topic, the worse this problem would be.

Second, you can ask a *filter* question early in the interview to identify those who lack needed knowledge. A "general knowledge" filter question (#1 in the five-question sequence mentioned earlier) might take the form, "How would you define the term 'unit rule'?" If a person says the rule requires 75 per cent attendance for a quorum, you could avoid asking him to assess unit rule impact.

At times, you may even ask those with little knowledge to express opinions. Such opinions may not tell you much about the *issue* (possible impact of deleting the unit rule), but they do provide some information on *respondent biases* (a blast against innovations in party procedures, even if based on little information, suggests the respondent is a conservative at heart).

The filter question itself may yield newsworthy answers. In our example, widespread failure to define "unit rule" would strongly suggest that recent debates about party procedure have not affected workers in your area.

Far too many journalists and pollsters are content to find out whether people favor or oppose a course of action. They do not stop to ask how intensely they favor or oppose it, or how well *informed* they are about it.

Avoid asking someone to tell you whether he is well informed. It's rather embarrassing to admit ignorance, and many people won't do so. Questions should force him to *demonstrate* his level of information by providing some facts or a definition.

Reducing Embarrassment. Failure to answer correctly can prove embarrassing, and this may harm rapport. Fortunately, this problem is generally minor if the respondent feels at ease and is highly motivated to go on.

Questions can provide face-saving reasons for negative or wrong answers. This technique is often used in studies of newspaper or magazine readership. It's embarrassing to admit that you do not read Time, Newsweek or the New York Times. A question might be worded roughly as follows to soften the blow:

> Some people read Time, others Newsweek; and still others rely on their daily papers for the news. Do you happen to read Time every week?

This question implies that the daily newspaper and Newsweek provide news, so a person failing to read Time need not feel like a moron. The guy who reads Time will generally say yes, but a non-reader can answer no without much embarrassment.

Sometimes *indirect* questions reduce embarrassment. Take the query, "Do you now subscribe to Time or are you planning to do so in the near future?" People who are subscribing will be glad to tell you so. Those not now subscribing may lie about their future plans. However, the opportunity to do so gives them a face-saving alternative to claiming that they subscribe. Thus the question should give a pretty accurate estimate of current subscriptions.

Indirect questions of this sort can appear devious, and they can also be vague. It's wise to use them with extreme care.

Still a third approach is to imply that many people don't know about the unit rule, read Time Magazine, or the like. One author has described this as the "everybody's doing it" technique. In a humorous vein, he proposes the example, "Lots of people are killing their wives these days. Did you happen to kill yours in the last week or two?"

An "everybody's doing it" question can be dangerous. The wording is designed to encourage a yes answer, and it's assumed that this encouragement will offset possible embarrassment from such a response. It's often unclear, however, whether the two tendencies are equally strong and therefore cancel out.

Probing. Every now and then an interviewee will go off on a tangent. In discussing the performance of Nixon's administration, for example, he might launch into a tirade about Watergate, the 1964 campaign or the President's alleged 1952 slush fund.

As he continues on this theme, you should let him go within limits. What he has to say about these issues may be quite relevant to your story. Also, an abrupt effort to stop him and "move him back on the track" may irritate him—he wouldn't go on unless he has strong feelings that he wants to get off his chest.

There comes a time, however, when you must regain control of the interview. You probably don't have all day, and you really want answers to your questions, not just his.

The need to tread carefully may be especially great where a person feels very strongly about the topic discussed. Our hypothetical respondent who talked at length about Watergate, for example, is probably a strong anti-Nixon man. He's apt to go on pursuing tangents for some time unless the reporter waits for a pause and moves in with a question something like this:

> That's very interesting. Before I forget, however, let me clarify your feelings about Nixon's administration. Would you say that his performance has been very good, pretty good, good, fair or not good at all?

Such a question is called a *probe*. Its purpose is to get a respondent back on the topic or to obtain a more detailed, clear answer about something that has already been mentioned.

It's extremely important that probes be neutral. One may be tempted to play along with an interviewee's mood by saying something like this:

> What you said a while ago indicates that you feel Mr. Nixon's performance in the White House has been very poor. Is that a fair statement, or did I misinterpret?

A person can hardly say no to such a loaded question. Pollsters often avoid such problems by simply repeating a question that had been asked earlier but not answered clearly. While generally good, this may not work if you ask the same question two or three times without getting a satisfactory response. Then you'd need to reword the question to avoid badgering your respondent.

You may help rapport by telling your respondent that his comments are very interesting. Also, you might say that you would like to explore the respondent's own point further after you have made sure of where he stands on your particular question.

A skilled interviewer can *ad lib* his probe questions without fear that the wording or tone of voice will be leading. It's almost impossible to anticipate every probe that you'll need, so you cannot write out all possible probe questions in advance. Of course, you can make a note on how you will probe after questions that prove somewhat complex or sensitive.

Saying Goodby. When you have asked your last question, it's sometimes appropriate to ask the news source if he thinks of other things which might be covered. This helps insure that he'll get anything which bothers him off his chest. Also, it corrects any feeling on his part that he may have been badgered or given little chance to say his piece.

Make arrangements to call back if necessary. Then thank him for his time, and promise to send him a clipping of the resultant story unless you feel sure he'll see it routinely. You may want to promise that he can see the story when it's written *if* you feel it contains technical, easy-to-misinterpret statements. As noted earlier, however, letting the source check a story in final form is rare in the newspaper business.

This concludes our discussion of the interview setting itself. Much of what we have said to date stems from interviewing practice by public opinion pollsters. We now turn to some particular problems that a reporter faces.

Some Special Concerns of the Reporter

Like the pollster, a reporter must gain cooperation and obtain frank, accurate, precise answers. However, he does face some problems more often than a polltaker does, and these merit special mention.

First, he is usually in a hurry. He often has little or no time to do background research or polish and pre-test a list of questions. He must "think on his feet," following up leads as they come up without asking unclear or loaded questions.

There is no easy formula for success here. Experience helps. So does basic knowledge of the topic discussed. A reporter who is new in town will be ill-equipped to ask incisive questions about urban renewal or graft in city government.

Second, it's sometimes necessary to interview a hostile or reluctant news source. Lincoln Steffens, a "muckraking" reporter who wrote for McClure's and other magazines around the turn of the century, gained particular renown in this area.[8]

Much of Steffens' success stemmed from his skill in making political bosses and gangsters feel at ease. The famed muckraker was careful to avoid badgering or insulting news sources. He did several exposes on George Cox, a Cincinnati political boss. Yet he claimed to have made Cox feel "trusted" during interviews.[9] Even a hostile source will apparently cooperate if he respects a reporter's integrity, honesty and open-mindedness. It also helps, of course, if he appreciates the power of the reporter's paper.

Another interviewing must is *flexibility*. Even as a crusading reporter, Steffens reportedly worked hard to avoid "cynicism, blanket condemnations, or evasion of moral judgments. Such attitudes, he thought, ... could be shunned as obviously dangerous by informants."[10]

Steffens' own varied contacts with presidents, kings and crooks apparently helped him feel something in common with almost any news source. Talking with a person in his own language can do wonders in making that person feel at ease.[11]

Each news source has a unique personality. Lonesome folks want company, and they are apt to yearn for idle chit-chat that might anger a busy executive. Egotists sometimes feel a need to brag. A good reporter will humor such sources—letting them have their say as much as possible without completely losing control of the interview.

At times, Steffens had to resort to threats in seeking information, according to Stein. In fact, his mere presence was a kind of threat. Sources who knew him to be a knowledgeable insider—very apt to detect and pounce on gaps in a story—would seldom hold back.[12]

Threats to get information somewhere if a given source won't provide it should be used only as a last resort. Even when making

TOOLS FOR GATHERING INFORMATION 133

such a threat, a reporter may be able to give assurances that his story will do justice to all sides of a controversy. Such assurances reduce hostility. And when a news source is angry, he's apt to say what he feels he must and no more.

In one of the few studies dealing specifically with journalistic interviews, Bennett trained speakers to practice two types of evasion—hardline and softline—in addressing a high school journalism class. The hardline evader would abruptly refuse to answer a question with a remark such as "no comment" or "ridiculous." The softline speaker, on the other hand, would beat around the bush, maintaining a friendly manner and throwing out irrelevant comments.

Ratings of speakers showed that the young reporters generally did not realize their questions were being evaded systematically. Of course, Bennett's reporter "guinea pigs"—largely untrained high school seniors—were doubtless more gullible than experienced journalists. However, the research pointed up the need to be alert and persistent when dealing with a crafty, evasive news source.

In the same study, reporters who asked lots of questions tended to take few notes and made relatively few errors in their notes. Apparently the thoughtful, critical students prepared a few questions and vigorously sought accurate, complete answers to these. Also, taking word-for-word notes may have led to errors and left little time for follow-up questions to fill gaps and reveal distortions.[13]

In practice, reporters differ greatly in their note-taking. A few show remarkable speed in jotting down every comment verbatim. Others barely take down the high points and key words during a speech or interview, then go into seclusion for a few minutes to provide more detail from memory right after they leave the room.

It's widely felt that taking too many notes can make the respondent feel neglected since your eyes seldom meet his. On the other hand, a fair amount of writing may aid rapport because it subtly tells the respondent that his comments seem important and you're determined to quote him accurately.[14] There is very little concrete evidence to support or reject these claims.

Our discussion of interpretive reporting (see Chapter 12) suggests that an interview or speech story should not include too many verbatim quotes. A few will add a personal touch and emphasize key points. But a story that's much more than about one-third direct quotes generally does a poor job of interpreting statements—of putting them in perspective.

This line of reasoning suggests a need to take verbatim notes only on points that seem very important. A good reporter can spot a good quote coming when just a few words have left the speaker's mouth. He then moves his pencil into action, noting the quote in detail.

Most reporters develop a kind of shorthand for use in note-taking. Only a fortunate few actually take formal shorthand. However, most use a few shortcut symbols, including some from basic mathematics and logic. Reporters vary greatly as to the symbols which they find convenient. One of the authors makes much use of the following symbols.

Symbol	Translation Into English
/	That which comes after the slash mark is assumed to be true or given.
>	That which comes before the symbol is numerous, large, growing, expanding. (Strictly defined, that which comes before this mathematical symbol is larger than that which comes after. However, this meaning can be extended in writing interview and speech notes.)
<	The opposite of the symbol just above. The entities just before the symbol are small or few in number.
&	And
∼	No, none, never
A ⊃ B	If A is true, then B is also true.

Another common practice involves the shortening of words through several means. For example, it is very common for reporters to drop the vowels and sometimes other letters in words, producing in their notes things like tchr (teacher), brd (board), scl (school), spkr (speaker). Also they may use a type of phonetic spelling: B (be), B4 (before), no (know). Finally, it's common to write many abbreviations, standard and otherwise: educ (education), com (committee), comm (communication), pres (president), secy (secretary).

Use of such a system of note-taking is likely to produce something like this: M opnt sys elect me & sv mny. lts lk at rec. Wre $100,000 n dt. On rd 2 bnkrpsy. The reporter who developed this system then could produce the following in his story: "My opponent says 'Elect me and we'll save money.' Let's look at the record. We're $100,000 in debt, on the road to bankruptcy."

The point is this: If you don't know formal shorthand or notehand, develop your own system. Without such a system, the process of taking notes could be a duty you'll never be able to manage effectively.

To repeat, it's wise to get to a typewriter immediately after an interview. Where the comments gleaned were long and complex, one might retype his notes as nearly verbatim as possible. Unclear points—and points requiring further research and interpretation by the reporter—will come to light in this process. Also, main and subordinate points will fall into place, and the story itself will tend to take shape in the reporter's mind. In fairly brief, straightforward interviews, retyping notes before you write a story might take enough time to incur the wrath of an impatient city editor.

Tape recorders have become available at fairly reasonable prices. While sometimes handy in covering speeches, recorders create some problems in the interview setting itself. For one thing, they may make some respondents feel uncomfortable and reticent. On the other hand, they can help insure one that he will be quoted accurately. More study is clearly needed in this area.

When it comes to writing the interview or speech story, a recorder can also be a help in some cases but a hindrance in others. Certainly, the reporter doing an in-depth piece with no pressing deadline may improve his accuracy by replaying a tape to check for errors. However, someone writing a fairly substantial story in minutes will almost have to go from notes. He'll have no time to fool with a recorder.

Certainly, it seems unethical to bug a respondent's home or office—even if the recorder is a small one hidden on the interviewer's person. Where it's done, recording should be open and above board.

Telephone Interviewing. While the basic principles we have discussed apply to telephone interviewing, there are some clear differences between telephone and face-to-face.

For one thing, the phone interviewer must work quickly to establish rapport with his respondent. What's more, he must do this without the aid of a friendly smile and other nonverbal cues. He must explain why he's calling, what he'll be asking, and how much time he'll take right away. The respondent is apt to hang up if one pauses for idle chit-chat.

Second, the dictum that one should ask important questions early, valid in any interview, is especially important on the telephone. It's much easier to put down a receiver than to kick an interviewer out of one's home or office. (Where the respondent is highly interested and involved in the topic, of course, a phone interview can run a half hour or longer. Innovations such as the Wide Area Telephone Service make even lengthy interstate phone calls practical in some areas.)

Third, because of its brevity, a telephone conversation often affords little opportunity to follow up new leads. The interviewer must decide precisely what questions he'll ask before calling. Then he must generally be content to ask them, thank the respondent, and hang up.

A surprising number of clerks and secretaries fail to observe common courtesy in answering telephones. For example, many will not quickly identify themselves and their organizations. Others will demand a lengthy description of the caller and his mission before putting a call through to the boss. A reporter must learn to accept such lapses in good grace—and to avoid having them himself.

Sampling. Very often, a reporter wants to interview a few people and apply his findings to a larger sample or population. A specialized field of study called *statistical inference* can help him do this. While statistical inference is beyond the scope of this book, a few comments seem in order.

First, the size of a sample, while important, is not as crucial as many people think. Some observers ridicule the Nielsen Ratings for television programs because these ratings stem from no more than one or two dozen homes in a city the size of Cleveland, Ohio. Such complaints are groundless. Nielsen generally seeks to draw conclusions about the nation as a whole, not about Cleveland alone. And interestingly enough, statistical formulae prove that required sample size remains almost the same as population size increases once you get past a population of roughly a half million.

Certainly a sample of only a dozen people interviewed for a man-on-the-street story permits almost no conclusions about the larger population—no matter how carefully the sample is chosen. However, a well chosen sample of two or three hundred can sometimes yield meaningful results. (The precise sample size required varies greatly from case to case, and it depends on considerations that we can't cover here.)

A reporter often samples in a very general, crude sense. For instance, he may seek to get the feel of how the state legislature feels on a new bill, but he lacks the time to contact every state legislator. If he's sharp, he will try to reduce bias by insuring that all major groups in the legislature—the Democrats and Republicans, the farmers and city slickers, the rich and poor—are well represented.

In much the same vein, a campus reporter will have to watch himself in interviewing coeds. His natural tendency may be to talk with cute gals and ignore the plain Janes. Unfortunately, beauty probably correlates with gregariousness, which relates to many issues that a campus reporter is apt to study. That is, gregarious gals (heavy daters and belongers) may differ from bookworms in their views on Greeks, campus uprisings and other topics.

Location is also a factor when interviewing. A person who talks only to students entering the union building may get an overdose of heavy daters, grill hounds, protestors and other atypical groups. Work only around the library, on the other hand, and you're apt to wind up with too many bookworms and all-A students.

Reputable pollsters generally turn thumbs down on mail surveys. It's impossible to tell just who has filled out a mail questionnaire (Mom may do it even though Dad was designated in the sample). Failure to understand a question generally becomes apparent in a personal interview, but not in a mail survey. And perhaps most important, roughly 5 to 25 per cent of those in a general population sample will usually bother to fill out and return the document. That leads to bias because the few who respond tend to differ greatly from the many who don't (in particular, responders tend to feel strongly about the issue, and to be well-educated). Therefore, results cannot be applied with confidence to a larger population.

In rare cases, a mail survey may work well because respondents are very highly motivated to fill out a questionnaire and return it. This holds where a population is highly specialized (for example, the General Motors Board of Directors) and the topic is important to them (the corporation profits tax).

As we've seen, one is generally well-advised to do some background reading before he talks with potential news sources. We now turn to some general guidelines useful in deciding what and where to read.

Some Useful Resource Materials

The library can be a pretty forbidding place to the college freshman or cub reporter who does not know where to start looking.[15]

To begin with, it's easy to get discouraged when you begin with a subject catalogue. Most large libraries do have a card catalogue listing major books and publications by topic. However, such listings tend to be gross—each one with a large number of entries. For example, the library at one major university has 760 separate entries under the heading "taxation," enough to swamp a poor reporter with but a few hours in which to bone up before covering a speech on taxation.

Things would probably fall into place much more quickly if one were to call a local certified public accountant and ask for the title of a recent book summarizing, in lay language, major issues in taxation. With the growth of paperback publishing, such books have come out by the thousands. Very few topics are so obscure or technical that no author has treated them in a brief, readable way.

Chances are such a recent book will have a bibliography with titles of many related books and articles. As he reads further, the newsman will find himself pursuing certain aspects of the topic because they tie into local circumstances—and because they simply seem interesting. Such narrowing, in turn, will help single out other materials.

If he proceeds far enough, the researcher will find that each new article or book refers largely to items he's already read. This gives a feeling of mastery over the subject matter—and it probably means the reporter is set to interpret comments well and ask intelligent questions.

Perhaps the most useful single library resource for an observer with little specialized expertise is the *Readers' Guide to Periodical Literature.* The Readers' Guide indexes articles in over 100 familiar and oft-used magazines. Articles are listed by subject and by author.

The Readers' Guide comes out in paperback twice a month. Issues are eventually "cumulated" into one alphabetical list covering longer periods of time and bound into hardcover books.

A somewhat similar publication, very helpful in covering political and current-events topics, is the *New York Times Index.* Published twice each month and cumulated into a single volume at the end of the year, this publication gives thorough coverage befitting the Times as a "newspaper of record."

A single speech may appear in the Index under six or eight different alphabetized subject headings. Also, the Index is very useful in checking spelling of new nations, sports records, the membership of Senate committees and other facts which may seem obscure but could be crucial in a given situation.

A somewhat less detailed but very useful resource on current events is *Facts on File,* a weekly digest of world news found in most major libraries. This digest covers news under such headings as World Affairs, National Affairs, Finance, Economy, Science and Education. Also found are events in the arts, books published, theater openings, key obituaries and the latest in sports.

A few more specialized reference sources are the following:

1. Almanacs such as *The World Almanac and Book of Facts* give a wide variety of facts including chronological lists of major events for

TOOLS FOR GATHERING INFORMATION 139

a given year, population and election statistics, and even distances between major cities. These volumes occupy an important place in most newspaper morgues or reference libraries.

2. The voluminous *Dictionary of American Biography* has scholarly, objective accounts of major happenings in the lives of the great and the near-great. Another possibility is *Who's Who in America*.

3. *Encyclopaedia Britannica* is generally thought to be the most comprehensive of all encyclopedias. Here experts write in a readable yet scholarly way about topics ranging from the Civil War to cancer.

4. Publications of the *United States Bureau of the Census* surely qualify among the most potentially useful but often neglected volumes in any library. Of particular value is the *Statistical Abstract of the United States,* published annually with summary figures on the industrial, social, political and economic organization of the country. *Statistical Abstract* deals with the current year, a companion publication called *Historical Statistics* with the past. Other Census Bureau publications of interest are the *County and City Data Book,* with figures on local areas, annual estimates of population and economic trends, and many specialized reports based on the national census conducted every 10 years.

5. The *Dictionary of American History* is a six-volume publication reporting on a wide variety of topics—many generally not associated with history. Entries include "baseball" and "tin pan alley." Articles are concise and have brief, helpful bibliographies.

6. John Bartlett's *Familiar Quotations* is one of several collections of its type which can help one spice up a story. Bartlett's is arranged chronologically by author and has an excellent alphabetized keyword index.

The above are but a few helpful maps for picking one's way through the confusing jungle of published material now available. In addition, specialized indices such as *The Education Index* and *Sociological Abstracts* abound.

In the newsroom itself and away from the library, perhaps the most often-used reference volumes are the city directory and that old standby—the telephone directory. The phone book is often the more accurate of the two in spelling names and keeping addresses up to date, but many persons have unlisted phone numbers. In these cases, the city directory is quite necessary. It lists residents in order of street addresses—a highly useful feature if the reporter has only a last name and an address, or if he has only a name common to several residents. The city directory also may well list residents' occupations.

Summary and Conclusions

Asking questions and recording answers seem at first glance like rather routine, mechanical tasks. Reporters tend to take the interview for granted as a way of getting information. However, studies show that interviewing is a delicate tool, with answers depending about as much on the question asker as on the answerer.

The first step in preparing for an interview is to learn about the topic and the person being interviewed. This helps gain the respondent's respect by showing that you aren't just another hack writer. Also, careful preparation helps you control the conversation so you will leave with the important questions asked.

It's important to be polite and considerate. The first minute or two of interviewing time generally focuses on making a respondent feel at ease. A little light banter and a clear explanation of why you are seeking the interview will help here.

Several tips on question wording should help the body of the interview go smoothly.

First, strike a balance between *open-ended* and *structured* questions. Questions should be open enough so a person can give his unique slant. At the same time, they should be structured enough to guard against gaps in your information once you get to the typewriter. The right balance depends partly on the topic and the person interviewed.

Second, word questions clearly and in a matter-of-fact way. Unclear items may yield no meaningful answers at all. Loaded, emotional ones can almost force a person to express a pro or anti position, regardless of how he actually feels.

Third, be alert to points that need further exploration as they come up. Politely ask *probe* questions to get the interview onto the specific topic that you want to cover, while also leaving room for some meandering.

Note-taking practice varies among reporters. It's important to take careful notes while also looking up fairly often at your respondent. Typing a full set of notes immediately after you leave an interview can pay, especially where statements are involved or vague.

It's important to make sure that you interview a representative sample of citizens, councilmen or legislators if you want to say anything about the views of these bodies. Sampling is a specialized area of study. However, common sense can often help insure that a reporter talks to a fairly representative sample of the population he's interested in.

TOOLS FOR GATHERING INFORMATION   141

In doing background research, it's often helpful to start with such reference sources as *The World Almanac and Book of Facts, Facts on File* and the *New York Times Index*.

LIST OF REFERENCES

1. Cantril, Hadley, *Gauging Public Opinion* (Princeton, N.J.: Princeton University Press, 1944), p. 109.

2. Hyman, Herbert H., "Problems in the Collection of Opinion Research Data," *American Journal of Sociology* 55:362-70, 1950.

3. Ray, Michael L., and Webb, Eugene J., "The Kennedy News Conferences and Question Duration Effects," *Science* 153:899-901, 1966.

4. Hyman, Herbert H., *Interviewing in Social Research* (Chicago: University of Chicago Press, 1954), pp. 83-99.

5. Parry, H.J., and Crossey, Helen M., "Validity of Responses to Survey Questions," *Public Opinion Quarterly* 14:61-80, 1950.

6. Cited in Eugene J. Webb, and Jerry R. Salancik, "The Interview and the Only Wheel in Town," *Journalism Monographs*, no. 2, November 1966, p. 33.

7. Cited in Robert L. Kahn and Charles F. Cannell, *The Dynamics of Interviewing* (New York: John Wiley and Sons, 1957), p. 141.

8. Stein, Harry, "Lincoln Steffens: Interviewer," *Journalism Quarterly* 46(4):727-36, Winter 1969.

9. *Ibid.*

10. *Ibid.*

11. *Ibid.*

12. *Ibid.*

13. Bennett, Roger E., *A Study of Variables in the Interviewing Process,* M.S. Thesis, Ohio University School of Journalism, 1970.

14. Webb and Salancik, *op. cit.*, p. 37.

15. For a useful discussion of resource materials, see Mona McCormick, *Who-What-When-Where-How-Why Made Easy* (Chicago: Quadrangle Books, 1971).

CHAPTER 8

The Specialist at Work: Beat Reporting

The reporter who covers a beat is a specialist who has a somewhat greater responsibility than the general assignment reporter.

Both kinds of reporters must have the same devotion to accuracy and speed, of course, but the beat reporter goes beyond the basics. He covers the same general area day by day, and he must become an expert in his field if he is to cover it effectively. The city hall reporter, for example, probably knows more about city government than most of the people actually employed by it.

A general assignment reporter, on the other hand, covers just about anything; most of his work is specifically assigned by his editor. The job may be dull one day and excitingly impossible the next. It's a perfect job for gaining a liberal education. The general assignment reporter, in a week's time, may find himself covering speeches, obituaries, the weather, dinner meetings, police news, political rallies, labor relations, elections and—of course—people, ranging from congressmen and governors to scientists and industrialists to the man on the street. The job may even include coverage of his newspaper's promotional gimmicks, such as one less than fondly remembered by one of the authors—in which he had to sort through children's entries of names for the zoo's new baby kangaroo and pick a winner.

General assignment and beat reporters differ in the scope of their coverage; there also is a difference in how they go about their duties. Whereas the general assignment reporter is usually told just what stories to cover, the beat man has a specific day-to-day assignment—responsibility for his beat and all that happens on it. The editor does not give him a list of possible stories; the reporter should know his beat better than his editor does.

In other words, the beat reporter must necessarily exercise more news judgment than his general assignment colleague. The beat reporter must weigh the importance of the possible stories from his beat and attempt to cover everything newsworthy in descending order of importance. It may be excusable for him to miss some small items, but he cannot omit any significant story.

Although beginners sometimes break into a beat rather quickly, it is customary to assign the beats to experienced people, in line with their own interests and aptitudes. Someone who finds court procedures boring is not likely to be given the courthouse beat; the reporter who does not enjoy the uncertainty and unplanned excitement of police news should not be assigned there.

Once a reporter is assigned to a beat, he is likely to stay there for a substantial period of time, hopefully several years at least. It takes time and experience to learn the intricacies of a beat, and a newly-assigned beat man is not apt to be effective immediately. Even if he does not miss any major stories, his coverage will not be as knowledgeable as it will be after months or years on the beat.

The beat reporter, even more than the general assignment man, must be able to demonstrate a unique competence as he goes about his work. Once a reporter has mastered accuracy, speed and newspaper style, the actual writing of the story is often the easiest part. *Getting* the story—at least a good story—is what in many cases takes initiative, nerve, patience, quick thinking and, sometimes, a strong stomach.

Two key points can sum up what the beat reporter must learn before he can cover his beat competently:

1. He must know his beat—its functions, procedures, limits and relationship with the overall community structure.

2. He must know the news sources on that beat—who they are, what they do, what they're like and how to handle them effectively.

The first point will be discussed more specifically as we examine several of the beats later in this chapter.

Point 2 is more important than it may seem at first glance. The reporter must, of course, know who holds what position within his beat. He should know as many people as possible by sight and should go out of his way to circulate among them and cultivate them—even those who can rarely provide information, since they may someday hold the key to a major story.

Ideally, a reporter knows *everyone* on his beat, from the custodian to the man at the top. However, until he has handled the beat for a long period of time, this perfection is not likely. The reporter will naturally begin by getting acquainted with the most newsworthy people on the beat; if he covers city hall, his first contacts should be the mayor, department heads and councilmen. As he gains time on the beat, he will get to know more and more people.

Eventually, it will be vital for the reporter to cultivate the friendship of the "little" people on his beat. Chances are, he will have to get to know some of them fairly early, just to get past them to see the top brass. Most of the time the people in the lower echelons of the beat won't be able to provide stories, but they are often valuable in giving tips which *lead* to the important stories. Many a big story has originated from a whispered comment: "Why don't you ask the mayor about . . . ?"

The reporter's knowledge of his sources and his relationship with them will have a strong bearing on how well he covers his beat. After all, he will spend as much time with them, in their own bailiwicks, as he will with his own colleagues in the newsroom; the beat reporter cannot do his job from the security of his own desk.

Handling one's news sources can become a study in amateur psychology. The reporter's job is to get information, as accurately and completely as possible, and he must know how to deal with his sources if he is to accomplish his duties. This is not to say he should lose his own personality by going into an act or by being a hypocrite; nevertheless, news sources differ considerably and must often be handled differently.

Suppose you find that a certain city official is reluctant to reveal information to reporters. Perhaps he has been irritated too often by garbled stories, inaccurate quotations, or what he considers unjustified editorial criticism of his office, and he has decided it is safer to say as little as possible to the press. If you want to change his attitude and turn him into a valuable news source, one approach would be to spend some time every day or so merely chatting with him—no note-taking, no probing, no stories. Eventually he may be tempted to "test" you by offering a relatively minor news item about his department. At that point, you should take great pains to write the little story as accurately and inoffensively as possible; it should not be difficult. A few instances like this and the reluctant news source will learn to trust you and will see to it that any important news about his office is directed your way. He may even become so confident in your fairness and ability that he will not be offended if you find it necessary to write a story which reflects somewhat adversely on his realm.

Another method of dealing with a specific kind of news source requires that the reporter have a retentive memory, at least on a short-term basis. Some sources who seem to enjoy talking with a reporter, even when they know he is going to write a story about what they say, freeze up if the reporter takes out his pencil and paper and starts scribbling voluminous notes. Such sources then slow down to a stilted, weigh-every-word pace. In these cases, the experienced reporter keeps the pencil and paper in his pocket. He talks with the news source until he has gained the necessary information, then leaves and seeks a quiet corner where he can quickly jot down the details before he forgets them.

Still another way to handle a news source might be termed the "hard sell." It can best be applied to persons holding elective office who adopt a high-handed attitude toward a specific reporter or the press in general. One of the authors recalls a mayor who favored a reporter for one newspaper to the exclusion of all other newsmen; no other reporters got major stories from the mayor's office, and important announcements were timed for release to the advantage of the favored reporter's deadlines. The author, working for the other newspaper, informed the mayor that the practice would have to stop or the mayor's name would no longer appear in that newspaper unless it was something unfavorable—and a mayoralty election was not far away. Politicians are quite image-conscious, particularly around election time, and the situation improved. (The mayor lost the election anyway.) Purists might call this practice resorting to threats, and in a way it is, but temporary hard-nosed tactics are sometimes necessary to permit a complete, balanced coverage in the long run.

News sources sometimes conveniently forget to inform reporters when a newsworthy event happens. A truly observant reporter will be able to get some of these stories anyway. The mayor and councilmen in a small city held an "executive session" one night and did not tell the city hall reporter about it. But when the reporter passed the council chambers the next morning he noticed cigar ashes piled high in several ashtrays. He confronted the mayor and pried loose a major story about the otherwise secret meeting.

One of the dangers of beat reporting is that the reporter is bound to become friendly with some of the people he is covering day after day. (The good reporter also makes his share of enemies.) Although the reporter may take a dim view of some of his sources, he probably will like and respect a number of others. This personal contact and its ramifications can test a reporter's fairness and objectivity to the limit. The conscientious reporter is aware of this danger and learns to cope with it.

What about "off-the-record" information? Every reporter, particularly on the beats, will face this problem. Sooner or later, one of your sources will respond to your question by saying, "I'll tell you all about that, if you'll keep it off the record." There are three reasonable ways to deal with such a situation:

1. If immediate publication of the information would jeopardize something obviously worthwhile (such as national security, a pending police investigation or a surprise party for an honored citizen), the reporter should respect the request. He should accept the information off the record to keep himself informed in preparation for the time when it can be *on* the record.

2. If the news source can and will promise that you will be given the green light to use the information *before* it is given to any other media, you may decide to keep it off the record temporarily.

3. If the off-the-record request is for the bureaucratic convenience of the official himself (you can soon learn to tell when this is the case), you can ask him not to give you the information—you'll try to get it elsewhere *on* the record.

In any case, once the reporter gives his word to keep something off the record or to respect a confidence, he *must* honor the agreement. The reporter who breaks confidence with a news source probably will never again receive significant information from that source and others. Generally, it is better to lose a story than to risk the loss of your effectiveness with your sources in the future.

What about the "don't use my name" request? Ideally, the information in a news story should be attributed to an identified source, but in practice it is customary occasionally to attribute information to "a high-ranking government official" and the like. If you trust the veracity of your news source, and if you see a good reason for his anonymity (the likelihood of trouble from his superiors, for example), it is generally permissible to hedge on the attribution. Many good stories have resulted from the reporter's prerogative of granting anonymity to his sources, and many states have "shield laws" (see Chapter 11) which make it difficult to require a reporter to reveal sources of information. However, unspecific attribution should not become a standard practice; it should be weighed carefully on its merits in each case.

Some news sources may try to run your business (since they may think you are trying to run theirs). Almost everyone, qualified or not, considers himself knowledgeable about what a newspaper should or should not do. Remember that you and your editors, based on journalistic knowledge and experience, will make the decisions about what is published and how it is written. It is up to you to make your sources understand this very clearly.

Integrity plays a major role in the success of the beat reporter. The reporter should be an honest man, even if he must occasionally deal with someone who isn't. Honesty may not win you the affection of some news sources, but it is likely to win their respect—and that is even more important than affection when it comes to doing your job.

Beat Organization

Beats constitute specialization. The bigger the newspaper, the bigger the staff (generally), and consequently the bigger the opportunity for specialization.

The small town daily paper may have a couple of general assignment reporters and a police beat reporter. A somewhat larger paper may add a city hall reporter and a combination courthouse-county government reporter. Increasing in size, the latter may be split into separate beats, with further addition of a schools or education beat and a suburban beat.

When one reaches the huge metropolitan newspaper, the beat specialization takes on extreme diversity. Specialist reporters may cover science, medicine, the arts (or only one of the arts), space, agriculture, religion, social change. The individual newspaper expands and creates its beat list in relation to what it thinks best serves its readers.

Bear in mind again that most beat reporters start their careers as general assignment reporters. If you are interested in science writing and hope to become a specialist in that field, don't be discouraged if you have to spend some time as a general assignment reporter first.

Let's look at a few of the specific beats to be found on most newspapers of moderate size. The structure, however, can vary considerably even among papers with similar circulations.

Police

As pointed out in an earlier chapter, a police beat reporter is concerned to a large extent with spot news—accidents, fires, crime—involving cold facts about occurrences.

Contrary to the stereotype of bygone days, the police reporter does not (or should not) spend most of his time hanging around the police station. Nothing much, beyond the recording of reports, really happens there. Of course the reporter spends some time checking the day's reports and chatting with police officials; but the information for many of his stories can be obtained by telephone, and the good police reporter does not have to call the station to find out everything that happens—in many cases, the police call him.

Furthermore, he does not chase police cars to the scene of every accident or zoom after every fire truck. He goes to the big ones—the ones that may justify more detailed, personalized, knowledgeable coverage than a police report would offer. (And contrary to legend, few reporters nowadays conduct their own investigations of crimes.)

Most police reporters have a series of telephone "checks" which they make at intervals throughout their shifts. They routinely call the list of numbers to determine whether anything is happening—city police, state police, fire department, sheriff's office, coroner and the like. In this way, many of the small stories can be taken care of, and the reporter is alerted to major stories within a reasonable time. If something big is happening, he leaves the office and goes to the scene.

An experienced reporter, well-known and respected by police, often is notified and invited to accompany officers on an important task, such as a vice raid. This is not a result of the reporter always making the police "look good"—rather, it is a matter of mutual respect. After all, no decent reporter deliberately sets out to make anyone look good—or bad.

Beyond the basic checks and keeping track of routine stories (and there are many of these in the course of a police reporter's day), he must often cover a big story, such as a multiple murder or a huge fatal fire. At that point, much of his routine work is taken over by a general assignment reporter.

Since many modern readers want more than spot news, a good police reporter will write a number of in-depth stories from his beat. Perhaps the city's traffic accident rate shows a tremendous increase for the current year; the reporter may write a comprehensive story trying to determine why. Perhaps politics is riddling the police department and is causing morale problems and inefficiency; a story should reveal the background, the causes, the implications, the possible solutions.

Excitement, of course, is a relative phenomenon, but most newsmen would agree that the police beat is more exciting than most. The police reporter cannot plan his day by listing the events he will cover; he can't say, "I have to cover a fire an hour from now"—the fire hasn't started yet, and nobody knows it will. The reporter may be enjoying a cup of coffee one minute and be speeding across the city two minutes later to the scene of a murder.

This uncertainty appeals to many reporters; to others it does not. Furthermore, the police beat (like police work itself) is apt to center on the unfortunate and undesirable elements of life, and this often makes the beat intolerable for some kinds of people. Not all reporters will find satisfaction in viewing charred buildings, mangled bodies or handcuffed suspects as a day-to-day routine for a long period of time. Your experience with police stories as a general assignment reporter should let you know whether the police beat itself would be your cup of tea.

City Government

The kind of government a city has—and the kind of people running it—will have a vital influence on the desirability of that city as a place to live. But far too few citizens show more than a minimal interest in government below the national level. Many do not inform themselves sufficiently to vote intelligently, and many others do not vote at all.

Part of the blame for municipal apathy can be attributed to civic laziness, but part might well be directed at city hall reporters who do not take the trouble to make their beat interesting to the readers.

The reporter who merely skims the surface and reports the obvious can thoroughly bore his readers. Yes, it is important to report zoning changes, a routine city council agenda and personnel appointments—but these are relatively unexciting except to the people directly involved.

City Hall can be dull indeed, if one does not view it with perspective and attempt to zero in on the issues. It is up to the city hall reporter to interest his readers, and it can be done.

City government, even in smaller cities, has become relatively complex. The reporter must understand the intricacies of his beat—the organizational structure of the city and its operation. He must learn who does what, and how. He must know how to look at the city budget and decipher it in a meaningful way for his readers. He must be aware of changes in city government's approach—new functions and services, streamlining, modernization—and let the public know about them.

And, beyond the government's operation itself, the reporter must be conscious of political manifestations which influence that operation.

This political side of the beat, with the conflict which characterizes politics, also can be complex. If the mayor is Republican and the city council Democratic, the conflict is obvious. But even if it is a one-party city, the cliques and factions within a party can be as tension-ridden as the more usual interparty strife. (Political factionalism tends to be individual and personal in small cities but is likely to be based, in large cities, on bureaucratic party structures.)

The organization of a fairly typical city government might be something like this:

I. Executive branch—the mayor and his staff
   A. Department of Public Works
      1. Bureau of Streets
      2. Bureau of Water
      3. Bureau of Sewage Treatment
      4. Bureau of Engineering
   B. Department of Public Safety
      1. Bureau of Police
      2. Bureau of Fire
      3. Bureau of Health
   C. Department of Public Property
      1. Bureau of Parks
      2. Bureau of Recreation
      3. Bureau of Public Buildings
   D. City solicitor (the city's legal office)
   E. City personnel office
   F. Assessments and zoning
   G. City treasurer and/or tax collector
   H. City controller (the financial director)

II. Legislative branch
   A. City Council
   B. City clerk's office

III. Authorities and commissions: These groups, tied with varying looseness to city government itself, are semi-independent organizations concerned with specific functions, such as parking, urban renewal, human relations, public housing, airport and planning.

Not all of these offices need be checked daily, once the reporter has enough contacts to be reasonably sure of not missing anything of consequence. The reporter probably will make daily checks of the mayor, department heads, some bureau chiefs, the city clerk and councilmen. Beyond these, the reporter will be guided by what he knows is happening within the normally less newsworthy offices.

The point is this: The city hall reporter is responsible for everything on his beat (except for the functions covered by the police reporter). It is up to him to build up control of the beat to the point where he misses nothing newsworthy, whether spot news, in-depth reports on trends within the government or accounts of political turmoil affecting the city.

County Government

Covering county government is similar in many ways to the city hall beat. The reporter operates in much the same way—understanding the government structure and learning who the important news sources are. Like the city government reporter, he spends some time each day going from office to office, gathering stories.

The principal difference is in the emphasis of county government itself. Its functions generally differ somewhat from those of city hall. The county may not have its own water and sewage treatment facilities, for example, relying instead on the individual municipalities within its borders for those services.

Many counties, depending on the states in which they are located, will have such divisions as health departments, solicitors, road maintenance crews, planners, law enforcement (generally the sheriff's office), engineers and assessment offices—and often these will overlap the jurisdiction of their municipal counterparts.

However, rather than a single chief executive (mayor) and legislators (city councilmen), the county is more apt to have a board of commissioners or supervisors, who act as both administrators and legislators.

In many cases, county government seems less active and perhaps more archaic than city government, and the county may exert less direct influence on the citizen than does the government of the municipality in which he lives. For this reason, and because county government often operates from the courthouse, one reporter sometimes has the responsibility for covering both county government and the courts.

Nonetheless, if county government does need to be modernized and made more relevant to public needs, it would seem that full, fair coverage is necessary to promote reader awareness of what the county does, how well it performs and what it should be doing.

Suburbs

Not too long ago, many of our suburbs were semi-rural areas with a lot of open space, somewhat in limbo between the parent city and the overall county government.

Now, however, suburbs have become giant barnacles clustered around most cities; they are built-up, complex and semi-municipal in their own right. Many are almost self-sufficient, particularly in the sense of municipal government. Some have their own business communities, their own public services (streets, water, sewers, police, fire departments).

Suburban residents may be considerably less diverse than those within the city limits; it is felt that suburbanites as a group may be better educated and more civic-minded than the general public. If so, it is quite possible that suburban reporting might justifiably be a bit more detailed and technical than coverage of other beats.

There has been a growth of full-fledged suburban newspapers which give a local flavor to complement the metropolitan papers read by most suburbanites. And, some city newspapers publish special editions aimed at suburban readers.

Most city papers, however, assign reporters to cover suburban activities, often centering on suburban government. Not only does the suburban resident want to know about the city's news—he also wants coverage of some kind for his own home area.

The suburban beat reporter can find peculiar problems on his job. For one thing, suburban government often is fairly new, and its leaders have not become accustomed to being news sources; they may be quite honest but nevertheless more hesitant to reveal the suburb's "business" to reporters. It probably will take more persistent digging to get important stories.

Furthermore, a newspaper in a medium-sized city may assign one reporter to cover all the city's suburbs (or neighboring small towns). The mere logistics of physically visiting each suburb's governmental offices on a day-to-day basis can be virtually impossible. It amounts to the reporter's having a half dozen economy-sized beats rolled into a single huge one.

If a city's suburbs are sufficiently large and news-producing, the newspaper may establish bureaus in the most important ones. A bureau might consist of a rented office with desk, typewriter, telephone and reporter. That reporter would then be responsible for his suburb and would phone his stories to the newspaper.

Courts

Just as judicial organization varies among the states, so does court coverage vary among newspapers.

As pointed out earlier, some newspapers assign one reporter to cover "the courthouse"—including both the county courts and county government. Often that same reporter, if the paper has no beat man at the federal building, will also be responsible for federal court when it is in session. Perhaps he also will cover municipal court sessions if he thinks a case will eventually make its way into the county courts. The reporter who is responsible for all of these areas has his work cut out for him.

In larger cities, this conglomeration of responsibility is more likely to be divided among several reporters.

All beat reporters must become experts in their own areas, but the court reporter probably requires more technical knowledge than most of the others. The law, of course, is not written for easy understanding by laymen; court proceedings and terminology are not well-understood by the general public. The court reporter must translate documents from "legalese" into ordinary English. He must write accurate, interesting news stories about sometimes dull-appearing, complex court actions. He must be able to talk with lawyers and judges and understand what they are saying.

The reporter, furthermore, must know the law itself. He cannot approach every trial or every document without any knowledge of the pertinent law. If he is covering a voluntary manslaughter trial, for example, he should know how that differs from murder and from involuntary manslaughter, and he should know the applicable penalties.

The court reporter (and the police reporter) should have a good understanding of what is involved in prejudicial pre-trial publicity—and what constitutes contempt of court.

As on other beats, the court reporter must cultivate his sources and learn who is most likely to have the answers to his questions. Getting to know people can help a reporter on any beat. One of the authors, even though he was only substituting on the court beat, gained a private interview with a man who minutes before had been convicted of murder; the story resulted primarily because the author knew the deputy sheriff who was escorting the prisoner back to his cell.

Schools

A few years ago, a newspaper that assigned a reporter specifically to the city's schools might have called this "covering the school board." And that's just about all it was—covering the school board as a government unit in charge of the school district.

Many papers have expanded their horizons in this area. The school board beat has become the education beat, and the reporter does not confine himself to the administrative aspects of the schools. He writes, in addition, stories about developments in education itself, what teachers and students are doing and innovations in the classrooms.

It has become, for many reporters, a three-sided beat:

1. The education reporter must be concerned with the government side of the schools—what the board is doing in regard to budgets, taxes, hiring, policies and politics. This means going to school board meetings and keeping in touch with individual board members.

In some cities, the school district has a larger budget and employs more people than city government. Schools are big business and, unfortunately, in some areas they are "big politics" as well. Reporters are often surprised to find that patronage and nepotism can be so prevalent in an educational structure, particularly when many schools are governed by unpaid and "nonpolitical" school board members.

2. The reporter must talk frequently with the people who are actually operating the school district on a daily, full-time basis—the superintendent of schools and the business manager. They are concerned with applying board policies and with the overall functioning of the schools, the superintendent from the educational side and the business manager from the nonprofessional side (maintenance, purchasing and the like).

3. The reporter will have to go to the principals and the teachers to learn what is really going on in specific schools and within the classrooms themselves. Some news stories will originate there, but the reporter will often find a myriad of ideas for feature stories at this level.

Education constitutes a complex beat whose nature provides more opportunity than usual for features and in-depth, interpretive stories. The beat is generally considered a highly interesting one because of its diverse nature.

A Word About Elections

On election nights, the dividing line among the beats can become quite indistinct, particularly for the staff of a morning newspaper. Most of the beat reporters will make cursory checks of their own bailiwicks before making themselves available to the editor for special election duty.

Many of the beat reporters will be interested in the election as it applies to their specific beats—the city hall reporter for results of contests for city government positions, the suburban reporter for the tallies for his areas, and so on.

But chances are that the working assignments for election night will not completely reflect the reporters' specific interests. During the hectic evening, most of the beat men and general assignment reporters will be working on one thing: the election. The police reporter alone may find himself going about his normal duties (and hoping that two big stories don't break at the same time).

Several reporters are likely to be sent to the courthouse, where returns are coming in. One or two will telephone the counts back to the newspaper office. Others will talk with election officials, party leaders and candidates who congregate to see the results as they trickle into the courthouse.

Still other reporters may be sent to the headquarters of each political party, where tabulating processes often are faster (though perhaps less accurate) than at the courthouse.

And some reporters may remain at the paper and telephone suburban and outlying areas for their specific contests.

Gradually, as results approach finality, many of the reporters will return to the office and start writing stories about specific election battles. At this point, the beat organization may re-establish itself to some extent, with the city hall reporter writing the story about city races, the county reporter covering the county government contests, and so on.

Most reporters consider election night one of the busiest shifts of the year.

Summary

The beat reporter is responsible for one major area of his newspaper's coverage. Whatever the beat, the reporter is—or must soon become—a specialist in his realm.

To do his job well, the beat reporter must know the beat itself and the news sources on it. He builds up his proficiency gradually, learning more and more about the structure and functions of the beat and cultivating the cooperation of his sources. Once he has mastered the beat, it will be rare for any significant news to escape his attention.

The beat reporter typically does two kinds of things. One is covering spot news; the other is gathering possibilities for interpretive and feature stories to be worked on after deadline has passed.

Whether he covers the police beat for a small city paper or urban renewal for a metropolitan giant, the beat reporter is the newspaper's expert in his field. For the reporter who thoroughly enjoys his beat, it is one of the most rewarding and satisfying jobs in journalism.

CHAPTER 9

Rewriting: The Second Effort

A reporter spends much of his time writing—that's obvious. Not so apparent to the beginner, perhaps, is the fact that the reporter is apt to devote substantial attention to rewriting.

The rewriting performed in a newspaper office can take various forms:

1. Rewriting one's own work.
2. Rewriting public relations releases.
3. Rewriting readers' contributions.
4. Rewriting the work of other reporters.
5. "Rewriting" a story from the telephoned notes of another reporter.
6. Preparing new leads or writing new material to be inserted in an already written story.

Some newspapers have full-time rewrite men who spend all of their time at their desks. They are expected to be even more proficient than reporters themselves in spelling, grammar and usage. And they are expected to question dubious statements and check possible factual errors, often by consulting newspaper files and reference volumes or by telephoning news sources.

On other newspapers, deskmen (copy editors) sometimes double as rewrite men, and there is often a fine line between editing and rewriting. Some stories, although obviously needing attention, can be salvaged with skilled use of the editing pencil and pastepot.

Many papers, however, do not have regular rewrite men, and most of the rewriting is performed by the reporters themselves.

Rewriting Your Own Story

Not all stories are rewritten, of course. The good reporter may scratch out a word or phrase, transpose a couple of paragraphs or insert a few words before turning in his story—but he rarely will have to do it over, and he rarely will have the time.

Even the best reporters, however, can do an occasional sloppy job (and the good reporter will recognize it as such as soon as he finishes it) and will have to reorganize the story entirely.

More frequent than this is something called the "false start." Once a lead is written, the rest of the story often simply falls into place. But writing the lead can be difficult, because the reporter wants it to be "just so." It is common to see a reporter start to type a story, pause with a frown after the first paragraph or two, rip out the paper and start again. This may happen several times before he is satisfied with the lead. There is nothing wrong with this process as long as it is not a chronic practice with every story one writes.

Most editors, however, will descend indignantly on the reporter who tries to retype every story before he turns it in. Some students, unsure of their ability to think at the typewriter, try to write the first few paragraphs in longhand before starting to type—and this certainly would not be tolerated by an editor; again, the time element just does not permit such dilly-dallying.

Few stories require complete rewriting by the reporter himself. Once he has a satisfactory lead and has completed his story, he can type an insert paragraph if he has forgotten something (pasting it in at the appropriate place), or he can repair the story satisfactorily with a number of minor changes and corrections without redoing it entirely.

Rewriting Public Relations Releases

Not all news is gathered firsthand by reporters.

Every newspaper receives vast numbers of public relations releases, most of them by mail. Many reporters have wished they could exchange their salaries for the money spent on postage to get bales of useless mail to the newspaper office.

This is not to say that all PR releases are useless. Some are quite valuable in a news sense. If the PR story has a local angle, it probably will be rewritten and published. But many releases are sent indiscriminately to hundreds of papers whether there are local angles or not, and these almost always are tossed into the wastebasket. (Some are never even opened, since editors soon learn to recognize valueless material.)

Where a local angle does exist in a PR release, the story—generally a rather short one—will be rewritten to emphasize it. Furthermore, a good reporter would often want to go beyond the information contained in the release; by obtaining additional facts, he may produce a much better story.

Many editors are finding that public relations writers are steadily improving. Some releases—often from institutions or businesses which have frequent contact with the newspaper—can be used as submitted, verbatim.

If the PR man served as a newspaper reporter for a couple of years before entering public relations, chances are that he knows how to write a usable news story. News writing course work in journalism schools also helps to improve the quality of public relations writing, once the student aspiring to public relations realizes that much of his work will involve *writing* to the specifications of the media.

Assuming, however, that the release is worth using but must be rewritten, the reporter's job is to put the story in newspaper style and structure. He must bear in mind that the release may have an ax to grind, and all subjective material must be removed.

One of the chief faults of many PR releases is the PR writer's eagerness to bolster the egos of his superiors. Consequently, the release might start like this:

> Thomas R. Chollingford, President of the Amalgamated Rope Industries, Inc., announced today the appointment of two new Vice Presidents for the growing firm.
>
> Aimed at streamlining the firm's Sales and Engineering departments, the appointments will bring better services to customers, Mr. Chollingford said.
>
> Named Vice President for Sales was Thornton G. Thudberry, while Willis F. Johnson was appointed Vice President for Engineering.

And then it would go on to give background about the appointees. But the release has an awful lead (Chollingford is not the important item), it uses "Mr." when most papers do not, it capitalizes titles standing alone, and it contains some very subjective and unnecessary comments ("growing firm" and "better services to customers").

The story, newsworthy enough in itself, might be rewritten this way:

> Two new vice presidents have been appointed by the Amalgamated Rope Industries, Inc.
>
> Thornton G. Thudberry is the new vice president for sales, and Willis F. Johnson is vice president for engineering, President Thomas R. Chollingford announced today.

Rewriting Readers' Contributions

Readers occasionally submit news items, usually of minor importance but worth using in many cases.

Perhaps proud parents send in an item about a son's graduation:

REWRITING: THE SECOND EFFORT

      Mr. and Mrs. James Thompson, 695 Pittsfield St., announce the graduation of their son, William, from the University of Vienna, Austria, last week with a degree of Bachelor of Fine Arts.

      William, a lifelong resident of this city, is a graduate of Rosewood High School, where he was valedictorian, Class of 1966. He is an extremely talented sculptor and plans to follow this pursuit as a career.

Then the item might go on for several more paragraphs, extolling William's talents and detailing his background.

Many stories sent in by readers are far worse, writing-wise, than the one above. However, it still requires rewriting, both for organization and for style:

William Thompson, valedictorian of Rosewood High School in 1966, received a bachelor of fine arts degree last week at the University of	Vienna, Austria. Thompson, son of Mr. and Mrs. James Thompson, 695 Pittsfield St., plans a career as a sculptor.

Notice that the first words of the rewritten story are not "Mr. and Mrs. James Thompson." As proud as the parents may be, the story is not about them. Notice also that unnecessary words, style variations, and opinionated comments ("an extremely talented sculptor") have been eliminated.

A reporter can expect to rewrite many small items such as this, particularly on smaller papers.

Rewriting Other Reporters' Stories

Journeymen reporters with extra time on their hands sometimes are asked to rewrite the work of beginners. This is not a desirable practice except under extreme deadline pressure, because the cub reporter should be made to rewrite his own story and learn from the experience.

Furthermore, few beginners will be asked to rewrite the work of another reporter, but the occasion will arise when the young reporter gains more experience in the job.

Perhaps the story in question includes all the facts, but they are not presented in logical news story sequence. Perhaps it has a buried lead—the real lead being lost in the middle of the story. Or, perhaps it is simply a horribly written story which cannot be saved by mere editing. The harried editor tosses it to an experienced reporter for rewriting. Later, hopefully, when the deadline has passed, the editor will have a chat with the beginner and explain what was wrong with his story and what was done to correct it.

It should be mentioned that rewriting can be overdone. Changing a story should not occur simply for the sake of change. Ideally, the original writer should be consulted to preclude the possibility of incorrectness through altered facts or improper emphasis.

Here is part of a story that must be rewritten completely:

> City Council met last night and took action on several important matters.
>
> The first important item was the hiring of 15 new policemen. This brings the police department to a strength of 87 men.
>
> Councilmen also agreed to establish a canine corps of seven dogs. Training of dogs and handlers within the police department will begin next month.

> Council voted to allocate $50,000 for paving of streets in the new Mayfield subdivision, although the funds will eventually return to the city from liens against affected properties.
>
> Members discussed the inadequacy of the city's sewage treatment plant and agreed to hire a consulting firm to study the facilities and recommend the necessary modernization and expansion.

The story probably would then go on to provide further details about each item. But the terrible lead and the scattered itemization above certainly need rewriting:

> A strengthening of the police department—by the hiring of 15 new men and the establishment of a canine corps—was approved by City Council last night.
>
> Councilmen also agreed to hire a consulting firm to study the sewage treatment plant and allocated funds for street paving in the new Mayfield subdivision.
>
> The hiring of 15 new policemen will bring the force to a strength of 87 men. The training of seven dogs and their handlers will begin next month.
>
> (... further details here on police department items ...)

> Council members discussed inadequacies in the sewage treatment plant and voted to hire experts to recommend possible modernization and expansion.
>
> (... further details here on the specific consulting firm and what the "inadequacies" are ...)
>
> The Mayfield paving project, for which $50,000 was allocated, will not be a city expense in the long run, because costs will be assessed against affected properties through liens.
>
> (... further details here on the paving, including specific streets if known ...)

Many stories, although they are adequately written, can be improved by rewriting. The facts remain the same, but a spark is added to the writing itself.

Two examples follow to illustrate this kind of improvement, courtesy of Duane W. Bowler, editor of the Billings, Mont., Gazette.

First, the reporter's original copy:

REWRITING: THE SECOND EFFORT

An uncontrolled blaze destroyed a farm home 14 miles west of Billings about 9 a.m. Thursday morning. Yellowstone County Deputy Sheriff Roy M. Bulger said the fire could have swept nearby grass areas and destroyed other buildings on the ranch had a slight wind been blowing.

The two-story, 8-room home belonged to Miller Thatcher, a rancher of that area. Mr. and Mrs. Bruce Kraft and their five children were living in the home at the time. Bulger said one of Kraft's children admitted playing with fireworks in the home. It has not been officially determined if this was the cause of the fire.

Mrs. Kraft said she was separating milk when one son ran to tell her of a fire upstairs. She rushed her three sons out of the house, grabbed her 2 1/2-month old girl from a crib and told one of the boys to take her to a neighbor's house. Mrs. Kraft said she tried to fight the blaze with a garden hose but it was "too smokey." She said she gathered what small personal items she could and put them outside before her husband noticed the blaze roaring from the rooftop and came rushing from the field where he was working to save what things he could.

"We grabbed everything we could before it got too hot," Mrs. Kraft said. "We got our refrigerator out but I don't know if it's going to work. It's all burnt and melted." She said they had no insurance on personal effects. Thatcher said the home was not insured. He said they would build a new home or move a house to replace the charred structure.

Thatcher, a father-in-law of Kraft, said the family is living with them until they can move into another home. Thatcher and Kraft are farmer-ranchers.

Because the home was out of city limits, no fire fighting equipment was dispatched. An O'Donnell Fire Service truck was nearby to check spreading of the flames to grass and bush areas.

And the improved version that appeared in print:

A Fourth of July fire sent a farm mother and four of her five small children fleeing from their burning two-story home 14 miles west of Billings Thursday morning.

Mrs. Bruce Kraft battled the second-story blaze with a garden hose before smoke and flames drove her back. The eight-room house was destroyed.

Kraft was cultivating beans, Mrs. Kraft was separating milk, their three boys were playing upstairs, their baby girl was in her crib and 2-year-old Naomi was playing in the yard when tragedy struck about 9 a.m.

Dallas, 10, broke in on her work to tell his mother of a fire upstairs. Mrs. Kraft hurried Dallas, Mark, 9, and Lester, 8, out of the house and grabbed baby Ruth from her crib. She told Mark to take Ruth to her brother-in-law's home, the Bill Kraft place a quarter of a mile away.

Then she started her losing battle against the flames. When smoke and flames forced her back, Mrs. Kraft hastily gathered up what belongings she could to carry them outside.

Meanwhile, her husband saw flames roar through the roof and rushed home.

"We grabbed everything we could before it got too hot," Mrs. Kraft said. "We got our refrigerator out but I don't know if it's going to work. It's all burned and melted."

Mrs. Kraft said the family had no insurance on its belongings. The dwelling, owned by her father, Miller Thatcher, was not insured either, she said. The Krafts moved in with Thatchers until they are able to find another home.

Roy H. Bulger, deputy sheriff, said had there been a wind the fire would have swept through the grass to destroy other ranch buildings and destroy field crops. An O'Donnell Fire Service truck stood nearby to check the spread of flames to grass and bush areas.

Bulger said the cause of the fire had not been determined. He said the parents told him one of the boys admitted he had been playing with fireworks in the home.

Not only does the rewritten version have an added spark—it is better organized, has more clarity and adheres more closely to journalistic style and correctness.

The second example, first in the reporter's original version:

HELENA—Welfare authorities hope Montana's new child abuse reporting law will result in a central state registry of parents who physically abuse or wilfully neglect their children.

Steps are being taken to draw up an agreement under which county officials will report abuse and neglect cases to the State Welfare Department.

Joseph H. Roe, the department's director of child welfare services, says this would permit the department to set up a central file of all reported instances of child abuse in the state.

"Such a registry is important for detection of repeaters and for preventive intervention in child abuse cases," Roe said in an interview. "It could aid doctors, hospitals, law enforcement and social agencies in their joint efforts in dealing with child abuse."

The 1965 law requires doctors, nurses, teachers and social workers who have reason to believe a child under 18 has been subjected to physical abuse or wilful neglect to make a detailed report to the county attorney. The county attorney is required to order an immediate investigation. The law also grants immunity from civil and criminal liability to the person making the report, unless it was made maliciously.

The law has produced no dramatic results so far. A check of county attorneys in several of Montana's larger cities indicates there has been little or no increase in the number of child abuse cases reported, although Roe says he has received a number of inquiries about the law from those required to make the reports.

Lewis and Clark Deputy County Atty. William F. Crowley said he feels there is a reluctance to report abuse cases despite the immunity provided by the law.

"I'm sure a lot of it goes on, and we would be anxious to investigate if we could just get the cases reported," Crowley said.

Montana's law was in response to a startling nationwide increase in physical maltreatment and deliberate neglect of children by their parents. The bill had the support of the Montana Medical Association, the State Welfare Board, the Montana Conference of Social Workers, the Governor's Committee on Mental Health and Mental Retardation, the American Legion and others.

Dr. David G. Gil, an assistant professor at Brandeis University in Waltham, Mass., was in Helena recently to discuss Montana's new law with state welfare authorities. Brandeis, a graduate school for advanced studies in public welfare, is undertaking a nationwide survey of child abuse for the U.S. Children's Bureau and the Child Welfare League of America.

Gil said current figures indicate about 200 American children are murdered and more than 1,200 are injured every month by abusive parents and guardians. He said the rate of child abuse cases is increasing faster than the population growth.

Gil wants to find out why. Are children becoming more provocative? Are parents becoming more vicious? His survey will try to determine what type of people abuse their children. It will include interviews with doctors, hospital personnel, law enforcement officers, welfare officials and with abusive parents themselves.

Roe's concern is less with punishing these parents than with protecting the children from physical abuse and malnutrition. The important thing, he says, is to get the children away from abusive or neglectful parents and then try to get psychiatric help for the parents.

"What's the use of stockpiling these people in prison when there is a possibility we can rehabilitate them?" Roe asks.

He told of a stepfather who attached a 220-volt electrical circuit to the index fingers of a 1 1/2-year-old girl and burned both those fingers off.

"It took eight months to get the child ready for adoption because she had so much abuse," Roe said.

The father was found to be a dangerous psychopath.

In northeastern Montana a few years ago a little boy was hospitalized with a broken leg and the attending physician tipped welfare authorities to keep an eye on his parents. Sometime later the father took the boy to a Bozeman hospital for treatment of a leg fracture that had occurred 11 days earlier. The Bozeman doctor was so incensed by the obvious case of abuse that he called Roe personally. Both parents were sent to Warm Springs.

All abuse cases are not beatings. Roe recalled the case of a girl who had been kept in an apple box for nine years and developed curvature of the spine.

He told of a sawmill worker and

his wife who took the body of their youngest child to a mortuary. The undertaker suspected malnutrition, and an autopsy provided he was right. The couple had four or five other children. An investigation revealed that they, too, were poorly fed.

It was a case of the parents hogging the food and not leaving enough for the kids, Roe said.

Roe feels the main weakness of Montana's law is that there is no specific provision for reporting fatalities resulting from child abuse.

Also, he says it is probably impossible to write legislation covering "emotional deprivation" of a child. Children can be damaged, he says, by parents who feed and clothe them well and treat them well physically but who, by overprotection or other reasons, deny them a normal adolescence.

Not a bad story. But the rewritten version is far more likely to elicit reader interest in what the editor rightly regarded as a problem deserving public attention:

HELENA—The stepfather attached a 220-volt electrical circuit to the index fingers of a 1 1/2-year-old Montana girl. It burned off both those fingers.

A little boy from Northeastern Montana suffered too many broken legs.

A girl was kept in an apple box for nine years. She developed curvature of the spine.

An undertaker suspected a sawmill worker's child died of malnutrition. The parents hogged the food. There wasn't enough for the kids.

These are actual cases of child abuse in Montana.

Elimination of these and lesser abuses is what welfare authorities hope to achieve with Montana's new child abuse reporting law.

Welfare is establishing a central state registry of parents who physically abuse or wilfully neglect their children. Agreements will be reached under which county officials will report abuse and neglect to the State Welfare Department.

"Such a registry is important for detection of repeaters and for preventive intervention in child abuse cases," said Joseph H. Roe, child welfare services director.

"It could aid doctors, hospitals, law enforcement and social agencies in their joint efforts in dealing with child abuse."

There's other help, too, if used.

A 1965 Montana law requires doctors, nurses, teachers and social workers who have reason to believe a child under 18 is abused or neglected to make a detailed report to the county attorney. The prosecutor is required to investigate immediately. The doctor, nurse, teacher or social worker reporting gets immunity from civil and criminal liability.

Billings and Yellowstone County authorities note no material increase in child abuse reporting under the new law. County Atty. John Adams commented "the medical profession has always been very cooperative when there is a possible case of child beating. But neglect is another matter." Yellowstone has 50 to 60 hearings a year.

Similar reports are heard from other larger cities.

Montana's law came in response to a startling nationwide increase in physical maltreatment and deliberate neglect by parents. The bill had general support. Nobody admits to approving of child abuse and neglect.

Nationally, the figures leave one sick. Current figures indicate about 200 American children are murdered and more than 1,200 injured every month by abusive parents and guardians. Dr. David G. Gil of Brandeis University in Waltham, Mass., said child abuse is growing faster than the population.

He visited Montana recently. He wants to know reasons for the increases.

Are children becoming more provocative? Are parents becoming more vicious?

Gil will talk to doctors, hospital personnel, law officers, welfare workers and with abusive parents themselves to find out.

Director Roe of the child welfare services is concerned less with punishing parents than with protecting children.

He said the important thing is to get the children away from the abusive or neglectful parents—and then get psychiatric help for the parents.

"What's the use of stockpiling these people in prison when there is a possibility we can rehabilitate them?" asked Roe.

What about the child with the electrically burned fingers? The father was found to be a dangerous psychopath.

The parents of the boy with too many broken legs both were sent to a mental hospital.

Roe feels there's a weakness in Montana's law. It lacks specific provision for reporting child abuse fatalities.

He also knows it is probably impossible to write legislation covering "emotional deprivation."

Children can be damaged, he said, by parents who feed and clothe them well, treat them well physically, but who by overprotection or other reasons deny them a normal adolescence.

Rewriting From Telephoned Notes

After some practice, most reporters can go to the scene of a story, take notes, call the office, and dictate a story without typing it first. The story is drafted in the reporter's head—he "sees" it there and simply "reads" it in story form to the person taking it down on the typewriter in the office. Generally such stories, even major ones, are not complicated.

Under deadline pressure, with a still-developing story, the newspaper may want to publish the available facts without waiting for a complete account of the event. In such a case, the reporter is likely to phone notes to the office, presenting the information in merely conversational form to the rewrite man, who then writes the story itself.

Later, when the event is over, the reporter himself probably will return to the office and write a complete story for later editions.

Occasionally a story covered by several leg men simultaneously must be pulled together by the rewrite man. If the story is big enough, the editor may send several reporters, each of whom is assigned one aspect of the story. The rewriter then takes the bits and pieces telephoned by all of these reporters and blends them into one major story. This is a complex task and is not the kind of thing a beginning reporter would be expected to do.

New Leads and Inserts

News is constantly changing. The story which appears in a newspaper's early editions may have to be updated as events move along. Yet the original story may have a substantial amount of content which will hold up. Consequently, it may be necessary only to write a new, up-to-date lead, delete some outdated material and insert copy on new developments.

Reporters sometimes update their own stories; on other occasions a reporter on a later shift will update a story written by another reporter.

And, new leads and inserts frequently are written for stories which come in on the wire. Perhaps you discover that someone from your city is missing in an earthquake in Turkey. You probably would use the comprehensive wire story about the event itself, but you would localize the lead and insert material about the local resident within the story.

Summary

Rewriting can take many forms. It can involve copy written by you or a colleague, items brought in by persons not employed by your newspaper, or stories which did not need rewriting until new developments made it necessary to update them.

Whatever kind of rewriting is done, and whether it is done by a reporter or a full-time rewrite man, the aim is the same—to make the story better in some way. It may need improvement in timeliness, in localization, in its accuracy, or in the writing itself.

CHAPTER 10

Humanizing the News

Newspaper reporters and editors have tended to define certain things they do as "feature stories." Journalism professors and students frequently talk about "feature stories." Everyone seems to accept the terminology, but there is little agreement on what it means. A "feature story" is somewhat like the taste of an apple or the sound of a breeze rustling through the trees. Everyone can recognize it, but no one can define it precisely.

This is not to say that everyone who uses the term is wrong, but that it's difficult to specify such a type of story because almost all copy in your daily newspaper can be a "feature story." What most of us call a "feature story" is, quite simply, a story written in a particular manner. Thus, what is a feature to one reporter may be "straight news" to another. The distinction depends primarily upon the reporter's approach to the presentation of the facts, the points he chooses to emphasize and the writing style he uses.

The difference is more than semantic. We call this chapter "Humanizing the News" to emphasize that we're talking about a process, not a static object. Thus, what we tend to call a feature story is the result of the process of inserting the human element into any story and the utilization of certain writing techniques. That human element involves many things, but most of them can be lumped under two broad characteristics: human interest and incongruity.

"Human interest" denotes any event or idea that appeals to people more or less naturally and not necessarily because it has significance to their everyday activities. It is somewhat standard to say that there are three main categories of human interest—sex, children and animals. While these topics do seem to interest people, so do other themes such as self-interest, sympathy, corruption, progress, conflict, disaster, hero-worship, adventure, spirituality and success.

Any human interest element must be solidly based in human emotion. Notice that each of the elements in the above list can be tied directly to some emotion, some potentially very strong and natural human feeling. A common mistake is to assume that when one speaks of emotion with regard to the feature writer, the reference is primarily to sorrow or tragedy. But human interest is much broader; in fact, the emotion of joy, especially when involved with humor, probably appears more frequently in modern newspapers than sorrow or tragedy. There was a time when newspapers concentrated on the "tear-jerker" type of story, but such emphasis is not as great today.

Another element which feature stories usually have, in addition to emotion or human interest, is incongruity, or the unexpected. This involves a set of circumstances in a story in which the result our experience would lead us to expect does not occur. It is related to the "whodunnit" story or the suspended interest and surprise ending organization. People like the challenge of guessing the ending, and they enjoy being surprised. In fact, the element of incongruity makes up the essence of most jokes.

Incongruity also plays a role in the actual writing of the feature story, for the reporter can add considerably to the effectiveness of the story if he has enough skill with his language to make it work for him in surprising the reader. Perhaps the most obvious example of this type of skill is the use of the pun. Even though the first response to a good pun is a groan, most people appreciate a person who has such talent with the language.

Let's now take a case in which such situation incongruity and verbal incongruity combine in the hands of a skillful reporter to produce an eye-catching feature lead. First, a summary lead based upon the results of a trial in a municipal court:

> Bert Cedrick, 32, of 14 Bartholomew Lane was sentenced to 30 days in city jail by Police Judge Oakley Addis yesterday after he and another man were picked up for fighting outside the Inside Inn.

This is a very straightforward, summary statement, containing all the "five W's and H." But it is the lead of an unimaginative reporter who missed a good opportunity from the hearing. The fight had been over ownership of a battered brass cornet. In an effort to determine who actually owned the instrument, Judge Addis had asked each of the two men to play it in court. Cedrick couldn't, and the other man, Raymond Ogden, could. Ogden's sentence was suspended. Another reporter, recognizing the unexpected quality of such a procedure and adding to this his own skill with the language, wrote this lead:

> The charge wasn't piracy in a case before Police Judge Oakley Addis yesterday, but it had something to do with activity on the high C's.

This second lead is sharp and interesting. It shows some imagination. The reporter who has the ability to recognize such situations and to use them effectively in his writing will be more likely to hold the reader's interest.

Types of Feature Treatment

Depending upon the amount of newsworthy information which featurized stories contain, they can be classified generally into two categories: strictly human interest and newsfeatures. Let's look at these separately.

Strictly human interest stories are written for entertainment and need not contain information which is newsworthy by the usual standards. Such stories—often called "brighteners" or "brights"—simply are interesting because they are amusing, tragic, pathetic, happy—in brief, because they elicit some emotional response from the reader. Very frequently, these stories will be in the form of anecdotes which have unexpected, humorous endings. As such, they usually are written as concisely and to the point as possible.

The following four stories have purely human interest functions:

MIAMI (AP)—Poor Zero Zzyzz, he has lost his cherished position—last in the Miami telephone directory.

September's issue has a new low man among more than a half million Southern Bell subscribers: Vladimir Zzzyd.

Zzzyd, a horticulturist who breeds seeds, is currently operating in North Carolina but is a permanent resident of Miami.

The name is Russian and the native of eastern Poland moved to the United States in the 1920s. Now in his 60s, Zzzyd spent much of his life in Pennington, N.J.

Now that Zzzyd—rhymes with "kid"—has replaced Zzyzz—which rhymes with "fizz"—he'll be at the bottom until somebody ousts him.

Another traditionally female-only bastion has fallen to the demands of men's lib.

Fathers have invaded delivery rooms across the country and in Smyrna last week the men struck another blow for equality. They showed up at a baby shower.

It was a "Liberate Your Mate" stork shower given by Mr. and Mrs. Philip Carnes in honor of prospective parents, Mr. and Mrs. Jim Wooten.

From the start, the guests could tell it was not going to be a run-of-the-mill baby shower. Instead of the traditional fare of tea and cookies, the hosts served champagne. And not all the gifts were pink and blue booties and gowns.

The father-to-be opened one box to find something to ease some of the upcoming nights of walking the baby—a fifth of liquor.—Reprinted with permission from Atlanta Constitution

CLEVELAND, Ohio (AP)— Anthony Asher of suburban Rocky River wants to get into politics.

"And you've got to start somewhere," he says.

So he erected a $2,000 sign near Memorial Parkway that says: "What about this guy ASHER?"

Asher, 34, who said he also is thinking of establishing a Cleveland address, said he may run for either mayor of Cleveland or county commissioner.

SAN FRANCISCO (UPI)—When a motor vehicle department clerk asked Loren Furness why he needed a new driver's license, he replied that an elephant had eaten the old one.

Noticing the clerk's mystified expression, Furness explained that he was a keeper at the San Francisco Zoo and had dropped his wallet in the pachyderm area. An elephant named "May" snapped it up, and ate it.

Human interest stories like these appear in newspapers frequently, but newsfeatures provide the greatest number of examples of humanizing the news. This is because the newsfeature is a story which has both newsworthiness and human interest or incongruity and which has been written in the "feature way." It could have been written as straight news if the reporter had elected to write it that way. But an enterprising reporter has spotted the fact that the information contains both news and human interest and has adopted his writing style to take advantage of both.

A good example of this type would be a situation in which, say, a 5-year-old boy gets separated from his parents at the local swimming pool. A frantic search begins. The pool is evacuated, and police and firemen begin searching the area. Announcements about the missing boy are made over the local radio stations. When the boy is found, he has walked several miles and is within two blocks of his home. His mother says he has taken a route which the family seldom uses. This story has news value, and it could be written in the inverted pyramid form with a summary lead. But it also has human interest and an element of the unexpected. The good reporter, therefore, would combine these elements with the information and emphasize the human interest factors while also providing needed information. Thus, he has satisfied the requirements of the straight news story and the feature story. He has written a newsfeature.

Note how all of the following examples use human interest and a casual writing style in the presentation of a news story:

To be a successful NARC (undercover narcotics agent), you have to stay cool, walk tough, remain with the scene no matter what, and above all, know where it's at and what's happening at all times.

Wearing a shaggy beard, the right kind of sun glasses (you can peek out, but the world can't peek in) and making good body moves doesn't hurt either, one undercover agent for the West Virginia State Police Criminal Intelligence and Narcotics Strike Force proved in Charleston yesterday in a car on Kanawha Boulevard.

Sauntering up to three young men who seemed to be doing more inhaling than exhaling on a pipe they shared, the agent asked, "What's happening, man?"

"Grass, man," one youth replied.

"State police, man," the bearded, sunglassed NARC told the startled trio.

Lodged in the Kanawha County jail today pending a hearing before Harry Ashwell on charges of possession of marijuana were Larry P. Kendall, 20, of Cottle, Russell B. Harrison, 22, of Fenwick, and John Carpenter, 21, of Richwood, all students at West Virginia Tech, state police said.—Reprinted with permission from Charleston, W. Va., Daily Mail

SAN FRANCISCO (UPI)—There was no question about what to serve when Frank Epperson celebrated the 50th anniversary of his famous invention with his grandchildren.

Epperson, 78, a retired real estate man, slurped a Popsicle along with the youngsters.

A half century ago, Epperson patented the "frozen drink on a stick" after experimenting with various molds and determining that glass was the best material to freeze them in.

He received a royalty on Popsicle sales from 1923 to 1929. But he sold his rights after the stock market crash because he needed cash for his real estate ventures.

"It has given a lot of simple pleasure to a lot of people," he said with pride at his San Francisco Bay area home. "And I've enjoyed being part of it all."

Epperson said the original idea came by accident—when he was 11.

He had mixed some then-popular soda water powder in a pitcher and left it on the back porch overnight with a stirring stick in it. The temperature dropped to record lows that night in 1905 and young Frank had a stick of frozen soda water to show his school friends the next day.

He forgot all about it until the early 1920s when the stick-less ice cream bar became a popular success.

Epperson decided a frozen dessert on a stick—being more convenient and less messy—would do even better and started experimenting.

Epperson, whose 28 grandchildren are all Popsicle addicts, originally called his confection the "Epsicle."

There are two stories about how the name was changed. One is that the frozen drink made a "pop" sound as it came out of the glass mold; the other, that someone described it as a frozen lollipop.

The inventor sold his rights to Popsicle Industries of Englewood, N.Y., whose licensees now produce nine billion of the bars annually, with orange still the favorite flavor.

The company paid tribute to the product's golden anniversary by presenting Epperson with a plaque honoring his original patent.

BY BOB OLMSTEAD
Chicago Sun-Times

CHICAGO—Now you may think a piano is a musical instrument.

And the dictionary may define the piano as a musical instrument.

But the Chicago Board of Education recently spent $183.75 researching the question and has come to the firm legal opinion that it's not.

The question came up when Mrs. William L. Rohter, a board member often critical of what she considers sloppy accounting practices, noticed that the school budget lists pianos as furniture, not as musical instruments and therefore not as teaching materials.

This is crazy, said Mrs. Rohter. A piano's a musical instrument. Everybody knows that.

Even Webster's New International Dictionary, second edition, says: "Piano: a stringed instrument of percussion..."

Not so, said the board of education. A piano's a piece of furniture and always has been.

Mrs. Rohter went to the Chicago school's music director and asked him, "What do teachers do with a piano?"

He looked at her rather strangely and said, "Why, we teach music with it."

Armed with this expert opinion, Mrs. Rohter went back to the board of education and demanded that it change its mind and its budget. The board said it would research the question.

At a recent board meeting, during a discussion of legal expenses, Mrs. Rohter complained that she had learned that the school's legal department spent $183.75 to find out what a piano is—but never told her the answer.

A legal aide dug around and handed her a two-page opinion which concluded that a piano is a piece of furniture because the budget has always classified it that way.

The significance of all this—if any—is that the money for a piano could come from two different tax funds—the building fund and the textbook fund.

A year ago, the school system's accounting practices were criticized by its own accountants, Arthur Andersen & Co., as being so arbitrary as to be nearly useless in reflecting reality.

Mrs. Rohter maintains that—if the piano example is any indication—the budget's conductor may have changed, but the melody lingers on.—Reprinted with permission from Chicago Sun-Times

They don't fool around in the Mountain State of West Virginia.

As boldly as they can say it, representatives of the West Virginia Department of Commerce have announced they will arrive in Detroit Sunday to "lure" manufacturing plants away from Detroit.

They describe the Detroit area as being "particularly hard hit by labor difficulties and the typical overall problems that beset a manufacturer in an urban environment."

The visit by West Virginians has been preceded by letters from Gov. Arch A. Moore Jr. to every major industry in the Detroit area.

The letters extended personal invitations from the governor to meet with the industrial development salesmen and to consider the "many advantages offered new manufacturers in West Virginia."

West Virginia has also placed advertising in newspapers in advance of the sales trip.

West Virginia's industrial development director, Alex Lawrence, said this will be the first time a "blitz trip" has been conducted in Detroit.

"Our state has the proximity to the growing eastern and southern markets that industrialists want and a new highway network which gives us a very salable item," he said.

The visit by out-of-state industrial development salesmen to Detroit and Michigan is nothing new.

Many cities and states have expert teams of industrial development salesmen visiting the city and state, according to Robert Sweany, vice-president of business development for the Greater Detroit Chamber of Commerce.

"This is a very common practice, but most of the out-of-state salesmen talk to our industrialists about expanding plant facilities in their states because they realize much of Michigan's industry won't leave the state.

"They don't try to steal them.

"The blatant announcement by West Virginia to steal our Detroit industry, therefore, is most unusual.

"It does point up one thing—that Michigan should take an example from West Virginia people and have a much more aggressive and extroverted industrial sales promotion ourselves."

The blitz by West Virginians comes after four bodies disclosed recently that Michigan's industrial executives are unhappy with the state's climate for business and industry.

The studies of attitudes of Michigan industrialists indicated that many of them would not build their factories in the state if they had to do it over again.

They blamed racial tension, crime problems, high taxes, high labor rates and workmen's compensation and unemployment compensation laws for their disenchantment with the state.

Apparently officials of the West Virginia Department of Commerce have also read the reports.—Reprinted with permission from The Detroit Sunday News

This notion of types of feature stories could be carried further, being more specific and giving subtypes to cover the many situations in which the reporter is likely to find an opportunity for a feature story. But the fact is that almost any story can be a feature story if the reporter is alert enough to recognize the elements and skillful enough to write in the feature manner, placing information and human interest in the proper perspective. A touch of the human element can add interest to almost any news story if presented judiciously.

Humanizing Your Writing

Now let us turn our attention to the techniques used in humanizing the news. It's at the same time very easy and frightfully difficult, because almost anything goes. The feature writer has almost complete freedom, and he's welcome to try his wings.

In feature writing, rules are deliberately broken or new ones created if the situation calls for it. The latter part of that sentence, however, is very important. When rules are broken, it has to be for more reason than that the reporter wants to break them. It must be done to serve a specific function; it must add some element to the story which is needed. And, like the clown on a tightrope, the reporter must first have a very firm grasp of the rules before he can break them effectively. In newspaper writing, creativity simply for the sake of creativity and not for the benefit of the reader usually produces copy which is ineffectual. It represents a forgetting of the purpose of the newspaper, to communicate with the reader, not to satisfy the reporter's own personal whims. Good writing—especially feature writing—is naturally restrained, purposive writing.

But if the reporter knows the rules and has a reason for breaking them, he may, for example: write his stories in first, second or third person instead of the usual standard third person; use slang in his stories in direct contrast to straight news; provide a summary statement at the end of his story, a practice not acceptable with the inverted pyramid; use any form of story organization which seems most acceptable, usually avoiding the inverted pyramid. These are only examples; the list could run through all the rules of newspaper writing except that of accuracy.

Let us now be more specific about the "feature way" of writing in the context of feature leads, language, writing style and story organization.

Feature Leads. At this stage, it would be well to remember that the "five W's and H" summary lead has two primary functions: (1) to summarize the story by giving the essential fact or facts of the story; and (2) to attract attention. Of the two, emphasis is on No. 1, the summary of the story. It is expected that attracting attention will be accomplished by the content of such a summary.

The feature lead, on the other hand, seeks to serve the same two functions, but reverses the order of their importance. That is, it seeks, first, to attract attention and stimulate interest through a variety of techniques and, second, to provide information about the story itself. Because of this, the only content requirement of a feature lead is that it, at a minimum, give a *hint* of what the story is about. There must be some direct connection between the lead and the story itself, naturally, but this connection can be a very loose one. One would not, for example, write a lead simply for the purpose of attracting attention (perhaps a joke) and then launch into a story which was not related in any way.

As an example, we might remember the lead on the police court story presented earlier. It has as its main purpose to attract attention, and the information it provides the reader is minimal. It tells only that the story concerns something that happened in police court (we're not sure what) and that it involved Police Judge Oakley Addis in some way. In spite of this limited amount of information, however, the lead is very likely to attract the reader into the story, if for no other reason than to find out what the story is all about.

Other examples of leads which might do the same thing for the same story are the following:

> A short tune ended on a sour note for Bert Cedrick yesterday in police court before Police Judge Oakley Addis.
>
> Lady Justice faced the music in police court yesterday, including some sour notes, but in the end she reached her decision by playing it by ear.
>
> Bert Cedrick is singing the blues in jail today because he couldn't play them on a cornet yesterday in police court.
>
> Bert Cedrick has been in jail before, but he never thought he would get 30 days just because he wasn't musically inclined.

Note that each of these leads, in spite of different approaches to the subject, makes some reference to the incongruity of the situation. Note also how most of them use a familiar idea or statement in a somewhat different or unexpected context. And note that they are all short. Brevity is indeed a virtue when writing feature leads. Good writers have found that the short, compact, to-the-point lead is much more effective than one which rambles on and on. Human interest and incongruity have their greatest impact when presented in a concise manner. Consequently, it is seldom that a good feature lead will exceed three typewritten lines.

It may be that the lead examples above would be inappropriate for some kinds of story organization. Some of them may contain too much information, for example, for the reporter who wants to deliberately withhold the unexpected happening until the end of the story. In such suspended interest stories, the writer simply uses his lead to set the scene of what follows, ordinarily chronological arrangement of information. He then, step by step, directs his readers toward a logical conclusion and throws in the unexpected element as a surprise ending.

It was stated earlier that leads are the most difficult part of the story to write, and this is especially true for feature leads. Even the most experienced reporters frequently go through a number of false starts before they find the lead which satisfies them. Sometimes a reporter, under pressure of a deadline, will use a lead which he feels is not quite right. But if he has time, he will work with the lead until the proper idea and wording fall into place. It all boils down to allowing your imagination to play upon the human interest or incongruous elements in the story, then seeking the correct words to express the ideas you formulate. If words and ideas mesh, you're ready to move into the body of the story; if the idea comes, but not the words, don't be afraid to toss out that idea and seek another; if the idea won't come, write a lead which may be acceptable although not quite what you would like, then complete the story and return to rework the lead if time permits. The point is that feature leads take work; good feature leads usually are made, not born.

Feature Language. Differentiation between feature and news writing is very evident in the type of language which the reporter uses. This does not mean common usage of profanity or vulgarities, for most reporters still must tailor their language for family readership. But it does mean that the language in a feature story usually is more relaxed, more casual, than in straight news. A feature story should be written in as near conversational style as you can create. It should sound like a story being told by someone to a group. Just imagine yourself, in the case of the police court story, saying to a friend, "An interesting thing happened in police court yesterday," and then simply telling the story.

Such conversational style can involve many things. It may mean the use of incomplete sentences or, for the right reason, improper grammar. It may mean the use of slang, colloquialisms or a particular dialect (although it is only fair to warn the beginning reporter that writing in dialect is extremely difficult and is not effective unless done properly). Sometimes, it will involve using such obvious conversational gimmicks as "It seems that . . ." This, for example, might fit very well at the beginning of the second paragraph of the police court story, following the lead with: "It seems that Bert Cedrick and Raymond Ogden were in police court charged with disturbing the peace. . ." The reporter also might find some reason to use nonwords such as "uh" or "ah" to indicate pauses in the speech, or he might deliberately stop in mid-sentence, then start again, to indicate a false start: "I really want . . . uh . . . I mean, I think I would like . . . at least, it sounds like an interesting idea to me."

It's important to remember that selection of common, well-known words and simple sentence structure are musts for conversational style. Most people speak this way. And, when judicious, but limited, use of other techniques is added, the result stands a good chance of being effective. But don't overdo such use of conversational gimmicks to create an effect. Too many reporters have a tendency to place too much emphasis on the gimmicks and too little on word choice and sentence structure. The result often is a very forced, uncomfortable, virtually unreadable and certainly unacceptable piece of writing.

It's appropriate to mention verbal irony again as a part of the conversational approach to feature writing. If a play on words, such as a pun, suits your purposes and if you have a good one, then it is a legitimate tool for the feature writer. Sarcasm and satire also fit into certain situations, although they must be used very carefully, and the feature writer must avoid misusing his freedom of subjectivity. Understatement and overstatement also can add considerably to a feature story. The following lead, for example, uses understatement very effectively, to provide an eye-catching quality:

> Officers Karl Macklin and Barry O'Dell knew that something was out of the ordinary yesterday when, driving along Westbranch Avenue, they saw two lions trotting toward Koon's Butcher Shop.

Even though all of these techniques are available to the feature writer, he must use them with caution. They tend to be most effective when used verbally because the speaker can use inflection—a shifting of his tone of voice—to indicate his real meaning. But no such device is available in written communication, so the reader may not understand the real intent. When the feature writer is using irony, a pun, sarcasm, satire, understatement or overstatement, he must make certain that his meaning is very clear to the reader. Lack of understanding or misunderstanding by the reader destroys the effectiveness of any type of writing.

In brief, language plays a very important role in the effectiveness of feature writing, and the reporter should use a variety of techniques to achieve a conversational approach. But he remembers at the same time that everything must be done for a reason; thus, verbal techniques must be very carefully chosen and used cautiously. The good reporter knows that nothing can make a story sound more amateurish than over-reliance on techniques for their own sake.

Writing Style. Important to the presentation of straight news, writing style is crucial to the feature story. It includes the relaxed, casual approach discussed earlier; it also includes a greater reliance upon short direct quotations and greater amounts of dialogue. But the general point to remember is this: Feature writing must be dramatic writing; that is, it must be written in a style which is compatible with the mood of the content. This idea is borrowed from music. In a sense, all music is mood music since it elicits some psychological response. Rapid-moving, staccato music tends to create a psychological atmosphere of excitement, of movement, of haste. Slow music utilizing greater flow creates the mood of peace and quiet, of meditation, of relaxation.

Writers of novels and short stories have been applying this technique for years. They know that language and sentence structure and even paragraph structure can convey a particular mood if handled correctly. What they have discovered is that long sentences which flow smoothly seem to create an atmosphere of thoughtfulness, of deliberation, of calm. On the other hand, if one wants to convey an atmosphere of haste, quick action and rapid movement, he uses short, staccato phrasing with much punctuation. In this way, writing style can team with content to create the proper mood for the story.

As an example of such pacing in short-story writing, let us review a brief passage from William Faulkner's "Barn Burning":

> *Then he was free. His aunt grasped at him but it was too late. He whirled, running, his mother stumbled forward on to her knees behind him, crying to the nearer sister: "Catch him, Net! Catch him!" But that was too late too,* the sister (the sisters were twins, born at the same time, yet either of them now give the impression of being, encompassing as much living meat and volume and weight as any other two of the family) *not yet having begun to rise from the chair, her head, face, alone merely turned,* presenting to him in the flying instant an astonishing expanse of young female features untroubled by any surprise even, wearing only an expression of bovine interest. *Then he was out of the room, out of the house,* in the mild dusk of the starlit road and the heavy rifeness of honeysuckle, the pale ribbon unspooling with terrific slowness under his running feet, *reaching the gate at last and turning in, running, his heart and lungs drumming, on up the drive toward the lighted house, the lighted door. He did not knock, he burst in, sobbing for breath, incapable for the moment of speech;* he saw the astonished face of the Negro in the linen jacket without knowing when the Negro had appeared.

The variety of rhetorical pacing within this one paragraph and even within individual sentences lends to it a quality which feature writers should seek. In the first place, although Faulkner's sentences are very long and complex, they are broken up into short phrases and contain much punctuation, thus creating the mood of breathless excitement which he intended. This can best be seen in the italicized

HUMANIZING THE NEWS

portions, especially at the beginning and near the end of the paragraph. In the middle, especially the parenthetical statement in the second sentence, are passages which do not convey such excitement, but moments of meditation. The ability to use a dramatic style of writing this way helped make Faulkner a great writer, although the newspaper writer seldom will make such extensive use of a Faulkner-type style.

But these principles do fit the newspaper story—especially the feature—very well. Notice, for example, how the writer of the following interesting, but unspectacular, story used the same techniques, although in a more modest fashion:

LEAD: Designed to catch interest and give hint of what story is about	For Blackie, a hard-working Labrador Retriever, it was all a matter of first things first at Lake Whahoo early yesterday.
Setting the scene for the narration	One of the participants in an ill-fated duck-hunting expedition, William Steppe of 42 N. Charles St. related the unusual experience this way:
Still setting the scene, this time for main action of the story	Shortly after daybreak, Steppe, Blackie and the dog's owner, George R. Stanley of 2 Barberry Lane, were in a small boat on the lake.
Taking a slow pace in effort to show the relaxed moment of the story	Five ducks had been bagged in the early morning hours before things slowed down. The sky was empty so Steppe and Stanley relaxed, laid down their guns and started to light cigarettes while Blackie gazed intently at the sky.
Speeding up tempo, using short sentences to emphasize the speed and excitement of the situation	Suddenly, a lone duck appeared on the horizon. The two men grabbed their guns, took quick aim, fired...but missed. Blackie became excited. In his readiness to retrieve, he tipped the boat over. Dogs, men and five dead ducks were dumped into the icy waters.
Slowing down again, to emphasize pace and to build suspense	Although weighted down by their heavy clothing and very, very cold, the two men managed to reach the capsized boat. They clung to it.

Slowly building to the climax	But Blackie knew what to do. In a very businesslike manner he went about his job, carrying the five dead ducks individually to shore. Only when all had been retrieved and were safely on the bank did he return to the boat to see what could be done for the men.
Punch line, presentation of the climax	The men were almost exhausted when Blackie took hold of a rope attached to the front of the boat and pulled them ashore.
Tag line, reporter's conclusion, seeking to subtly emphasize incongruity	Steppe and Stanley are in pretty good shape today, although both are suffering from colds and Stanley barely missed a case of pneumonia. Blackie? He's fine, and there's a possibility he may enjoy a sirloin steak for his efforts. The men haven't quite been able to make up their minds yet.

One final point about writing style is that the feature writer is allowed more leeway to be somewhat subjective in the treatment of his material. He is much more likely, for example, to be descriptive to the point of presenting some degree of personal opinion. He may reach conclusions about a subject or an individual in a feature, such as the tag line in the Labrador Retriever story. He may even go beyond subjectivity at times, even to the extent of presenting material which, if taken literally, is untrue. For example, take a feature about an immigrant who was called home suddenly by the death of his mother whom he had not seen for 30 years. There was no time for obtaining a passport by the conventional means, but through the efforts of his employer, friends and government employes, he was soon flying across the Atlantic on his way home. The writer of the story wrote: "Yards of broken red tape trailed after the plane."

This freedom to use untruth can be carried only so far. In this example, the statement is so obviously not intended to be taken literally that the reporter is not likely to get into difficulty. But he must be very careful. He never has the right to create facts. He must stick with the situation as it is, avoiding any degree of fiction except that which is rhetorical and is bound to be understood that way by the reader. Accuracy applies to feature stories just as much as to straight news writing.

Story Organization. This will be brief because there are few guidelines. A story can be organized in any logical manner which satisfies the reporter's purpose. To say there are few rules, however, is not to say there is no organization. It means simply that the reporter decides the best pattern in which to write his story and then organizes his facts according to that pattern.

This may involve use of the inverted pyramid, although incidences are rather rare. It may be suspended-interest organization in which the writer deliberately withholds the important element for the end. It may be pure chronology. In some cases (usually longer stories), the reporter may elect to use "flashbacks" as he seeks to tie present with the past. The only requirement is that it be logical so that the sequence is clear to the reader. If the reporter accomplishes his purpose and the reader can follow his description to that purpose, the organization is just right for the story regardless of what form it has taken.

Postscript

Feature writing requires greater thought and effort by the reporter than the standard news story. It does this because he must make several subtle decisions about leads, language, style and organization. There are few guidelines to which he can refer. Thus, don't be misled into thinking that feature writing is fun because it is easy; it is fun, but primarily because of the challenge which the reporter must face. If he overcomes this challenge, then feature writing is extremely satisfying.

And the reporter who develops the talent to use the principles of feature writing in all his stories will have a most valuable tool. Much of what is dull and uninteresting in some news stories stems from reporters' inability to use techniques which would make those stories interesting. Of course, straight news writing, being what it is, cannot be written in precisely the same way as a feature story. But a more casual style, a more informal approach, skill in language choice, use of drama and an appreciation for human interest all could add to the readability and interest of most regular news stories.

CHAPTER 11

The Journalist and the Law

The First Amendment to the U.S. Constitution may say that "Congress shall make no law . . . abridging the freedom of speech, or of the press," and the Fourteenth Amendment may place that same restriction on state and local governments, but those amendments don't mean that law has no impact on the journalist.

For example, the First Amendment never has been interpreted as forbidding libel legislation. Obscenity statutes outlaw publication of certain materials. Copyright laws both protect and restrict the press. Publications must meet requirements to use the mails for distribution. Broadcast journalists face government controls that the print media do not have to worry about.

The law also can be a tool to be used to the journalist's advantage. With it, he can pry public information out of uncooperative public officials, gain access to meetings, and protect confidential sources and information.

And the law itself often is news. Journalists who understand it can do a better job of reporting about crime, police activities, government affairs and courtroom events.

Libel

The most widely known restriction on journalism is libel legislation. Basically, libel is "any written publication that is injurious to the reputation of another" (Black's Law Dictionary). The concept, however, extends beyond the print media to such forms of communication as film, pictures, signs, cartoons and, in most jurisdictions, broadcasting. Libel is more serious than and distinguished from slander (spoken defamation) because of its permanence or wide distribution. It must include defamation (injury to reputation), publication (communication to one or more persons), and identification of the defamed party. Truth is not always a defense.

This chapter was authored by Katie Sowle, an attorney, and Tom Price, a free-lance writer, both of whom have taught part-time in the Ohio University School of Journalism.

There are two types of libel—"libel per se" and "libel per quod."

Libel per se is injurious on its face, such as a charge of criminal conduct. It varies with society's attitudes, according to time, place and circumstances. For instance, calling a person a Communist was not considered libel per se until emotional anticommunism became widespread in the 1950s. In the past, in certain parts of the South, calling a white person black was considered libel per se.

Libel per quod is not injurious on its face, but circumstances can make an otherwise innocent comment libel per quod. For example, to refer to a woman as a mother would not be libel per se, but if she were unmarried it could be libel per quod.

In libel per se, damages are presumed and the jury fixes the amount. In libel per quod, the plaintiff must prove damages. Where malice is proved, punitive damages also may be awarded. In libel per se, malice is assumed, but proof of actual malice can result in even higher damages being awarded by a jury. A jury can award much higher damages than any actual financial loss suffered by the plaintiff. At times, a judge can lower a jury-determined damage award, but loss of a libel case still can be ruinously expensive for a news medium.

All who take part in publication of the libel can be held responsible, including the source of the libelous information, the reporter and the publisher. Some jurisdictions hold that a newspaper is guilty of libel for publishing a libelous wire service story. Accurately reporting what someone else said does not relieve a newspaper of responsibility if the statement is libelous. A misleading headline can be libelous, even if the story it tops is not.

The status of the defamed party is crucial in libel cases. Journalists have much more freedom in criticizing and reporting about government officials than they have when dealing with ordinary private citizens. Other public figures also have less libel protection than private individuals. And an ordinary citizen can become a public figure by actions or circumstances beyond his control which thrust him into public view.

In the all-important *New York Times v. Sullivan* case (1964), the U.S. Supreme Court ruled, "The constitutional guarantees require, we think, a federal rule that prohibits a public official from recovering damages for a defamatory falsehood relating to his official conduct unless he proves that the statement was made with 'actual malice'—that is, with knowledge that it was false or with reckless disregard of whether it was false or not."

A private citizen, however, not only does not have to prove "actual malice" in a published falsehood but even may win a libel suit stemming from a truthful publication. In roughly half the states, truth is a defense only when published with good motives and for justifiable ends. Even in jurisdictions where truth is a defense, the often difficult burden of proving truth belongs to the defendant. Key aspects of the case would be the actual newsworthiness of the item and the medium's motivation for making the item public. Mr. Jones' love affair with Mrs. Smith, even if true, may not be a safe subject for a newspaper report.

Traditionally, "fair comment" has been a defense against libel in expression of opinion about the public work of a person in public life. "Public figures" include politicians, government officials, artists, entertainers and others who place their work before the public eye or who exercise public power. "Fair comment" protects only the journalist's comments about the public figure's public works (such as an artist's paintings), not aspects of his private life unrelated to his public actions. And the comments must represent the commenter's honest belief or opinion and must not be grounded in malice.

The "New York Times Doctrine" allows even more freedom for reporting on and commenting about public *officials*. The doctrine applies to purported statements of fact as well as expressions of opinion, and it significantly redefines malice.

Several landmarks were established in the Times case. It is impossible to libel units of government, and in the Times case the court held that a government official cannot claim to have been libeled by an "impersonal attack on governmental operations." Even if identified, the public official must prove that the defendant knowingly published a false statement or acted in "reckless disregard of whether it was false or not."

In *Rosenblatt v. Baer* (1966), the Supreme Court said the "public official" designation applies "at the very least to those among the hierarchy of government employees who have, or appear to the public to have, substantial responsibility for or control over the conduct of governmental affairs." Candidates for public office have been included in the scope of the Times Doctrine, as have participants in public debates "of grave public concern." And court decisions indicate that just about every detail of an elected official's (and candidate's) life is related to his public work, unlike a simple "public figure" who has at least some private affairs not exposed to "fair comment."

Two close and highly criticized Supreme Court cases extended

Times Doctrine coverage to "matters of public interest" and "matters of public or general concern," but this extended doctrine is not stable and the court recently agreed to review an appeal from a lower court that had followed the doctrine.

The extension occurred in the 1967 *Time, Inc. v. Hill* case, when the Supreme Court, in a 5-4 decision, applied the Times Doctrine to a New York right of privacy case involving "false reports of matters of public interest." In a 1971 libel case, *Rosenbloom v. Metromedia, Inc.*, the court—voting 5-3 with one justice not taking part and the majority issuing three separate opinions—extended Times Doctrine coverage to, in the words of the three-member plurality, "all discussion and communication involving matters of public concern, without regard to whether the persons involved are famous or anonymous."

Also unstable is the definition of "matters of public interest" or "of public or general concern." In 1972, the court dismissed a newspaper's appeal from a lower court decision that a person who signed an appearance bond for another person charged with a Peeping Tom offense was not involved in an event of public or general concern. The accused Peeping Tom failed to appear for arraignment and the newspaper erroneously identified the person who signed the appearance bond as the defendant in the case.

Although there is no such thing as libel of government, there are group libel, corporation libel and trade libel.

A group can be libeled only when it is so small that its individual members can be identified. In 1952, U.S.A. Confidential reported, "Some Neiman models are call girls—the top babes in town... the sales girls are good, too—pretty, and often much cheaper—20 bucks on the average." In *Neiman-Marcus Co. v. Lait,* a federal district court ruled that the nine models employed by the store were eligible to sue but the 30 sales girls acting in behalf of the 385 employed by the store were ineligible because their group was too large for individual identification.

Corporations and partnerships are eligible to sue for libel damages, as are unions and nonprofit organizations. The guidelines are basically the same as those applying to individuals, with the same distinctions between public and private figures. It would be easier for the local garden club to win a libel suit, for example, than for the Democratic party to win such a suit.

Trade libel is a form of unfair competition in which property or goods are disparaged to the financial disadvantage of their owner. Falsehood, malice and actual damage must be proved.

Prosecutions for criminal libel are disappearing from the American scene, but criminal libel statutes continue to exist in many jurisdictions. Underlying the doctrine of criminal libel is the theory that the defamation would tend to provoke breach of the peace. Truth could be irrelevant, although many jurisdictions allow truth as a defense.

In 1952, the Supreme Court upheld, 5-4, an Illinois criminal libel statute in a case involving a "hatemonger" who circulated literature that defamed blacks. The decision was highly criticized as threatening to approve suppression of unpopular expression. In 1964, the court applied the then-new New York Times Doctrine in overturning a Louisiana criminal libel statute that imposed criminal sanctions for criticism of official conduct of public officials. In 1972, the court ruled that criminal libel can be sustained "only when it is limited in application to words that have a direct tendency to cause acts of violence."

Libel of the dead can be prosecuted only under criminal statutes.

Qualified Privilege

"Qualified privilege" permits fair and impartial reporting on judicial, legislative and other public and official proceedings and documents—even if the reporting would be libelous in other circumstances. Fairness is defined in terms of accuracy, good faith and absence of malice. Privilege protects the reporter even if he knows the statement he quotes to be false.

Privilege is based on the theory that any member of the public, if present, could observe the proceedings or documents for himself and the reporter functions as the public's eyes and ears. Privilege is grounded in common law but is statutory or constitutional in most states, and its details differ from jurisdiction to jurisdiction.

Generally, privilege covers trials, legislative meetings, police arrest records, court records, and other governmental meetings and documents. In some states, privilege extends to all public, not just governmental, meetings at which public issues are discussed. Some decisions have extended it to reports on executive sessions and on secret documents obtained by reporters through irregular channels.

But, as with all libel-related matters, the reporter must exercise care when seeking the protection of privilege. Privilege has been applied to reports of a senator's corridor press conference after an executive session of a congressional subcommittee and to a formal interview with a state attorney general. Privilege also has been extended to official pronouncements of government officials.

But casual conversation with an official at a social gathering is not privileged. And many states require that substantial judicial action be taken before privilege applies to court records. A suit filed with a clerk of courts, for example, might not be privileged until the defendant is served or some other official court action is taken. Clear identification in the news report of the privileged proceeding, document or official also is advisable.

Mitigating Factors

Retractions, apologies, corrections and publication of replies are not defenses for libel, but they can be mitigating factors in determination of malice and assessment of damages, as can proof of a plaintiff's bad reputation or of a defendant's basing a libelous report on usually reliable sources.

Obscenity

Journalists are restricted also by obscenity statutes, under the theory that obscenity and pornography are not protected by the Constitution. Obscenity statutes vary from state to state, but they can be no stricter than what the Supreme Court will allow. The Supreme Court's definition of obscenity is, of necessity, subjective and likely to change with time and with the changing composition of the court itself

Currently, the leading obscenity decision is *Miller v. California,* together with four companion cases (1973). In *Miller,* a 5-4 decision, the majority of the court said the "basic guidelines" for determining obscenity must be:
"(a) whether 'the average person, applying contemporary community standards,' would find the work, taken as a whole, appeals to the prurient interest; (b) whether the work depicts or describes, in a patently offensive way, sexual conduct specifically defined by the applicable state law, and (c) whether the work, taken as a whole, lacks serious literary, artistic, political, or scientific value." "Community standards" may be local standards which could differ from community to community.

Knowledge that material is obscene is a prerequisite for a distributor to be convicted of violating obscenity statutes. But a distributor specializing in "adult books" could be presumed to have such knowledge.

Sales and promotion methods can lead to conviction "where the purveyor's sole emphasis is on the sexually provocative aspects of his publications" (*Ginzburg v. U.S.,* 1966). Composition of the audience also can be a key factor, the court recognizing that a publication obscene to one group may not be obscene to another. (*Mishkin v. New York*, 1966).

Postal Regulations

The Postal Service may seize any mail it considers to be obscene. If the sender objects, the Postal Service must conduct a hearing and the sender has the right of appeal. Postal regulations also forbid publications using the mails for distribution to publish information about lotteries, information about how to obtain foreign divorces, and "any matter advocating or urging treason, insurrection, or forceable resistance to any law of the United States."

Constitutional doctrine, however, might limit the effectiveness of these regulations should a publisher lose a second-class mailing permit because of them and appeal his loss to the courts.

Copyright

Journalists are both restricted and protected by copyright. They are restricted from plagiarizing other journalists' work, but their own work also is protected.

Copyright is provided for in the U.S. Constitution, and plagiarism also can be prosecuted as unfair competition. A specific news article, as a literary product, is copyrightable, but the news content itself is not. Also copyrightable are photos, cartoons, maps, columns, interviews, special series and other features. Copyright protection also has been extended to broadcasts and motion pictures.

Quotation from a copyrighted work for "legitimate purposes" is permitted, the test being whether so much of the work is reproduced as to cost the author his audience. Paraphrasing or rough copying may constitute copyright infringement.

Although "news," as such, cannot be copyrighted, the Supreme Court has held that a news medium does have certain property rights to information it gathers. In 1918, the court ruled that the International News Service (INS) was guilty of unfair competition for picking up, rewriting and then transmitting AP-transmitted news in direct competition with its rival press service.

The key in this situation is competition—INS would be permitted use of AP-gathered news after enough time had elapsed to eliminate the competitive aspect of the practice, and a publication in one section of the country could pick up news from a publication in another section as long as the two publications were not seeking the same audience.

Each whole section of a publication may be copyrighted, with the understanding that some portions of it may not be protected, and individual items may be copyrighted. Copyright is obtained simply by entering the word "copyright," the symbol © or the abbreviation "copr.," with the name of the copyrighter and the date of first publication. A work need not be registered with the U.S. Copyright Office to be copyrighted, but it must be registered before suit can be filed under federal copyright statutes. Copyright cannot be registered until after publication, although common law copyright protects unpublished work.

To register a copyright, the author should write to the Copyright Office for proper forms, then return the completed forms along with $2 and two copies of the published work. Book copyright registration also must be accompanied by a notarized affidavit testifying that the book was printed from type set in the United States or from plates made in the United States from type set within the United States.

Copyright may be assigned, granted or mortgaged by an instrument signed by the holder and may be bequeathed in a will. Assignment does not have to be registered, but an unregistered assignment would be void against any subsequent registered assignment, so it is advisable to register.

The copyright endures for 28 years from the date of first publication and may be renewed for an additional 28 years. Afterward, the work enters the public domain.

Covering the Courts

Most journalists will never enter court as parties to lawsuits, but many will be expected to report on court activities. To be a successful courtroom journalist, a reporter must know how the judicial system functions and the rights of and possible restrictions on the press in that process.

Because extensive prejudicial news coverage of an alleged crime can threaten a defendant's right to a fair trial, the law and journalism professions have clashed repeatedly over the "fair trial-free press" issue. There is a basic constitutional assumption that trials are public affairs, and this greatly limits the powers of courts to restrict press coverage of judicial affairs. The Sixth Amendment guarantees that "in all criminal prosecutions the accused shall enjoy the right to a speedy and public trial." But the Supreme Court has not firmly ruled that the press cannot be restricted in certain ways. And questions exist about whether the defendant could have his trial closed to the public at his request and whether the public trial guarantee applies in civil suits.

So far, the only challenged attempts by judges to close trials to the press and public have not been upheld; neither have attempts to forbid reporting on court proceedings held outside the presence of the jury or attempts to clear the courtroom to prevent press coverage. But the Supreme Court has not made a final determination of whether a judge ever could do so, and some traditionally secret proceedings do exist in some jurisdictions (such as juvenile court activities and certain domestic matters).

Because of the uncertain nature of the open trial situation, and in light of the traditional prejudice in favor of public proceedings, a journalist would be wise to appeal to a higher court should a judge ever attempt to restrict reporting on court proceedings. Probably, accurate, complete reporting on all stages of the judicial process is protected by the Constitution and common law. For unfair reporting or editorializing, however, journalists might be convicted of contempt of court if their actions presented a clear and present danger to the administration of justice and the conduct of fair trials. Journalists can be restricted by the court's power to regulate conduct within the courtroom (hence, near-universal bans on photography and broadcasting within the courtroom), but judges cannot prevent dissemination of public information to the public.

In most jurisdictions, the criminal judicial process begins with arrest, which is a public record. The defendant then has a preliminary hearing, at which the judge can try a misdemeanor and determine whether an accused felon should be bound over to the grand jury. The grand jury, meeting in secret, decides whether to return an indictment against the defendant. If indicted, the defendant goes before a trial judge and enters his plea. Following possible pre-trial motions, the trial is conducted before a jury or before the judge alone, at the defendant's choice. Stages of a jury trial include jury selection, opening statements by the prosecution and defense, prosecution evidence, defense evidence, prosecution rebuttal, closing statements by both sides, the judge's instructions to the jury, jury deliberation, the jury's verdict, sentencing and possibly appeals. All but the grand jury and petit jury deliberations are open to the public.

Open Meetings, Public Records

Laws providing for open meetings and public records vary from state to state and exist at the federal level. Legislatures and administrative agencies determine what government proceedings and

THE JOURNALIST AND THE LAW

documents are open to the public. The Federal Freedom of Information Act, billed at its passage as a blow for open government, provides much less freedom of information than its title implies. Journalists have found themselves forced into court or climbing the ladder of bureaucracy to obtain information they assumed to be open to them under the law. Reporters refused access to government records or attendance at government meetings must look to the applicable federal, state or local legislation to determine whether what they want is public by law or at the discretion of the government officials involved.

Journalists who obtain restricted government information, except possibly in extreme circumstances, cannot be restrained from publication. They could face criminal prosecution after publication, but again only in extreme circumstances.

In the famous Pentagon Papers case, the Supreme Court said that "any system of prior restraints of expression comes to this Court bearing a heavy presumption against its constitutional validity." Thus, the court said, the government "carries a heavy burden of showing justification for the enforcement of such a restraint." The door to prior restraint and post-publication prosecution was left ajar, however, with at least the "clear and present danger" test as a restriction on government retribution.

Confidential Sources and Information

Another legal situation which varies from state to state and is of great importance to journalists is the reporter's right (or lack thereof) to protect confidential sources and information. Many journalists had assumed a constitutional right to refuse to reveal confidential sources and unpublished information, but in 1972 the Supreme Court ruled that no such protection exists. The court did, however, say that Congress could enact legislation to provide so-called "reporter's shield" protection and warned that the government could not subpoena reporters simply to harass and intimidate them.

As of mid-1973, Congress had not acted on the court's invitation and just 19 of the 50 state legislatures had provided shield protection, most of them allowing less than total immunity from subpoena. Of the 19 shield laws, all of which cover newspapers, 10 don't mention magazines or periodicals, two don't mention radio stations, three don't mention television stations, 18 don't mention broadcast networks, 17 don't mention cable operations, and seven don't mention news services or press associations. All 19 cover judicial proceedings, but five don't mention legislative bodies and three don't mention administrative agencies. Eighteen specifically protect sources of information, but only three mention information itself and only two mention the means by which the information is received. One, Michigan's law, protects any communication between reporter and informant but doesn't specifically protect the identity of the informant. Six of the states qualify the protection to some extent, usually using such general and subjective terms as "public welfare" and "public interest."

Again, the individual reporter would be wise to examine the law in his state to determine whether and to what extent he is protected.

Broadcast Journalism

The First Amendment does not protect the broadcast journalist to the extent it protects the print media. The justification for the different treatment lies in the theory that anyone with a mimeograph machine can publish while the number of radio and television channels available is limited.

The radio or television station, as a government-licensed operation, must abide by many government regulations. The ultimate punishment for failure to abide is loss of license.

The two most important regulations on broadcast journalists are the Equal Time and Fairness doctrines. The Equal Time provision requires that if a station permits one legally qualified candidate for government office to purchase time on the air it must allow all opponents to purchase equal time. If one candidate is given free time, all opponents must be given similar free time. Exceptions are granted for a "bona fide newscast, bona fide news documentary, bona fide news interview, on-the-spot coverage of bona fide news events."

The Fairness Doctrine requires a station to provide "fair and adequate treatment on controversial issues" to all sides of the issues. It is an "affirmative duty," requiring a station to seek out the conflicting views, not simply to broadcast them in response to an advocate's demand.

Stations are permitted—in fact encouraged—to editorialize. But they must provide opportunity for replies.

Current broadcast laws could be revolutionized by the development of cablecasting, with its vastly increased number of channels. Cable could destroy the foundation of the rationale for denying broadcasting First Amendment protections available to the print media.

Summary

The most important lesson a journalist can learn about the law is to consult an attorney—preferably a specialist in communications law—whenever an important legal question arises. The second most important lesson he can learn is that care, accuracy, fairness and common sense are the keys to avoiding violation of libel, obscenity, copyright, postal and other laws and regulations.

Basically, libel is "any written publication that is injurious to the reputation of another," but the impact of libel legislation varies with the status of the person defamed and the circumstances surrounding the defamation. Retractions, apologies, corrections and publication of replies are not defenses for libel, but they can be mitigating factors. "Qualified privilege" permits fair and impartial reporting on judicial, legislative and other public and official proceedings and documents—even if the reporting would be libelous in other circumstances.

Journalists and other mass communicators are restricted by obscenity statutes and postal regulations, but the Supreme Court has allowed such restrictions to apply only in limited ways.

Copyright both protects a journalist's work and prevents him from plagiarizing the work of others.

So far, challenged attempts by judges to restrict press coverage of traditionally public judicial proceedings have failed, but the Supreme Court has not made a final determination of whether a judge ever could succeed and certain proceedings (such as juvenile court activities in some jurisdictions) traditionally have been conducted in secret. A journalist facing judicial restrictions on his reporting would be wise to appeal to a higher court.

Laws governing open meetings, public records and protection of confidential sources and information vary from jurisdiction to jurisdiction. To know where he stands, the journalist must consult the laws of his state and locality.

Broadcast journalism faces more government control than the print media, under the theory that the limited number of radio and TV channels creates a public utility that should be licensed by the government. But the development of cablecasting could destroy the foundation of that theory.

CHAPTER 12

Beyond the Fundamentals

By the time he gets to this chapter, the reader should sense that many traditions have stood the test of time in American journalism. The reporter's heritage is a rich one. He takes great pride in *speed*—in scoring a beat. He knows that *courage* and *persistence* have been and always will be the real keys to Pulitzer Prizes. And he vigorously defends his *independence* from special interests (it's been said that a reporter isn't doing his job unless he has some enemies).

That said, society is changing, and journalism must change with it. There's little agreement as to just what changes should occur and who should make them. However, the debate is opening new vistas—many of them related to the phrase *interpretive reporting*.

Like most abstract words, interpretation is vague. Before we can try to define it, we must get some idea of where it comes from. This, in turn, requires a brief look at the press's role in society—past, present and future.

A Look at the Press in Society

Contemporary scholars distinguish among four theories or sets of beliefs about the press.[1] *Authoritarian* and *Communist* beliefs have few followers among American editors. Thus we will focus on the *libertarian* and *social responsibility* theories.

Libertarian Theory

For perhaps a century leading up to roughly 1915, the western world as a whole seemed to be thriving. Adam Smith's "every man for himself" economics gained in popularity among businessmen and academicians. Further, intellectuals developed great faith in man's rationality. This faith went along with the idea that man ought to express himself freely because the good and true will win out in free and open encounter with the bad, untrue and trivial. British philosopher John Stuart Mill argued for free expression because:

1. If we silence an opinion, we may be silencing the truth. That's because finding the truth requires combat among all available ideas in the "free marketplace."

2. A wrong opinion may contain a grain of truth necessary for finding the whole truth.

3. People will hold an opinion as an irrational prejudice unless they are forced to defend it. Prejudices are bad because they are irrational.

4. Unless commonly held opinions are contested from time to time, they lose their vitality and their effect on conduct and character.[2]

It was perfectly all right to the libertarian if work was primarily to make money. Smith's economics, along with faith in man's rational power, suggested no need to hold back. Man could look after himself, so journalists could pursue their own business interests with few pangs of conscience.[3]

All of this is not to suggest that American journalism in the 1800s lacked professional ethics and ideals. Pioneer editors like Joseph Pulitzer and James Gordon Bennett sought to influence the political system though strict profit-and-loss figures might suggest focusing entirely on sex, blood and gore. Also, many if not most libertarians recognized a need to discourage ill-founded character assassination[4] and to remain mum on occasion for the public good.[5]

The libertarian press enjoyed unprecedented guarantees of press freedom. Such special treatment stemmed from a deep-seated belief in the press as a watchdog needed to make democratic government "serve the interests of liberalism." Obviously, then, libertarians saw a newspaper as something very special, not just another business.

To the conscientious libertarian, the name of the game was accurate, complete reporting of facts. In covering a speech, one should describe events so a reader can feel as though he was actually sitting in the audience. The reader, it's implied, can do most of the interpreting.[6]

Early American editors placed great emphasis on editorial writing, too. They felt all arguments—opinionated and factual—should vie openly in the free marketplace of ideas.

Social Responsibility Theory

In the vernacular, Western civilization has "laid quite a few eggs" during the twentieth century. The "war to end all wars," which came to an end in 1918, proved to be merely a beginning. Civil rights movements, revolts against colonialism in Asia and Africa, and other forces of social change seemed to call attention to man's frailties.

In academic circles, such schools of thought as Freudian psychology, behavioristic or stimulus-response psychology and social Darwinism suggested that man is moved more by inner conflicts and drives, a desire to belong and a need to feel important, than by his brain.

Against this background, a group of scholars came together in 1947 to consider the role of the press in society. Working under the leadership of Chancellor Robert Hutchins of the University of Chicago, these scholars were the first to really articulate social responsibility theory.

It's important to remember that the Hutchins Commission did not start from scratch. Rather, it elaborated and pulled together principles long accepted by many press critics and newsmen. In fact, social responsibility theory is really a revision of rather than a sharp departure from libertarian thinking. Both theories contain many of the same ideas, but with different twists.

To begin with, the commission challenged the basic premise that man's wisdom will insure the victory of truth in open battle with falsehood. Not only is man a frail and often irrational being, but the world which he must seek to understand is becoming more and more complex. Furthermore, people in the Western world are very busy and have little time for thorough analysis of issues.

In view of all this, the reader needs help. The commission felt a truthful, comprehensive account of the news, while important, is not enough. "It is no longer enough to report the fact truthfully," the scholars emphasized. "It is now necessary to report *the truth about the fact.*"[7]

Criticism of old-fashioned methods has increased greatly in the last few years. There seem to be at least three arguments suggesting that what television commentator Eric Sevareid calls "flat, one-dimensional" reporting is sometimes unequal to its task.[8]

First, there is no such thing as pure objectivity. We have already developed this argument (see Chapter 2), and it seems patently obvious at first glance. However, editors tended to erect a very strict wall between fact and opinion by mid-twentieth century, often acting as though facts are somehow pure, ultimate and above reproach. Peterson comments that, when the Hutchins Commission met in 1947, objectivity of the press was no longer a goal. It was a fetish.[9]

A study of news columns reveals that the New York Times devotes much foreign news space to *procedures*—specific events and proposals advanced on disarmament and other issues. A Communist paper, on the other hand, stresses social issues and ends, not the procedural *means,* of the cold war. Gerbner suggests that a Communist would probably view the Times' coverage as opportunistic and superficial—as anything but objective. Objectivity, it's implied, is somewhat in the eyes of the beholder.[10]

Obviously a reporter must make decisions—even in writing a routine article. For example, an auto accident story will seldom if ever describe just how badly a license plate has been bent. The need to make even such choices as this precludes pure objectivity.

Second, meaningful reporting requires that the reporter provide relevant standards of comparison and make cause-and-effect statements. This requires thoughtful, somewhat subjective analysis.

Few, if any, facts have meaning, it's argued, unless they are interpreted in light of some standard of comparison or frame of reference.[11] A 6-foot-6 basketball star may look huge if we have just come from a midget show but very small if we have just watched Wilt Chamberlain play basketball. In the same vein, the Vietnam War was confusing partly because we have had no similar wars. Thus, we had no standard of comparison we could use with confidence in deciding whether daily casualty figures and battlefield gains were large or small. A reporter seemingly must try to provide such a standard or readers will feel very puzzled.

It's also obvious that an event often makes little sense unless one discusses the causes and implications of that event. And philosphers stress that cause-and-effect statements necessarily require subjective thinking. One cannot check the assertion that poverty causes riots with quite the same objective, scientific rigor that he can check a man's height.[12]

In general, it would seem, a depth story on a social issue should provide as much detailed discussion as possible on three fronts:

1. The cause of the problem (the past).

2. The extent of the problem (the present).

3. The solution or alternative solutions of the problem, as well as its impact on people. Such discussion involves prediction of the future, which a reporter obviously cannot observe directly before he writes a story. This in itself introduces an element of subjective analysis.

Third, traditional objective reporting can make the press vulnerable and sometimes destructive. Libertarian standards demand that a reporter report, with little comment, almost anything that interests lots of readers. Douglass Cater, a veteran Washington correspondent, notes that few reporters who covered the late Sen. Joseph McCarthy believed him. Yet what Cater calls the "frozen standards of journalism" required that the newsman pass on McCarthy's charges of Communist leaning to the public.[13] Publicity, perhaps more than anything else, made it possible for Senator McCarthy to spread fear at home and reduce American credibility abroad.[14]

In the wake of recent racial troubles, militant leaders like H. Rap Brown could get an audience—and a television camera—relatively easily. The pure libertarian journalist would feel little obligation to stress in his dispatches that Brown represented but a small minority of American Negroes. The social responsibility theorist would emphasize such a responsibility.

While critical of traditional methods, the social responsibility theorist has been somewhat vague in suggesting new ones. However, some trends are developing, and new issues are crystallizing.

The 1947 Commission on Freedom of the Press laid the groundwork by spelling out five goals for the press.[15] These requirements did not originate with the commission. Rather, they stemmed from the thinking of those who operate the media.[16]

1. The media must provide a forum for the exchange of comment gent account of the day's events in a context which gives them meaning." This simply reiterates that reporting a "fact," while necessary, is not enough.

2. The media provide a forum for the exchange of comment and criticism. A paper must report fairly on all sides of an issue. "Fairness" is admittedly hard to define. Few people would argue that a paper ought to give two candidates equal play when one of them is saying and doing most of the newsworthy things. However, a paper should work hard to cover all major sides of an issue—particularly those sides opposed to the paper's own views.

3. The media must give a representative picture of the various groups making up society, avoiding over-simplified, inaccurate stereotypes.

4. The media must present and clarify the goals and values of society. Recent scholarship suggests that reporting may promote conflict in some communities, consensus in others.[17] In fact, suburban and community papers tend to stress controversial issues much less than do crusading metropolitan papers.[18] The Hutchins Commission seems to imply an editor must decide which role is important in his particular situation.

BEYOND THE FUNDAMENTALS

5. The media must provide "full access to the day's intelligence." No area of public interest must be ignored simply because a paper finds it easy or expedient to look the other way.

These brief statements do little more than open the door for discussion of interpretive reporting. One characteristic of such reporting is its focus on *issues* rather than isolated *events*.

Interpretive Reporting—What Does It Require?

Historically, the "city side" staffs of most American newspapers have concentrated largely on reporting a large variety of events—fires, conventions, city council meetings, crimes, and the like—as they happened. While granting the need for such coverage, critics who lean toward social responsibility thinking feel a need to go beyond it.

For one thing, strict event reporting makes a typical newspaper page look like a rather chaotic hodge podge, with a story on war losses in some remote corner of the world right alongside reports of a new auto brake lining in Detroit and a newly crowned Miss America in Atlantic City. Such weird association, along with a lack of background on any one story, allegedly adds to the reader's feeling of confusion.

Second, "events" really do little to enlighten the public. The typical American has but a few minutes each day to spend with his newspaper. Perhaps he could learn more by reading about a few key issues than about fires, murders and the like. After all, understanding issues is presumably more crucial than reading of isolated fires and crimes when it comes to being a wise, active citizen.

Those who defend primary emphasis on "event" reporting reply that long, detailed stories simply won't sell papers. Furthermore, papers serve society partly by keeping an eye on the events around us, by acting as a kind of watchdog.[19] A paper that focuses on a few key issues while ignoring other things is bound to leave many blind spots. An opinion magazine like New Republic or Ramparts, which does focus on clarifying global issues, may stimulate and interest the reader. It does little to inform him.

Interpretive reporting has been suggested as an answer to the event versus issue argument. Advocates of this approach acknowledge that a paper must inform people about day-to-day events. At the same time, they say, special techniques and viewpoints are needed on complex stories.[20]

Contrary to some criticism, interpretation does not mean a retreat to subjective editorializing. Rather, it involves using special approaches to insure a kind of objectivity. We now look at several such approaches.

Some Tools of Interpretation

Taking Time to Dig Out Thorough Background. Freed from tight deadlines, a depth reporter may spend weeks or even months on a specific story. Some large organizations like The Associated Press assign several men to one story. After intensive study, for example, a campus riot may look like part of a nation-wide radical conspiracy if it turns out that the leaders of that riot had also been on campuses all over the country.

Reporting of this sort does not play down facts. It seeks to clarify relationships among them.

Making a Strong Effort to Discuss All Sides of an Issue. The strict "event" reporter would cover a speech and let it go at that. The interpreter would feel an obligation to put these facts in perspective by presenting the other side. Such library tools as *The Reader's Guide to Periodical Literature*, *The Education Index* and *Sociological Abstracts* can point to needed background reading. Also helpful are current events sources like *The New York Times Index* and *Facts on File*. This is discussed in Chapter 7.

Using Other Than Traditional Ways to Organize a Story. Certainly few if any journalists would advocate turning tradition upside down very often by using an upright pyramid or climax form with the punchline at the end. Very seldom will anticipation of an exciting ending hold interest through an entire story.

However, the interpretive reporter might question to some degree strict adherence to the inverted pyramid on all stories. Many newsmen justify the inverted pyramid on the grounds that people don't read far into stories on the whole, so important points near the end would get little readership. Critics sometimes reply that it's hard to tell which came first here—the chicken or the egg. Readers may get through only the first few paragraphs partly because long newspaper use of the inverted pyramid has conditioned them to believe closing paragraphs are trivial. Thus the inverted pyramid may perpetuate and help create the skimming behavior often cited to justify it.

As noted in Chapter 10, suspended interest leads have a place in journalism. So does chronological ordering.

At least two story formats have received less attention than they deserve. These are the "question and answer" and "written debate" formats.

BEYOND THE FUNDAMENTALS

In the "question and answer" story, one or more reporters interview one or more news sources. Both questions and answers are recorded, usually with a tape recorder. The story first fills readers in on the news source or sources, on their topic, and on why that topic is important. Then both questions and answers are printed verbatim.* Parenthetical remarks not in the interview itself may clarify points that readers can't easily understand.

U.S. News and World Report uses this format regularly. Question and answer stories there tend to have an informal, conversational air that may help retain interest. Also, verbatim quotation itself, along with emphasis on the source and his credentials, adds a ring of authenticity.

We have coined the expression "printed debate" to designate a story format which journalists apparently haven't gotten around to naming. Such a story begins by defining an issue and telling the reader why it's important. Also, early in the story, a proposed action to solve the problem is described. Then comes a detailed summary of pro (or anti) arguments about the proposal, followed by anti (or pro) arguments. If space permits, pro and anti sections of the story may appear side by side under separate subheads to emphasize the contrast between them.

The term "printed debate" seems appropriate because such a story resembles a traditional debate. There is one key difference, however. A "printed debate" story, unlike the typical debater, may reach no conclusion. Instead, it may present arguments and stop, leaving the reader to make his own analysis. (Of course, if arguments are many and complex, a concluding summary may insure that the reader comes away with a clear grasp of the important arguments and the alternatives among which he can choose.)

Educational agencies such as the Cooperative Extension Service have used materials printed in this form to stimulate group discussion. "Printed debate" stories certainly fit the classical libertarian notion of ideas vying in free and open combat. A slight variant is the story with two or more alternatives discussed, rather than the pros and cons of one alternative.

A story in "printed debate" form which also exemplifies several other approaches discussed earlier is given opposite.

---

*Some editors advocate removing incorrect grammar, slips of the tongue and meaningless phrases. Others object on the grounds that a politician's semi-literacy is of interest to readers. The present authors would insist that such editing be done only if the reader is informed about it.

SHOULD THE U.S. GOVERNMENT PROVIDE FREE BIRTH CONTROL COUNSELING AND INFORMATION ON A LARGE SCALE?

Since about 1967, federal efforts to provide birth control information have gained impetus. It's estimated that about 5 million low-income American women want but don't now have access to family planning assistance. President Nixon has recommended enough federal funding to serve all these people within five years.

There is some disagreement about the program's cost. Sen. Millard Tydings of Maryland has called for an annual federal investment of $360 million by about 1974.

In discussing this issue, we will ignore the broad philosophical question of government's proper role *in general*. We will look specifically at the pros and cons regarding government provision of family planning aid.

On the "Anti" Side

It's generally known that the Roman Catholic Church opposes the use of contraceptive drugs and devices. In addition, several other authorities have recently spoken out against evangelical promotion of family planning.

Promoters have consistently made some very dubious assumptions, according to Dr. Judith Blake, chairman of the Demography Department at the University of California, Berkeley.

For one thing, charges Dr. Blake, it's been suggested that poor people have been denied government aid in family planning because of a kind of upper-middle class "conspiracy of silence." Such a conspiracy, born out of middle class prudery, supposedly made the topic taboo in political circles until President Johnson and others tackled it head on in the 1960s.

The idea that birth control has long been taboo in America simply doesn't stand up under careful study, Dr. Blake claims. Pointing to 13 national polls from 1937 to 1966, she notes that:

1. As far back as 30 years ago, 75 per cent of American women approved of the government's making birth control available.

2. By the early 1960s, 80 per cent favored doing away with legal barriers and providing birth control information to anyone desiring it.

However, Dr. Blake charges family planning promoters with assuming too glibly that most or all American women want such help *for themselves*.

Pointing to eight national polls in 1943-64, she notes that low-educated folks were consistently somewhat more inclined than college graduates to reject making birth control help available.

Furthermore, she claims, uneducated, poor people specify larger "ideal family sizes" than do wealthy folks. In her view, government promotion of small families may be unethical where the people themselves want large families.

Even those who favor birth control itself have some reservations about letting a large federal bureaucracy promote it.

For one thing, contraceptives are a highly personal matter. Their use may be a godsend in one family situation but downright dangerous in another.

However, past experience suggests that a government bureaucracy, to survive, must show tangible results. Thus field workers may zealously promote family planning to reduce birth statistics without due regard for subtle, personal factors.

Opponents of publicly supported birth control also point to possible side effects of the pill. Some effects may require a long time to show up, and few women have yet been on the pill for more than a couple years. Much research is needed in this area.

A further argument is that family planning information in young hands may increase sexual promiscuity. Such freedom could contribute to a general permissiveness and lack of resolute character that's said to be sweeping the country.

In still a different vein, Dr. Blake feels contraceptive devices and techniques really touch only symptoms, not the root causes, of over-population.

What are the "root causes?" The Berkeley demographer points to several:

1. Role relationships and related, widely held beliefs about what's right and important. Our society considers it normal and right for couples to have kids. The childless couple is often seen as incomplete, unfulfilled.

2. Laws prohibiting homosexual behavior among even consenting adults. If legalized, such behavior might serve as an acceptable substitute for marriage and normal family life in the eyes of some people.

3. A tax policy which provides exemptions for dependents.

4. Broad socio-cultural patterns. In criticizing Robert Malthus' famous prophecies of world-wide over-population and famine, sociologists William Ogburn and Meyer Nimkoff say he failed to allow for cultural trends which reduced birth rates in the western world from 1860 to 1935. Increasing rates since 1945 are apparently in the same category. They have little to do with family planning as usually defined.

Thus far, we've discussed mostly what family planning and its promotion might mean to the parties directly involved. In contrast, many advocates in developing nations have defined planning as a patriotic duty to avoid famine for everyone.

Conceding such arguments may be valid in China and India, Newsweek columnist Henry C. Wallich strongly criticizes their application to the United States.

"By an international standard, the United States is underpopulated," Wallich asserts. "Per square mile, our population is minimal compared with that of European countries which seem able to maintain reasonable standards of public cleanliness, decorum and social efficiency."

The Newsweek writer also believes America's 200 million people have achieved a lot. This suggests they are not "the worst part of the world's genetic material." To limit U.S. population, therefore, would lower mankind's potential world-wide.

Third, Wallich contends that strong efforts to keep American population from growing will tend to widen the gap in living standards between ourselves and the developing nations. This, he warns, might tempt envious, haggard masses from these lands to attack America's shores.

Finally, while less important now than a century ago, numbers still influence a people's power. Indeed, says Wallich, Pope Paul VI may be on the right track if he is seeking to maximize Catholic influence by maximizing Catholics.

On the "Pro" Side

In several ways, opponents of a large-scale family planning program seem confused.

Dr. Blake, for example, claims many Americans favor making birth control information widely available. She cites this to disprove any "middle class conspiracy" which planning advocates allegedly use to justify a current crusade. However, her data can easily be interpreted to mean people want family planning help. She doesn't prove they already have it.

Certainly there is no denying that the birth of children to the unmarried and the poor has deeply disturbed many Americans.

Out-of-wedlock births now number 318,000 per year, 44 per cent of them to teenagers. Abstract moral questions aside, these births have several documented, unfortunate consequences:

1. Forced teenage marriages are more common than ever before. And they are far less apt to endure than marriages of mature men and women. Resulting divorces cause pain and maladjustment for thousands of kids.

2. People who must earn a living while in their teens have little chance for further education. As a result, many are all but forced into lives of poverty.

3. Parental resentment toward unwanted children often robs them of the warm, stable home environment they need. This leads to life-long personality disorders.

Turning from the young to the poor, 15 million American children now live in poverty by census definition. That includes more than half of all children in families of five or more.

Dr. Blake and others who subscribe to the "culture of poverty" myth (that the poor want and therefore should have large families) do not offer convincing proof. For one thing, they cite data stemming largely from poll questions asking respondents to name an "ideal family size." However, there's a difference between such an abstract figure and the size of family a respondent personally desires. Studies focusing on the latter type of question show conclusively that poor people *do not*, on the whole, want larger families than the others. Yet in 1960-65, poor Americans had an annual fertility rate 50 per cent greater than that for the rest of the populace.

When criticized for their ethics, planning advocates insist a massive government program would increase, not reduce, individual freedom.

BEYOND THE FUNDAMENTALS 205

The well-to-do have long enjoyed expensive planning aids, they say. Providing comparable help for everyone would not force it down anyone's throat. Participation would be strictly voluntary.

Also, there is little evidence that the pill increases sexual promiscuity.

At Stanford, Michigan, Cornell, Yale, California and Washington, coeds can obtain contraceptives on request. Almost without exception, officials at these universities insist students remain responsible in their sexual attitudes and behavior.

Conceding that much remains to be learned about "the pill" and its side effects, family planning officials insist one must weigh these dangers against social and medical costs of having unwanted children. The result differs from case to case, and each family should have expert help in making up its own mind.

Turning to the realm of national policy, Wallich's claim that the U.S. does not share an overpopulation problem with China and India has also been rejected. For example, Dr. P.K. Whelpton, director of the Scripps Foundation for Research in Population, says the nation has already passed its optimum for good living.

Whelpton feels the world can keep 4 or 5 billion people alive by 2000 A.D. (Demographers forecast 6 billion by then) "on a level of living like that of India or China today."

However, he warns, if we would like the best of living for Americans, we should aim for from 25 to 75 million fewer persons than we had even in 1956.

Robert and Leona Rienow, a man-and-wife team of biological scientists, note that many anti-pollution and conservation crusaders blame our deteriorating environment on waste and neglect of Mother Nature's bounty.

While basically valid, as the Rienows see it, such breast beating obscures the importance of plain overcrowding. The fished-out stream, unbearable noise, and countless other annoyances stem largely from packing too many people in a small area.

Recent research shows that animals can't stand crowding. Even when they get plenty of water and food, many rats in a small area lose their sanity. Apparently city folk who yell at most anything and ignore brethren lying in the street are little different.

Emphasizing Consequence As a News Element. In discussing news judgment, we have noted that many newsmen over-emphasize prominent people and bizarre happenings, as well as blood, sex and gore. Also, newsmen on the whole pay too little attention to events happening more than 24 hours before deadline.

Almost by definition, the interpretive reporter would look askance at these tendencies. His reason for being is to aid understanding—to clarify a story's consequence—rather than to titillate readers.

Of course, it does little good to report in depth if your stories go unread. No experienced newsman would completely do away with soft news. However, a surprising number of journalists seem to ignore the fact that one can both inform and entertain at the same time. Historians like Bruce Catton and novelists like Ernest Hemingway surely do both.

Telling the Reader About News Sources

Today's journalist—perhaps even more than his libertarian forefathers—needs to let the reader know about news sources. Only with such knowledge can one decide when he needs to take a story with a grain of salt.

Problems in this area are multiplying. Journalists need to quote experts more than ever. At the same time, politicians and others in responsible positions are becoming more and more reluctant to be quoted.

On the other hand, as we have seen, issues are becoming more complex. And the more specialized and complicated a story becomes, the more readers must rely on experts to decide whether conclusions are true or false. For example, most Americans will probably admit they know little about guided missiles. Much debate has centered on missiles in recent years, generally dealing with costs, the danger of misfires and the merits of thick vs. thin missile systems. Most of us know we can't draw our own conclusions from what we regard as the "raw facts." We must rely almost entirely on Pentagon officials and scholars.

At the same time, expert sources have refused more and more to be quoted because they feel their reputations and programs may suffer. Attribution to people like a "reliable source close to the White House" and a "high ranking Pentagon official" have become commonplace.[2][1]

Such attribution generally tells the reader nothing about the news source's specific qualifications and very little about possible biases (one may feel, of course, that a missile story from a Pentagon source is somewhat one-sided). Reporters accept the practice simply because they feel it's better than letting the flow of news stop.

Journalists may solve this problem in part by describing sources' backgrounds and positions in some detail without naming names. To be sure, this isn't always easy. Many news sources are anxious to avoid identification by colleagues and rival bureaucrats who can decide who a "highly placed source" really is on the basis of very limited cues.

It's generally recognized that a reporter should establish his source's authority (or lack of it) by giving information on *qualifications* and *biases*. Anyone covering a rabble-rousing speech will surely rate a chewing out from his city editor if he fails to mention the speaker is a Communist.

While adhering to these practices, many newsmen should go much further than they do in providing background about sources. For one thing, they often need to be careful about the use of titles and biographical information which seem to suggest an argument is between *individuals* rather than *viewpoints* or *professional traditions*.

The authors once read of a symposium involving several experts with diverse backgrounds—all suggesting possible future developments related to the Vietnam war.

One speaker—a former State Department employe—noted that a technological innovation promised to greatly improve agricultural yields in Vietnam. This innovation, he suggested, might have a great impact on the post-war political and economic picture.

Immediately a distinguished professor of history on the panel rose to ridicule the role of such innovations. The professor went on to insist that the future political and social climate of Vietnam would depend largely on establishment of a political system in which all groups could play a part.

In newspaper accounts of this exchange, the history professor appeared to have the better of it. His title, distinguished professor of history, carried a great deal more prestige than did "State Department information officer."

Such emphasis on titles seems to miss the point. A truly well-informed observer would realize that this was not really an argument between two individuals at all. Rather the argument was between two professional traditions to which the speakers belonged by training and experience.

The State Department man was a member of a growing corps of professionals sometimes known as "change agents." These people—employed mainly by churches, foundations, governments and the United Nations—seek to help developing countries adjust to rapid economic and social change. Most if not all change agents have been trained to stress technological change as a key force within a nation.

The historian, by training, views the world quite differently. He tends to focus on political events, particularly on those which show continuity over time. Most historians, in fact, pay little attention to short-term economic changes. They are inclined to laugh at the possibility that a new crop variety would quickly alter a society's way of life.

A really good reporter would somehow let the reader know that our two debaters are really *professional traditions,* not *individuals*.

The State Department worker acted as a typical change agent, the distinguished professor as a typical historian. The implication that the historian had the edge because he was a distinguished professor is very misleading. The debate, as we've said, was simply not between two isolated individuals.

Perhaps traditional news story format is ill equipped to handle this matter. Few editors would stand still for devoting half a story to a discussion of source qualifications. A pair of "side bar" articles, one discussing historians and one on change agents, might be in order.

Should the Reporter Specialize?

We have suggested that a ghetto reporter will often need the help of specialists in various areas like the social sciences. This brings us to a matter which bothers many journalism students. How specialized should a reporter himself become?

As issues become more complex, the general assignment reporter with no special area of concentration often feels at sea. He simply cannot grasp what's going on at a symposium or even a city council meeting. Chances are that, even in covering an ordinary beat, he will tend to specialize and read up on certain areas.

On the other hand, journalists seem useful partly because they are generalists. In a typical community, most leading citizens have vested interests in school bond issues, PTA banquets and so on. The editor may be the only one who can stand back and place all these projects and interest groups in perspective. One of the authors—a former editorial writer—used to avoid joining groups because he felt his job required a detached view of everything and everybody.

One solution to this problem may lie in a close "team" relationship between reporter and editor. The reporter may tend to be a specialist—writing about complex matters in a way which the layman can understand. The editor may play the generalist role, using new techniques of headline writing, layout and typographic treatment to clarify relations among various stories.

To be sure, papers may require specialized editors (in society, sports and business news, for example) as well as generalist reporters.

To conclude our discussion of specialization, libertarian theory emphasized the newsman as generalist. Social responsibility thinking seems to call for cooperation among various generalists and specialists. Just how such cooperation might occur lies beyond the scope of this book.

A good reporter should probably be part generalist and part specialist. In college he should take a broad, liberal arts curriculum (in fact, he'll probably have to if he's studying at a reputable journalism school) which will add to his versatility on the job. In addition, however, he may be well-advised to concentrate in one or two specific areas in addition to journalism. Specialists like Alton Blakeslee, Associated Press science writer, and Lane Palmer, editor of Farm Journal, are among the best paid, most respected newsmen anywhere.

To this point, we have been discussing issues and techniques which have been widely considered for some time throughout a wide segment of what might be termed the journalistic establishment. We now turn to some newer, less widely accepted and perhaps more controversial trends sometimes lumped under the heading "New Journalism."

NEW TRENDS IN JOURNALISM

Precision Journalism—Use of Social Science Techniques

In Chapter 2, we noted a need to report frustrations, hatred and aspirations. It's difficult to measure such things objectively (that is, so people with various biases will agree on the results). Fortunately, the social scientist's techniques of sampling and surveying help. Long used in academia, these tools are just beginning to find a place in journalism.

The Detroit Free Press tried to go below the surface in covering the 1967 ghetto riots in the Motor City. Free Press staffers teamed with social scientists from the University of Michigan and elsewhere to study the rioters and what made them tick.

An initial survey in 1967 revealed great discontent—much of it directed against storekeepers and landlords. The Free Press described these poll results at length.

A year later, the Free Press and its co-workers repeated the survey, using social scientific techniques such as random sampling, indirect questioning about sensitive topics and computer analysis of data.

At first glance, the 1968 re-run seemed to imply things hadn't cooled off much in Detroit's ghettos. Much resentment was still there. However, the social scientist's refined analysis revealed a somewhat different view.

For one thing, the year between surveys had produced a growing separation between *black power* and *black nationalism* as general ways of approaching racial problems. Black power, the position held by most Detroit Negroes, involves lawfully but aggressively seeking political and economic power, as well as social equality. Black nationalism holds that the Negro can achieve his just due only by separating himself from and perhaps destroying white America.

The social scientists reasoned that unrest would be in the offing if black power advocates also had a tinge of black nationalism. However, the study showed little tendency for large numbers of even militant, aggressive protestors to advocate creating a black nation within a white nation. Black nationalists were not only rare, they were a breed apart. They did not seem to influence the thinking of most Negro citizens.

A study of Detroit Negro leaders found that genuine black nationalists had a small—though highly committed—following. Politicians, ministers and other leading citizens—like their followers—avoided mixing black power with black nationalism.

To sum up, Detroit ghetto residents were still very unhappy in 1968. They complained about some things even more loudly in 1968 than they had in 1967. However, some constructive shifts in Negro thinking seemed to be under way. A riot didn't seem likely in the near future.

What might a paper's role be in carrying out and reporting such a study?

Clearly, a reporter must recognize that he cannot do the study himself without special training or help. It's far from easy to draw and contact a representative sample of ghetto residents. And it's just about as hard to phrase questions that yield accurate information on a sensitive topic like why one threw a stone, set fire to a building or left his family.

Reporting figures from a large survey is only the beginning. Somehow one must make their human implications clear. Facts and figures are *denotative,* but the Kerner Commission asks journalists to express partly *connotative* meaning. Statistics do not tell us much about the ghetto resident's "difficulties, his burning sense of grievance," as the commission put it.

Some observers suggest that the traditional news story simply is not up to the task at hand. The reporter must take his readers step by step through a day in the life of some individual who wakes up to the scratching of rats and can't afford a noon meal.

The good feature or human interest writer sticks to the facts and avoids high-flown, vague words, as is shown in Chapter 10. Yet he selects and presents these facts so the reader will cry, laugh and feel hurt or angry, so he experiences the events reported in a personal way.

A widely acclaimed piece of social-science based reporting quite different from riot analysis was the book *The Real Majority* by Richard E. Scammon and Ben J. Wattenberg. These authors combined the insider's fascination with and insight into the political process (Wattenberg had worked for both President Johnson and Vice-President Humphrey) with the trained discipline and skepticism of an outside expert (Scammon has become a political researcher).

"Ordinary" campaign coverage in recent years has tended to give credence to several beliefs which, in Scammon's and Wattenberg's view, simply don't hold up under careful study. Space limitations preclude a careful summary, but we will take a brief look at how the authors approached two such beliefs.

First, it was often said during and soon after the 1968 campaign that *politics has become largely a contest between the radical young and their conservative "hard-hat" elders.* The press often portrayed dedicated young people as the prime force behind Sen. Eugene McCarthy's meteoric rise during the 1968 New Hampshire primary. Young Yippies and Hippies were arrayed against Mayor Daley's cops, many of them over 30, during the Democratic convention in Chicago. Middle-aged "hard-hat" construction workers supposedly beat up on young anti-war protesters. And so on and on.

Such impressions monopolized press coverage, apparently, because newsmen looked only at the surface—at certain unusual, bizarre events appealing to traditional news values.

Study poll data, say Scammon and Wattenberg, and a different picture begins to emerge. For example, one survey showed that young collegians differed more in various attitudes from blue-collar youth without college training than from older folks. And an October 1968 Gallup poll even suggested that people under 30 were at least as hawkish about America's role in Vietnam—perhaps more so—than were those over 50.[22]

A second widely held assumption was in 1968 (and still is) that, *in an era of TV and "image makers," issues really don't count for much during a campaign.* The Real Majority implies that this view—while perhaps not entirely false—is over-simplified. In fact, the authors argue, the so-called *social issue* has emerged recently as a major determinant of voting. This issue really embodies various matters such as drugs, morality race relations, law and order, and campus unrest.

Scammon and Wattenberg used poll data in various ways to support their claim that the social issue was becoming increasingly salient. Also, as good traditional journalistic "diggers" and analysts, they noted a social-issue trend in several 1969 mayoral races across the country. For example:

—A law-and-order candidate became mayor in normally liberal Minneapolis.[23]

—In Los Angeles, a black ex-policeman named Tom Bradley took a surprisingly soft line on law-and-order and thereby handed over that issue, along with the election, to incumbent Sam Yorty. As the authors see it, Bradley mistakenly accepted the liberal dogma that law and order is a code word for racism.[24]

—In the 1969 New York race, Mayor John Lindsay, a staunch liberal, got only 40 per cent of the votes in what the authors call America's most liberal city. In his celebrated attempts to cool the ghettos during the long, hot summers of 1966 and 1967, Lindsay had not taken time for follow-up visits and speeches to quell emerging unrest in Italian, Polish, Irish, Jewish and other so-called "ethnic" communities. Having thus ignored "middle America," Lindsay won his "victory defeat" only because two conservative foes split the anti-Lindsay vote.[25]

With this quick summary of "precision" journalism, we move to other branches of the really not-so-new New Journalism.

New Journalism

If you want to start a debate, walk into almost any newspaper office and proclaim that you are an advocate of New Journalism. Very quickly, your supporters will swarm to your side of the room, and the proponents of "established" or "traditional" journalism will move to the other side.

Unfortunately, much of the debate seems to center around the fact that most people—even its proponents—frequently don't know what New Journalism is. No one has written a handbook which explains it concretely and tells how to do it. Maybe no one can write such a handbook, for inherent in the term is the freedom to use different approaches. And it is this very factor which has made New Journalism seem like journalistic salvation to some and journalistic damnation to others.

One might define New Journalism with reference to a new type of writer, a type which includes Truman Capote, Tom Wolfe, Norman Mailer and Gay Talese, to name a few of the better known practitioners. Even though they are seeking to report factual events, these four have broken away from the traditional journalistic methods of presenting that information. Their styles are quite different, but they all use the techniques of the fiction writer in seeking to tell a story. All the traditional tools of the novelist—intimate description, dramatic presentation, dialogue, sometimes first-person participation—are used along with the usual journalistic methods in presenting a real-life situation.

New Journalists see their function as more than merely transmitting facts or ideas from one location or person to another. They seek to provide a complete picture in depth, in great detail, from more than one point of view and often from their own points of view. The idea is to permit the reader to better *experience* and enjoy the total situation because in such experience lies real truth. And New Journalists say this cannot result from what they believe to be strait-jacketed established journalism.

The major criticism leveled at New Journalism is that it is a subjective art in which the writer has great liberty to create facts, to comment upon them, to shuffle events around for dramatic or political purposes. Some critics—fairly or unfairly—see little difference between the New Journalist and the underground editor who refused to allow facts to stand in the way of presenting a political or doctrinaire point of view. They likewise are highly critical of the attitude toward factual accuracy expressed by some New Journalists: that real truth lies in the intentions and emotional tone underlying people's behavior and not in nitty-gritty factual situations; thus, these New Journalists have been quite willing to shrug off factual inaccuracies as long as the overall perspective is correct.

Critics say these attitudes are frightening. And, to the degree that such approaches are insisted upon, they are indeed frightening. Whatever the faults of the traditional notions of objectivity, the problems will not be solved by substituting the most dangerous and divisive faults of a purely subjective journalism.

However, few really would advocate either extreme. In fact, many New Journalists argue that opinion and dogmatism as such should be avoided. They define their function as giving the reader the fullest information upon which he can base his own conclusions. Indeed, even though they unanimously argue against traditional objectivity, many insist on a strict fairness in the presentation of material. They seem to be advocating greater freedom in the presentation of facts, not greater freedom in deciding what those facts are.

Some argue that New Journalism is not new, that it has been around for as long as there have been journalists. It's difficult to pinpoint the beginning of such a phenomenon, but it is generally felt that the underground press of the 1960s provided the early foundations upon which New Journalism has been built. New Journalism has gone through a whole series of types and has been called many things, each of which tends to mean something different. Among these are the following:

** **Alternative Journalism,** the main idea of which is to assure that a point of view neglected by the established media gets its opportunity for publication.

** **Advocacy Journalism** which screams for a particular cause and tends to be dogmatic and uncompromising.

** **Faction**, the use of fictional techniques of writing about factual events.

** **Reportage**, another term for the "new" non-fiction.

** **Saturation Reporting**, defined by Tom Wolfe in this manner:

> For years the basic reporting technique has been the interview. You have a subject to write about, so you go interview the people who know about it, you write down their answers and then you recount what they said.
>
> Saturation reporting is much harder. You are after not just facts. The basic units of reporting are no longer who-what-when-where-how and why but whole scenes and stretches of dialogue. The New Journalism involves. . .minute facts and details that most newspapermen, even the most experienced, have never dreamed of. To pull it off you casually have to stay with the people you are writing about for long stretches. You may have to stay with them days, weeks, even months—long enough so that you are actually there when revealing scenes take place in their lives. You have to constantly be on the alert for chance remarks, odd details, quirks, curios, anything that may serve to bring a scene alive when you're writing. There is no formula for it. It never gets any easier just because you've done it before.[26]

What will be the long-term contribution of New Journalism? Predictions are difficult, but one statement can be made with certainty: Even if the techniques of New Journalism do not become dominant (and it's a pretty safe bet they won't), the debate which has been stirred will have a significant impact on journalism.

Already, one can see many of the attitudes of the New Journalism permeating the established newsroom. Check the Pulitzer Prize winners; many could be labeled New Journalists. Read such magazines as Harper's, Atlantic, Esquire, New York and you will find example after example.

In fact, some will argue that the whole debate over "New" Journalism involves little more than semantics. They see no real differences among what are called New Journalism, Interpretive Journalism, Investigative Journalism and even Muckraking.

It should be pointed out that the demands on journalism are increasing in these very complex times. The public wants to know what is going on and expects journalists to provide that information. What one terms the journalistic response to those demands seems to dictate his position in the debate about the New Journalism. But in the long run, the goals of the old and the new journalism are the same—to adequately inform the people. Only time will tell which techniques will best accomplish that purpose.

Two words of caution must be stressed at this point. An individual who decides he is a New Journalist, who wants to adopt the techniques of New Journalism, *must* first have a basic understanding of the traditional techniques. One cannot reject something he does not understand, and New Journalism, if it ever is to be effective, must be a blend of both types of techniques, held together by the sweat of hours of research and writing. It also should be pointed out that while newspapers are not immune to the new journalistic techniques most of the best examples have appeared in magazines and books, two media which lack the time pressure and the space limitations of the daily newspaper.

New Journalism may well make a contribution to the profession, but its practitioners who define it as a license for slip-shod reporting and writing will not have a part in that contribution. And the chances are very good that the new techniques will not overcome the old, especially in newspapers. Much newspaper content will continue to be written as in the past, supplemented by examples of New Journalism.

Summary and Conclusions

In this chapter, we have raised a great many questions and fully answered very few. If nothing else, the reader should feel by this time that journalism is a changing profession which respects, yet is slowly breaking away from, proud traditions.

In closing, it seems important to note that the analysis of word meaning in Chapter 2 can help clarify the distinction between libertarian and social responsibility thinking.

The libertarian journalist was inclined to report the facts and let the reader do what he might with them. The best way to report a speech, it has been argued, is to give the reader much the same experience that he would have had if he were in the speaker's audience.

The editorial page presented opinion in libertarian journalism, and the news columns included a great deal of "human interest" material. However, neither editorials nor human interest seemed very relevant to the hard news of the day.

"Social responsibility" thinkers insist that we must report the news in a way which gives it meaning. To them, pain, hatred and love aren't neatly walled off and separated from the news of the day.

Rather, these connotative processes are part of the news as it occurs in American ghettos, the third world and elsewhere.

Newsmen, it's argued, must help ordinary citizens gain the wisdom needed to act as citizens. This obviously requires that the reporter have wisdom. It also requires that he write about things like a feeling of frustration without using vague, loaded words that have often led diplomats down the road to war and ivory towerish scholars down the road to confusion.

Precision journalism and other new trends discussed in this chapter are steps in a continuing process designed to aid the newsman in exercising his social responsibility.

Anyone still hazy about the distinctions between denotative and connotative meaning, and between libertarian and social responsibility thinking, might re-read parts of Chapters 1 and 2. And better yet, follow up on some of the background readings listed at the end of these two chapters.

LIST OF REFERENCES

1. Siebert, Fred S.; Peterson, Theodore and Schramm, Wilbur, *Four Theories of the Press* (Urbana: University of Illinois Press, 1963).

2. Mill, John Stuart, *On Liberty* (New York: F.S. Crofts and Co., 1947). Edited by Alburey Castell.

3. Siebert, Fred S.; Peterson, Theodore and Schramm, Wilbur, *op. cit.*, p. 52.

4. *Ibid.*, p. 54.

5. *Ibid.*, p. 58.

6. *Ibid.*, pp. 51-2.

7. *Ibid.*, p. 88.

8. Cited in Douglass Cater, *The Fourth Branch of Government,* (New York: Random House, Inc., 1959), p. 107.

9. Siebert, Fred S.; Peterson, Theodore and Schramm, Wilbur, *op. cit.*, p. 88.

10. Gerbner, George, "Press Perspectives in World Communication: A Pilot Study," *Journalism Quarterly* 38(3):313-22, Summer 1961.

11. Helson, Harry, *Adaptation Level Theory* (New York: Harper and Row, 1964).

12. Ray, Jack and Zavos, Harry, "Reasoning and Argument: Deduction and Induction," in Gerald R. Miller and Thomas Nilsen (eds.), *Perspectives on Argumentation* (Chicago: Scott, Foresman and Co., 1966), p. 69.

13. Cater, *op. cit.*, pp. 73-4.

14. Cater, *op. cit.*, p. 72.

15. Peterson, Theodore; Jensen, Jay W. and Rivers, William L., *The Mass Media and Society* (New York: Holt, Rinehart and Winston, 1966), pp. 113-7.

16. *Ibid.*, p. 110.

17. Olien, Clarice N.; Donohue, George A. and Tichenor, Phillip J., "The Community Editor's Power and the Reporting of Conflict," *Journalism Quarterly* 45(2):243-52, Summer 1968.

18. For full development of this thesis, see Morris Janowitz, *The Community Press* (Chicago: University of Chicago Press, 1967). Also see Jack Lyle, *The News in Megalopolis* (San Francisco: The Chandler Publishing Co., 1967).

19. Lasswell, Harold D., "The Structure and Function of Communication in Society," in Wilbur Schramm (ed.), *Mass Communication* (Urbana: University of Illinois Press, 1960), p. 118.

20. For a full development of this thesis, see Neale Copple, *Depth Reporting: An Approach to Journalism* (Englewood Cliffs, N.J.: Prentice-Hall, 1964).

21. For a stimulating discussion of the rules and customs governing veiled attribution to protect a new source, see Samuel J. Archibald, "Rules for the Game of Ghost," *Columbia Journalism Review* 6(4):17-23, Winter 1967-8.

22. Scammon, Richard M. and Wattenberg, Ben J., *The Real Majority* (New York: Coward, McGann & Geoghegan, Inc., 1971), p. 49.

23. *Ibid.*, pp. 230-3.

24. *Ibid.*, pp. 233-8. Bradley defeated Yorty in 1973.

25. *Ibid.*, pp. 240-5.

26. Wolfe, Tom, "The New Journalism," *The Bulletin* (American Society of Newspaper Editors), September 1970, p. 22.

APPENDIX 1

The Mechanics of Copy Preparation

To establish uniformity for ease of handling and to assure that all necessary production information is available, newspapers have tended to develop sets of procedures which reporters follow in the preparation of their copy. Although these procedures vary somewhat from newspaper to newspaper depending upon individual preferences, such differences tend to be minimal. Our purpose in this chapter is to present a generally accepted procedure to the beginning reporter, with some indication of areas in which slight differences might be expected.

Basically, the mechanics of copy preparation involves two areas: (1) the format of the typewritten page handed in by the reporter and (2) the symbols used by both the reporter and editors in making changes in the copy.

Copy Format

It is a matter of individual newspaper practice as to which of two systems the reporter uses relative to paper size. One system uses as many sheets of standard-sized (usually 8 1/2 x 11) paper as are necessary for the story. The other uses one long, continuous sheet of paper, the length of which depends upon the length of the story. The format discussed here will be for use on the standard-sized paper; the reporter who uses the long sheet will use the same system, omitting the middle steps.

In either event, most reporters will make carbons of their stories, either because of paper policy or so a copy of the story will be available for reference after the original has been turned in. Some reporters save the carbons for future reference, but they usually are thrown away after a clipping of the story has become available.

Figure A shows a four-take story, prepared in an acceptable, generally standard, format, one which will correspond reasonably closely to that of most newspapers. Let's look at its individual aspects.

Figure A

On the first page (or take), the reporter has first placed his name in the upper left-hand corner. Usually, this is just his last name. Single-spaced immediately below the name is the "slug," or identification, of the story. This represents the simplest word or series of words which can be used to distinguish this story from others. The slug in Figure A is "Cedwick speech," but, depending upon the story content, it could be "Bobcat baseball," "Smith obit," "City Council," "Auto Accident," or any other appropriate phrase. Whatever its content, the slug usually is as brief as the reporter can make it and still provide specific identification. For some newspapers, there are two other pieces of information provided with the name and slug. One is the date; the other is an indication of whether the story will be illustrated. If no mention is made, it will not be illustrated; if an appropriate phrase such as "With Art" is typed under the slug, the makeup men know they must plan for a picture. That picture will be labeled, "With Cedwick Speech" to show its proper placement.

After adequately identifying the writer and story content, the reporter then drops down at least one-third, sometimes as much as one-half, of the page before actually starting to type his story. The major reason for leaving this much space is to permit copy editors to insert the headline and provide the back shop with special instructions about setting the copy. It also provides room for a byline, which is provided by an editor if he determines that the story deserves one.

In typing the story, the reporter will at least double space and perhaps triple space, depending upon his editor's wishes. Some newspapers insist on lines of a specified length (usually 60 spaces), but all require that the reporter leave ample margins, again providing room for any special printing instructions. If line length is specified, it usually is to provide editors with some reasonable estimate of how long the story will run when it has been set. Most reporters pay little attention to the right margin, however, simply assuring that adequate space is left. Little effort is made in seeking to make the right margin even. In fact, most reporters, to eliminate a chance for confusion, will avoid hyphenating a word regardless of where the line ends. The left-hand margin is, of course, even, with a five-space indentation at the beginning of each paragraph.

If a story exceeds one page, the reporter provides an indication of that fact at the end of the page. Usually, this is accomplished by simply writing "more" at the end of the page, and, for reasons we shall discuss later, this "more" is circled. Many newspapers, additionally, require that a page end at a paragraph juncture. Having no paragraph split from one page to the next facilitates the setting of the story. This, of course, means that the reporter is not concerned about the amount of space left at the bottom of the page.

All pages after the first are opened in the upper left corner with the reporter's name and the slug. Then, there are two major ways to indicate a succession of pages, depending upon the newspaper's preference. One is to number each succeeding page as a "take." No number is placed on the first page, but the second is labeled, just under or next to the slug, as "Take 2," the third as "Take 3" and so on. Another system is based on the idea that the second page represents the first addition to the first page. Thus, it is labeled "Add 1," the third page "Add 2," the fourth "Add 3," and so on. Either system is acceptable and common, but the reporter should follow the practice of his paper.

Contrary to the practice on the first page, the reporter drops down only a few spaces before beginning typing on all succeeding pages. There is no need to provide space for a headline, byline and printing instructions.

When the reporter has completed his story, he assures that everyone knows it by using one of the several symbols which are available. The most common practice is to place a circled 30 at the end of the copy. There is disagreement over the origin of this practice, but it is commonly accepted to mean "the end" of a newspaper story. Other newspapers may use different symbols for the same purpose, two of the more common of which are ### and —0—. In some cases, the reporter is required to place his initial at the end, as in 30JBP, ###JBP or —0—JBP. Some papers even permit the initials to serve as the sign the story is completed.

Copyreading Symbols

Since several individuals are involved in the transmission of a piece of copy from the reporter into the newspaper columns, some standardized means of communication is necessary to indicate changes in the original version. The reporter may change his mind after typing the story or an editor may want to make a correction or change, and these desires must be understood by everyone who looks at that piece of copy. Thus, there has been developed a set of symbols whereby changes can be made in ways which are clear to anyone familiar with the symbols. There are minor variations, but such copyreading symbols have become pretty much standard throughout the newspaper world.

The beginning reporter would be wise to spend the necessary time

THE MECHANICS OF COPY PREPARATION

in learning these symbols as completely and as quickly as possible. Here are those which are most common:

Begin a paragraph	⌐The beginning reporter would be wise to spend the necessary time in . . .
Insert letter or word	Two men w̬re killed and another . . . Two men⟆killed and another . . .
Delete letter	City coµncil last night . . .
Change letter or word	With Harry Jo⤬es leading the way . . . With Harry ~~Jones~~ leading the way . . .
Make one-space separation	The real/problem . . . The real/problem ., . . The real/problem . . .
Transpose letters or words	He made the mot⟅n . . . He⟨only⟩won two games.
Set in lower case	He studied /Biology, /Math and /Sociology.
Set in capitals	He worked for the national observer.
Close up tight	Copyreaders mu⌒st know the symbols.
Close up but leave one space	Copyreaders must ~~serve~~ know the symbols.
Make elements continuous	He said he saw the three men⟩ ‾‾‾‾‾‾‾‾‾‾‾‾‾‾‾ ⟨who were injured.
Insert period	U⊗ S⊗
Insert comma	red⋀white and blue
Insert colon	. . . the following⋀(1) (2) (3)
Insert semicolon	a printer⋀and
Insert apostrophe	He read the reporter⋁s story
Insert quotation marks	⋁Oklahoma! is a musical
Insert exclamation mark	"Oklahoma⋀" is a musical
Insert hyphen	re⋀lect
Insert dash	He said⟨although no one listened⟩that he . . .

THE MECHANICS OF COPY PREPARATION

Abbreviate   (Governor) William B. Smith

Spell out   (Wm.) B. Smith

Spell out figure   (73)

Use figure   (twelve)

Let it stand (stet)   He was ~~not~~ guilty. *stet* (Avoid use of stet when possible. Best to rewrite the word.)

Transpose paragraphs   His body was recovered by police at about 5 a.m. today.

                                      The drowned man was identified as Timothy Brown, 42, of Centerville.

Omit paragraph   Terrorism appears on the upswing. And a tough guerrilla campaign is being waged throughout the area.

                                      ~~If the Communists choose to strike hardest in this area, they will have several factors in their favor.~~

                                      It is here that the enemy is closest to its prime manpower pool.

More copy to follow   (more)

End of story   (30)   (###)   —0—

NOTE: All items on the page which are not to be set in print, such as more and 30, should be circled. This includes the reporter's name, the slug, the page number and any special instructions to the printers.

APPENDIX 2

The Associated Press Stylebook

Compiled and Edited By
G. P. WINKLER

To Members of The Associated Press:

THE reason for any stylebook is to provide a uniform presentation of the printed word.

This stylebook places no restriction on writing initiative.

The first stylebook in 1953 was a compromise of widely differing views of the membership. In 1960, at the suggestion of newspapers, The Associated Press and United Press International collaborated on a common style for the news services.

When compilation of the stylebook was first undertaken, the membership responded with the cooperation that has been characteristic through the years. That cooperation continues every day.

More than a quarter of a million copies of The AP Stylebook have been distributed, attesting to the solid ground on which the cooperative effort was based.

We are appreciative of the hundreds of hours of effort by the membership and the Associated Press Managing Editors Association helping make this book the standard of excellence.

WES GALLAGHER
General Manager

Pages 224-274 used with permission of The Associated Press.

Contents:
I   Capitalization
II   Abbreviations
III   Punctuation
IV   Numerals
V   Spelling
VI   Miscellaneous
VII Markets
VIII Religious
IX   Sports
X   Teletypesetter
XI   Filing Practices

THIS book is for the guidance and benefit of those engaged in writing and preparing material for newspapers, and provides forms for presentation of the printed word.

It represents cooperation of the AP and UPI for the first time in an effort to standardize usages without limiting individual initiative or enterprise.

The effort in this book has been to provide generally applicable examples and to cover word combinations, slogans, phrases, etc., constantly being added to and becoming part of the language.

Where some point is not covered specifically, an authoritative reference work should be followed.

The Style Committee of The Associated Press Managing Editors Association, AP members, schools of journalism and the stylebooks of many newspapers all have contributed forms, ideas, suggestions and help in preparation of the book.

An insert may be printed and stapled in the center of this book to adjust usage to particular situations, unusual local spellings, to indicate variations from the common style, some points or subjects of particularly local application, business variations, goodwill admonitions.

Capitalization I

1.1 CAPITALIZE titles preceding a name: Secretary of State John Foster Dulles. LOWER CASE title standing alone or following a name: John Foster Dulles, secretary of state. EXCEPTION: Incumbent president of the United States is always capitalized. Do not capitalize candidate for president, no president may seize, etc.

1.2 CAPITALIZE government officials when used with name as title: Queen Elizabeth II, Premier Debre, etc. LOWER CASE when standing alone or following a name: Debre, premier of France.

1.3 CAPITALIZE Pope in all usage; pontiff is lower case.

1.4 CAPITALIZE foreign religious leader titles Imam, Patriarch, etc., but LOWER CASE standing alone or following a name. EXCEPTION: Pope and Dalai Lama, capitalized in all usage. (See Section VIII)

1.5 CAPITALIZE titles of authority before name but LOWER CASE standing alone or following a name: Ambassador John Jones; Jones, ambassador; the ambassador. (See 1.12, 3.31)

1.6 Long titles should follow a name: John Jones, executive director of the commercial department of Blank & Co. Richard Roe, secretary-treasurer, Blank & Co. (See 6.5)

1.7 LOWER CASE occupational or "false" titles such as day laborer John Jones, rookie left-handed pitcher Bill Wills, defense attorney John Jones. (See 2.14)

1.8 CAPITALIZE Union, Republic, Colonies referring to the United States; Republic of Korea, French Fifth Republic. (See 2.12)

1.9 CAPITALIZE U.S. Congress, Senate, House, Cabinet; Legislature when preceded by name of state; City Council; Security Council. LOWER CASE when standing alone: The legislature passed 300 bills.
The building is the Capitol, the city is capital.
Do not capitalize "congress" when it is used as a synonym for convention. (See 1.20)

1.10 CAPITALIZE committee in full names: Senate Judiciary Committee, House Ways and Means Committee, etc. LOWER CASE "subcommittee" in titles and standing alone, also "committee" standing alone.

In some shortened versions of long committee names, do not capitalize: Special Senate Select Committee to Investigate Improper Labor-Management Practices often is rackets committee, not capitalized.

1.11 CAPITALIZE full titles: Interstate Commerce Commission, New York State Thruway Authority, International Atomic Energy Authority, etc., LOWER CASE authority, commission, etc., standing alone. (See 2.1)

1.12 CAPITALIZE Supreme Court, Juvenile Court, 6th U.S. Circuit Court of Appeals, etc. (See 4.2) Specify which U.S. Court such as district, patent, tax, etc. It is Juvenile Court Judge John Jones and not Juvenile Judge John Jones.

1.13 CAPITALIZE Social Security (Administration, Act) when referring to U.S. system: He was receiving Social Security payments. LOWER CASE use in general sense: He was an advocate of social security for old age.

1.14 CAPITALIZE U.S. armed forces: Army (USA), Air Force (USAF), Navy (USN), Marines (USMC), Coast Guard, National Guard but LOWER CASE all foreign except Royal Air Force (RAF) and Royal Canadian Air Force (RCAF); French Foreign Legion, no abbreviation.

CAPITALIZE Marine, Coast Guardman, Swiss Guard, Evzone, Bengal Lancer, etc. LOWER CASE soldier, sailor, etc. NOTE: It is Coast Guardman (no "s") if member of U.S. Coast Guard.

CAPITALIZE Irish Republican Army (political). (See 1.20)

1.15 CAPITALIZE Joint Chiefs of Staff but LOWER CASE chiefs of staff.

1.16 CAPITALIZE holidays, historic events, ecclesiastical feasts, fast days, special events, hurricanes, typhoons, etc. Mothers Day, Labor Day, Battle of the Bulge, Good Friday, Passover, Christmas, Halloween, National Safety Week, Hurricane Hazel, Typhoon Tilda, New Year's (Day, Eve) but LOWER CASE: What will the new year bring? At the start of the new year, etc.

1.17 CAPITALIZE Antarctica, Arctic Circle but not antarctic or arctic.

1.18 CAPITALIZE specific regions: Middle East, Mideast, Middle West, Midwest, Upper Peninsula (Michigan), Southern (Illinois, California) Texas (Oklahoma) Panhandle, Orient, Chicago's near South Side, Loop, etc.

1.19 CAPITALIZE ideological or political areas: East-West, East Germany, West Germany. LOWER CASE mere direction: Snow fell in western North Dakota.

1.20 CAPITALIZE political parties and members but not "party." Democrat, Democratic, Republican, Socialist, Independent, Nationalist, Communist, Congress (India) etc. LOWER CASE democratic form of government, republican system, socialism, communism, etc.
CAPITALIZE Red when used as political, geographic, military, etc., descriptive.
LOWER CASE nationalist in referring to a partisan of a country.
CAPITALIZE Algerian Liberation Front (FLN) and Irish Republican Army (IRA). (See 1.14)

1.21 CAPITALIZE names of fraternal organizations: B'nai B'rith (no abbreviation), Ancient Free & Accepted Masons (AF&AM), Knights of Columbus (K. of C. as departure from 2.1). (See 2.5)

1.22 CAPITALIZE Deity and He, His, Him denoting Deity but not who, whose, whom. CAPITALIZE Talmud, Koran, Bible and all names of the Bible, confessions of faith and their adherents. (See Section VIII)
CAPITALIZE Satan and Hades but not devil and hell.

1.23 CAPITALIZE Civil War, War Between the States, Korean War, Revolution (U.S. and Bolshevik), World War I, World War II, etc.

1.24 CAPITALIZE names of races: Caucasian, Chinese, Negro, Indian, etc. LOWER CASE black, white, red (See 1.20), yellow. Do NOT use "colored" for Negro except in National Association for the Advancement of Colored People. Colored is correct in African usage.
Identification by race should be made when it is pertinent.

1.25 CAPITALIZE common noun as part of formal name: Hoover Dam, Missouri River, Barr County Courthouse. LOWER CASE dam, river, courthouse, etc., standing alone. CAPITALIZE Empire State Building, Blue Room, Carlton House (hotel), Carlton house (home), Wall Street, Hollywood Boulevard. (See 4.1)
Plurals would be: Broad and Main streets.

1.26 CAPITALIZE species of livestock, animals, fowl, etc., but LOWER CASE noun: Airedale, terrier, Percheron, horse; Hereford, whiteface, etc.

1.27 CAPITALIZE names of flowers: Peace rose, etc. If Latin generic names are used CAPITALIZE the genus (camellia, Thea japonica).

1.28 CAPITALIZE trade names and trademark names: Super Sabre Jet, Thunderjet, but Boeing 707 jet (jet descriptive, not part of name), Pan Am Clipper.
"Coke" is a registered trademark of Coca-Cola and is not a synonym for soft drinks. "Thermos" is a registered trademark. Use vacuum bottle (flask, jug) instead.
Use generic, or broad, term preferably in all trademark names.

1.29 Some proper names have acquired independent common meaning and are not capitalized. They include paris green, dutch door, brussels sprouts, etc. Check dictionary.

1.30 CAPITALIZE titles of books, plays, hymns, poems, songs, etc., and place in quotation marks: "The Courtship of Miles Standish." (See 3.26)
The words a, in, of, etc., are capitalized only at the start or end of a title: "Of Thee I Sing" and "All Returns Are In" as examples.

1.31 CAPITALIZE first word of a quotation making a complete sentence after a comma or colon: Franklin said, "A penny saved is a penny earned." (See 3.16)

1.32 CAPITALIZE names of organizations, expositions, etc., Boy Scouts, Red Cross, World's Fair, Iowa State Fair but LOWER CASE scout, fair standing alone.

1.33 CAPITALIZATION of names should follow the use of preference of the person. In general, foreign particles are lower case when used with a forename, initials or title: Charles de Gaulle, Gen. de Gaulle, but De Gaulle without forename or title. (See 3.5, 6.4)

In anglicized versions the article usually is capitalized: Fiorello La Guardia.

It is E. I. du Pont de Nemours and Du Pont; Irenee du Pont but Samuel F. Du Pont (his usage).

1.34 CAPITALIZE fanciful appellations: Buckeye State, Leatherneck, Project Mercury, Operation Deep Freeze (Deepfreeze, one word, is trademark.)

1.35 CAPITALIZE decorations, awards, etc. Medal of Honor, Nobel Peace Prize.

Abbreviations II

2.1 First mention of organizations, firms, agencies, groups, etc., should be spelled out. Exception: AFL-CIO. In names that do not have commonly known abbreviations, the abbreviation should be bracketed after the spelled name. Thereafter in the story the abbreviation may be used. Example:
The desire was expressed in the Inter-American Economic and Social Council (IA-ECOSOC) of the Organization of American States (OAS) in considering the European Economic Cooperation Organization (ECCO).
Distant Early Warning line (DEW line).
General Agreement of Tariffs and Trade (GATT).

2.2 ABBREVIATE time zones, airplane designations, ships, distress call, military terms, etc. EDT, CST, MIG17, B60, Military Police (MP), absent without official leave (AWOL), SOS (but May Day), USS Iowa, SS Brasil. (See 3.3, 10.12, 6.15)

2.3 ABBREVIATE business firms: Warner Bros.; Brown Implement Co.; Amalgamated Leather, Ltd.; Smith & Co., Inc. (See 3.40)

2.4 ABBREVIATE St., Ave., Blvd., Ter., in addresses but not Point, Port, Circle, Plaza, Place, Drive, Oval, Road, Lane. Examples:
16 E. 72nd St. (single "E" with period); 16 Gregory Ave. NW (no periods in "NW"); Sunset Boulevard, Main Street, Fifth Avenue (no addresses. (See 1.25, 4.1)

2.5 Lower case abbreviations usually take periods. The rule of thumb is if the letters without periods spell words, periods are needed. Examples: c.o.d., f.o.b., etc. However, m.p.h., a.m., p.m.
Periods are not needed in 35mm (film), 105mm (armament), ips (tape recording).
In news stories first mention of speed should be "miles an hour" or "miles per hour" and thereafter in story use m.p.h.

ABBREVIATE versus as vs. (with period).

2.6 ABBREVIATE states which follow cities (towns, villages, etc.), airbases, Indian agencies, national parks, etc. (See 3.23)

2.7 Standard abbreviations for states (rule of thumb is abbreviate none of six letters or less except Texas):

Ala.	Ill.	Miss.	N.M.	Tenn.
Ariz.	Ind.	Mo.	N.Y.	Tex.
Ark.	Kan.	Mont.	Okla.	Vt.
Calif.	Ky.	Neb.	Ore.	Va.
Colo.	La.	Nev.	Pa.	Wash.
Conn.	Md.	N.C.	R.I.	Wis.
Del.	Mass.	N.D.	S.C.	W.Va.
Fla.	Mich.	N.H.	S.D.	Wyo.
Ga.	Minn.	N.J.		

Do not abbreviate Alaska, Hawaii, Idaho, Iowa, Ohio, Maine or Utah. All states are spelled standing alone: He went to Minnesota at the turn of the century.

2.8 ABBREVIATIONS:

C.Z.	P.R.	V.I.	Alta.	B.C.	Man.	N.S.	
Que.	Ont.	Sask.	Nfld.	N.B.	B.W.I.	P.E.I.	

but obscure ones should be spelled in story, such as Prince Edward Island, etc.

2.9 B.C. as abbreviation of Canadian province must be preceded by town name; B.C., the era, must be preceded by a date.

2.10 ABBREVIATE U.S.S.R. and U.A.R. in datelines.

2.11 ABBREVIATE United Nations and United States in titles: U.S. Junior Chamber of Commerce (Jaycees as exception in abbreviation by letters), U.N. Educational, Scientific and Cultural Organization (UNESCO). (See 2.1, 3.3)

2.12 Spell United States and United Nations when used as a noun. U.S.A. and U.N. as nouns may be used in texts or direct quotations.

2.13 ABBREVIATE and capitalize religious, fraternal, scholastic or honorary degrees, etc., but lower case when spelled: B.A., bachelor of arts. (See 8.4)

2.14 ABBREVIATE titles and capitalize: Mr., Mrs., M., Mlle., Dr., Prof., Sen., Rep., Asst., Lt. Gov., Gov. Gen., Supt., Atty. Gen., Dist. Atty., in titles before names but not after names. Do not abbreviate attorney in: The statement by defense attorney John Jones, etc. (See 1.7)

2.15 Mr. is used only with Mrs., or with clerical titles (except in texts or verbatim quotes). (See 8.4, 8.9, 8.10)

2.16 Do NOT abbreviate port, association, point, detective, department, deputy, commandant, commodore, field marshal, general manager, secretary-general, secretary, treasurer, fleet admiral or general of the armies (but Adm. Nimitz or Gen. Pershing is correct). (See 2.21)

Do NOT abbreviate "guaranteed annual wage" and do NOT abbreviate Christmas.

2.17 ABBREVIATE months when used with dates: Oct. 12, 1492; but spell out otherwise as October 1492. Abbreviations for months are Jan., Feb., Aug., Sept., Oct., Nov., Dec. Do not abbreviate March, April, May, June or July except in tabular or financial routine where the abbreviations are Mar, Apr, Jun, Jly and spell May.

2.18 Days of the week are abbreviated only in tabular matter or financial routine where they are Mon, Tue, Wed, Thu, Fri, Sat, Sun. The proper word division for Wednesday is: Wednes-day.

2.19 ABBREVIATE St. and Ste. as in Sault Ste. Marie, St. Louis, St. Lawrence, etc. (except Saint John, N.B.). Abbreviate the mountain but spell the city: Mt. Everest, Mount Vernon; Abbreviate army post but spell city: Ft. Sill, Fort Meyer.

2.20 Do not abbreviate Alexander, Benjamin, Charles, Frederick, William, etc., as Alec, Alex, Ben., Benj., Chas., etc., unless person does so himself. Follow person's preference.

2.21 Military abbreviations:

ARMY

General	Gen.
Lieutenant General	Lt. Gen.
Major General	Maj. Gen.
Brigadier General	Brig. Gen.
Colonel	Col.
Lieutenant Colonel	Lt. Col.
Major	Maj.
Captain	Capt.
Lieutenant	Lt.
Chief Warrant Officer	CWO
Warrant Officer	WO
Sergeant Major	Sgt. Maj.
Specialist Nine	Spec. 9
Master Sergeant	M. Sgt.
First Sergeant	1st. Sgt.
Specialist Eight	Spec. 8
Platoon Sergeant	Platoon Sgt.
Sergeant First Class	Sgt. 1.C.
Specialist Seven	Spec. 7
Staff Sergeant	S. Sgt.
Specialist Six	Spec. 6
Sergeant	Sgt.
Specialist Five	Spec. 5
Corporal	Cpl.
Specialist Four	Spec. 4
Private First Class	Pfc.
Private	Pvt.
Recruit	Rct.

NAVY, COAST GUARD

Admiral	Adm.
Vice Admiral	Vice Adm.
Rear Admiral	Rear Adm.
Commodore	Commodore
Captain	Capt.
Commander	Cmdr.
Lieutenant Commander	Lt. Cmdr.
Lieutenant	Lt.
Lieutenant Junior Grade	Lt. (j.g.)
Ensign	Ens.
Commissioned Warrant Officer	CWO
Warrant Officer	WO
Master Chief Petty Officer	M.CPO
Senior Chief Petty Officer	S.CPO
Chief Petty Officer	CPO
Petty Officer 1st Class	PO 1.C.
Petty Officer Second Class	PO 2.C.
Petty Officer Third Class	PO 3.C.
Seaman	Seaman
Seaman Apprentice	Seaman Appren.
Seaman Recruit	Seaman Rct.

MARINE CORPS

Commissioned officers are abbreviated the same as Army, warrant officers the same as Navy. Noncommissioned designations are the same as Army except specialist and:

Master Gunnery Sergeant	Mgy. Sgt.
Gunnery Sergeant	Gunnery Sgt.
Lance Corporal	Lance Cpl.

AIR FORCE

Air Force commissioned officers are abbreviated the same as Army. Noncommissioned designations include:

Chief Master Sergeant	CM. Sgt.
Senior Master Sergeant	SM. Sgt.
Master Sergeant	M. Sgt.
Technical Sergeant	T. Sgt.
Staff Sergeant	S. Sgt.
Airman 1st Class	Airman 1.C.
Airman 2nd Class	Airman 2.C.
Airman 3rd Class	Airman 3.C.
Airman Basic	Airman

The Air Force also may designate certain other descriptions as radarman, navigator, etc., but such designations are not abbreviated.

The Navy has numerous ratings such as machinist, torpedoman, etc., and they are not abbreviated.

The Army, Coast Guard and Marine Corps also may describe personnel by specific duty in addition to rank.

Note: The period is used in several abbreviations, such as Spec. 1.C., in Teletypesetter in the absence of the diagonal or slash mark.

Punctuation III

Punctuation in printing serves the same purpose as voice inflection in speaking. Proper phrasing avoids ambiguity, insures clarity and lessens need for punctuation.

THE PERIOD

3.1 The period is used after a declarative or imperative sentence: The facing is Vermont marble. Shut the door.
The period is used after a question intended as a suggestion: Tell how it was done.
The period is used in summary form:
1. Korean War. 2. Domestic policy. A. Punctuate properly. B. Write simply.

3.2 The period is used for ellipsis and in some columnist material. Ellipsis: The combine . . . was secure.
Column: Esther Williams gets the role. . . . John Hay signed a new contract. Rephrasing to avoid ellipses is preferable.

3.3 The period is used in abbreviations: U.S., U.N., c.o.d., etc. (See Section II for variations)
3.4 The period separates integer and decimal: 3.75 per cent; $8.25; 1.25 meters. (See 7.1, 7.2, 7.5, 7.7)

3.5 The period is omitted after a letter casually used as a name, and where a person omits the period in his name:
A said to B that he was not watching.
Herman B Wells (his usage). (See 1.33)

THE COMMA

3.6 The comma separates words or figures:
What the solution is, is a question.
Aug. 1, 1960.   1,234,567
The comma serves in a series:
The woman was short, slender, blonde, well-dressed and old.
x, y and z.   1, 2 and 3.
The Selma, Ala., group saw the governor.

3.7 Do not use comma before "of": Brown of Arkadelphia.

3.8 Newspaper usage has, in most cases, eliminated the comma before "and" and "or" but this practice does not lessen the need for the mark in: Fish abounded in the lake, and the shore was lined with deer.

3.9 The comma is used to set off attribution: The work, he said, is exacting. It is used in scores: Milwaukee 6, St. Louis 5.

3.10 The comma is used to separate in apposition or contrast:
Smithwick, the favorite, won handily.
But: The car that failed had been ahead.

3.11 The comma is omitted before Roman numerals, Jr., Sr., the ampersand, dash, in street addresses, telephone numbers and serial numbers: Louis XVI, John Jones Jr., Smith & Co., ORegon 3-3617, 12345 Oak St., A1234567. (See 4.4)

THE SEMICOLON

3.12 The semicolon separates phrases containing commas to avoid confusion, and separates statements of contrast and statements too closely related:
The draperies, which were ornate, displeased me; the walls, light blue, were pleasing.
The party consisted of B. M. Jordan; R. J. Kelly, his secretary; Mrs. Jordan; Martha Brown, her nurse; and three servants. (Without the semicolons, that could be read as nine persons.)

THE APOSTROPHE

3.13 The apostrophe indicates the possessive case of nouns, omission of figures, and contractions.
Usually the possessive of a singular noun not ending in "s" is formed by adding the apostrophe and "s"; the plural noun by adding the "s" and then the apostrophe: boys' wear, men's wear.
The apostrophe also is used in the plural possessive "es"; Joneses' house.
The "s" is dropped and only the apostrophe used in "for conscience' sake" or in a sibilant double or triple "s" as "Moses' tablet."
In single letters: A's.

PUNCTUATION

3.14 The apostrophe is used in contractions: I've, isn't; in omission of figures: '90, '90s, class of '22. (See 4.3)

3.15 The apostrophe use or lack of should follow the official name of group, institution, locality, etc.: Johns Hopkins University, Actors Equity Association, Court of St. James's (variation of possessive ending).

THE COLON

3.16 The colon precedes the final clause summarizing prior matter; introduces listings, statements and texts; marks discontinuity, and takes the place of an implied "for instance":
The question came up: What does he want to do? (See 1.31)
States and funds allotted were: Alabama $6,000; Arizona $4,000, etc.

3.17 The colon is used in clock time: 8:15 p.m. (See 4.9)

3.18 The colon is used in Bible and legal citations:
Matt 2:14. Missouri Statutes 3: 245-260.

THE EXCLAMATION POINT

3.19 The exclamation point is used to indicate surprise, appeal, incredulity or other strong emotion:
How wonderful!   What!   He yelled, "Come here!"

THE QUESTION MARK

3.20 The question mark follows a direct question, marks a gap or uncertainty and in the latter use is enclosed in parentheses:
What happened to Jones?
It was April 13 (?) that I saw him.
The mark also is used in public proceedings, interviews, etc.:
Q. Were you there? A. I don't recall.
Exception: Where, in interviews, the question or answer is of some length, it is preferable to paragraph both Q. and A.

PARENTHESES

3.21 Parentheses set off material, or an element of a sentence.
It is not the custom (at least in the areas mentioned) to stand at attention.

3.22 Where location identification is needed but is not part of the official name: The Springfield (Ohio) Historical Society edition, etc. It is not necessary to bracket: The Springfield, Ohio, area population, etc.

3.23 Parentheses are not used around political-geographical designation: Sen. Theodore Francis Green, D-R.I., and Rep. Charles A. Halleck, R-Ind., were invited. (See 2.6)

3.24 Parentheses set off letters or figures in a series: The order of importance will be (a) general acceptance, (b) costs, and (c) opposition.

3.25 Where part of a sentence is parenthetical and the punctuation mark comes at the end of the sentence it goes outside:
He habitually uses two words incorrectly (practical and practicable).
Ordinarily the mark goes inside: (The foregoing was taken from an essay.)
Several paragraphs of parenthetical matter start with the opening mark on each paragraph and the final paragraph is ended with a closing parenthesis with the punctuation inside.

QUOTATION MARKS

3.26 Quotation marks enclose direct quotations; are used around phrases in ironical uses; around slang expressions; misnomers; titles of books, plays, poems, songs, lectures or speeches when the full title is used; hymns; movies; TV programs, etc. (See 1.30, 10.14)

3.27 Use quotation marks instead of parentheses around nicknames apart from the name: Smith, who weighed 280, was called "Slim."
Harold "Red" Grange.
The comma and period are placed inside the quotation marks. Other punctuation is placed according to construction:
Why call it a "gentlemen's agreement"?
The sequence in multiple quotations:
"The question is 'Does his position violate the "gentlemen's 'post-haste' agreement" so eloquently described by my colleague as "tommyrot"?'"

THE DASH

3.28 The dash indicates a sudden change. Examples:
He claimed—no one denied it—that he had priority.
It can be used instead of parentheses in many cases: 10 pounds—$28—paid.
If that man should gain control—God forbid!—our troubles will have only begun.
The monarch—shall we call him a knave or a fool?—approved it.

3.29 The dash is used after the logotype and before the first word of a story:
NEW YORK (logotype)—Mayor, etc.

3.30 The dash also is used as the minus sign in temperatures to indicate below-zero temperature: Duluth −12.

THE HYPHEN

3.31 The hyphen is one of the least correctly used, and most abused, marks. It is used properly to form compound words, to divide words in composition, in figures, in some abbreviations, and to separate double vowels in some cases.

The general rule for hyphens is that "like" characters take the hyphen, "unlike" characters do not.

A-bomb, U-boat, 20-20 vision, 3D, B60, MIG17, 3-2 (odds and scores), secretary-treasurer, south-southwest, north-central.

Exception: 4-H Club.

3.32 Adjectival use must be clear. (See 5.6)
The 6-foot man eating shark was killed (the man was).
The 6-foot man-eating shark was killed (the shark was).

3.33 Suspensive hyphenation:
The A- and H-bombs were exploded.
The 5- and 6-year-olds attend morning classes.

3.34 Ordinarily in prefixes ending in vowels and followed by the same vowel, the hyphen is used: pre-empt, re-elect. (Check dictionary for exceptions such as cooperate, coed, coordinates, etc.)

3.35 NEVER use the hyphen with adverb ending in "ly" such as badly damaged, fully informed, newly chosen, etc.

3.36 The hyphen also serves to distinguish meaning of similarly spelled words: recover, re-cover; resent, re-sent.

3.37 The hyphen also separates a prefix from a proper noun: pre-Raphaelite, un-American, etc.

3.38 The prefix "ex" is hyphened: ex-champion.

3.39 The hyphen has been abandoned in newspaper usage in weekend, worldwide, nationwide, etc.

THE AMPERSAND

3.40 The ampersand is used in abbreviations and firm names: Jones & Co., AT&T, etc. (See 2.3)

Numerals IV

In general, spell below 10, use numerals for 10 and above.

4.1 Numerals are used exclusively in tabular and statistical matter, records, election returns, times, speeds, latitude and longitude, temperatures, highways, distances, dimensions, heights, ages, ratios, proportions, military units, political divisions, orchestra instruments, court districts or divisions, handicaps, betting odds and dates (Fourth of July and July Fourth acceptable).

Use figures in all man or animal ages. Spell under 10 for inanimates: four-mile-trip, four miles from the center, etc.

Exceptions Fifth Avenue, Fifth Republic of France (See 1.25, 2.4), Big Ten, Dartmouth eleven.

The forms: 3-year-old girl, the girl is 3, 5 feet 2, 5-foot-2 trench, Washington won, 6-3; $10 shirt, seven-cent stamp, eight-hour day, five-day week, 60 cents (See 4.6), .38-caliber pistol.

6:30 p.m. or 6:30 o'clock Monday night (never 6:30 p.m. Monday night, or 6:30 p.m. o'clock). (See 6.15)

The vote was 1,345 for and 1,300 against.

The ratio was 6 to 4, but the 6-4 ratio.

It is 20th century but Twentieth Century Limited (train).

In series, keep the simplest related forms:

There are 3 ten-room houses, 1 fourteen-room house, 25 five-room houses and 40 four-room houses in the development.

$4 million but four million persons—the $ is equivalent of second numeral.

4.2 Numerals: 6th Fleet, 1st Army, 2nd Division, 10th Ward, 22nd District, 8th U.S. Circuit Court of Appeals.

Arabic numerals for spacecraft, missiles, etc.

4.3 Casual numbers are spelled:

A thousand times no! Gay Nineties. (See 3.14)

Wouldn't touch it with a ten-foot pole (but: The flag hung from a 10-foot pole—an exact measure).

4.4 Roman numerals are used for personal sequence, Pope, war, royalty, act, yacht and horse: John Jones III (some may prefer and use 3rd), Pope John XXIII, World War I, King George V, Act II, Shamrock IX, Hanover II. (See 3.11)

NUMERALS

4.5 Highways: U.S. 301, Interstate 90, Illinois 34.

4.6 In amounts of more than a million, round numbers take the dollar sign and million, billion, etc., are spelled. Decimalization is carried to two places: $4.35 million.
Exact amounts would be: $4,351,242.
Less than a million the form: $500, $1,000, $650,000, etc.
The same decimalization form is used for figures other than money such as population, automobile registration, etc. (See 4.1)
Spell "cents" in amounts less than a dollar. (See 4.1, 7.5)
See Section VII for exceptions in market routine.
In ranges: $12 million to $14 million (or billion) not $12 to $14 million (or billion).

4.7 The English pound sign is not used. Spell "pounds" after figures and convert to dollars. (See 3.28)

4.8 Fractions in Teletypesetter are confined to matrices of 8ths: ⅛, ¼, ⅜, ½, ⅝, ¾, ⅞. Other fractions require the hyphen 3-16, 9-10, 1-3, etc.
Fractions used alone are spelled: three-fourths of a mile.
If the diagonal or slash (/) is incorporated in Teletypesetter operation, that symbol will replace the hyphen in fractions other than 8ths. The "plus" sign now occupies that casting-machine channel in the agate font and the hyphen will continue to be used in the agate font for fractions other than 8ths.
Stories dealing with percentages use figures; an isolated one-time reference under 10 is spelled as: four per cent of the population is illiterate.

4.9 Time sequences are given in figures: 2:30:21.6 (hours, minutes, seconds, tenths). (See 3.17)

4.10 Metric measurements use the comma in three-figure sequences except that kilocycles and meters in electronics are printed solid unless 10ths are included and the 10ths are set off by a period.

4.11 Serial numbers are printed solid: A1234567.

4.12 Write it No. 1 boy. No. 2 candidate, etc.

Spelling V

The first preference in spelling is the short version in Webster's New International Dictionary with exceptions as given in this section; the U.S. Postal Guide; The U.S. Board of Geographic Names and National Geographic Society with exceptions as given in this section. The news services have agreed on some spellings where authorities do not agree.

5.1 The following list includes agreed spellings:

Algiers	Cologne	Kingstown	Romania
Antioch	Copenhagen	Kurile	Rome
Antwerp	Corfu	Leghorn	Saint John, N.B.
Archangel	Corinth	Lisbon	St. John's, Nfld.
Athens	Dunkerque	Macao	Salonika
Baghdad	Florence	Madagascar	Sofia
Bangkok	Formosa Strait	Marseille	Taipei
Basel	Frankfurt	Mt. Sinai	Tehran
Bayreuth	Genoa	Mukden	Thailand
Beirut	Goteberg	Munich	Tiflis
Belgrade	Gulf of Riga	Naples	Turin
Bern	The Hague	North Cape	Valetta
Brunswick	Hamelin	Nuernberg	Mt. Vesuvius
Bucharest	Hannover	Peking	Vietnam
Cameroon	Hong Kong	Pescadores I.	Warsaw
Cape Town	Jakarta	Prague	Wiesbaden
Coblenz	Katmandu	Rhodes	Zuider Zee

5.2 Where old and new names are used, or where quoted material uses a different form, one is bracketed: Formosa (Taiwan); Gdansk (Danzig), etc.

5.3 In Chinese names, the name after the hyphen is lower case: Chiang Kai-shek, Mao Tse-tung.
It is Peking People's Daily, People's Republic, etc.

5.4 Often used and frequently misspelled: (*preferred spelling)

adviser	consul	hitchhiker	restaurant
accommodate	copilot	homemade	rock 'n' roll
anyone	copter	home town	schoolteacher
Asian flu	council	impostor	sit-down
ax	counsel	ionosphere	skillful
baby-sit	disc	isotope	strait jacket
baby sitter	drought	judgment	strong-arm
baby-sitting	drunken	jukebox	subpoena
baritone	employe*	kidnaping	swastika
blond, male	embarrass	likable	teen-age
blonde, female, hue	eyewitness	machine gun	under way
box office	fallout	missile	vacuum
box-office sales	fire fighter	naphtha	wash 'n' wear
cannot	fulfill	old-timer	weird
cave-in	goodby*	per cent	wheel chair
chauffeur	good will, noun	percentage	whisky
cigarette	goodwill, adj.	permissible	wiretapping
clue	hanged	post office	X ray, noun
consensus	harass	propeller	X-ray, adj.

Disc is a phonograph record, National Council of Disc Jockeys is the trade organization.

It is drunken driving.

Be sure of words ending in ise, ize, and yse.
It is GI and GIs for persons, GI's and GIs' for possessive.

A consonant after a vowel and ending in a final accented syllable is doubled: corral, corralled; transfer, transferred; canal, canalled.

A consonant is not doubled when the accent falls on an earlier syllable: total, totaled; kidnap, kidnaped; channel, channeled; cancel, canceled.
It is bus and buses—buss is not a vehicle.

5.5 In compounding, meaning should be the guide. A great grandfather means he is great; a great-grandfather is lineage. Three-piece suits at $100 a piece would be $300 each; three-piece suits at $100 apiece would be $100 each.

It is right-hander, right-handed, left-wing group, left-winger but the left wing of the party.

5.6 "Air" is solid in airplane, airline, airport, airwave, airship, etc. Some corporate names divide airline: Eastern Air Lines (EAL), United Air Lines (UAL).

5.7 Some of the general rules for prefixes and suffixes:
all (prefix) hyphenated: All-Star.
ante, anti (prefix) solid: antebellum, antiaircraft—except in proper noun usage which is anti-American, etc.
bi (prefix) solid: biennial, bifocal.
co (prefix) usually solid: copilot, coed, etc.
counter (prefix) solid; counterfoil, etc.
down (prefix and suffix) solid: downstroke, touchdown.
electro (prefix) solid: electrolysis.
ex (prefix) hyphenated: ex-champion.
extra (prefix) solid: extraterritorial.
fold (suffix) solid: twofold
goer (suffix) solid: churchgoer.
in (prefix): insufferable; (suffix) hyphenated: stand-in
infra (prefix) solid: infrared.
inter (prefix) solid: interstate.
intra (prefix) solid: intrastate, intramural.
multi (prefix) solid: multimillion, multifaced.
non (prefix) solid: nonpartisan, nonsupport.
out (prefix) hyphenated: out-talk, out-box.
over (prefix and suffix) solid: overcome, pushover.
post (prefix) solid: postwar (but it is post-mortem).
pre (prefix) solid: predetermined, predawn.
self (prefix) hyphenated: self-defense.
semi (prefix) solid: semiannual.
sub (prefix) solid: subzero.
super (prefix) solid: superabundance, superman.
trans (prefix) solid: transatlantic, transcontinental (but trans-Canada with proper noun of country).
tri (prefix) solid: trifocal.
ultra (prefix) solid: ultraviolet.
un (prefix) solid: unshaven, unnecessary (but un-American with proper noun).
under (prefix) solid: underground, underdog, undersold.
uni (prefix) solid: unicolor.
wide (suffix) solid: worldwide, nationwide.

Miscellaneous VI

6.1 Engine is correct, not motor, in aviation; twin-engine, six-engine, etc. Exception: Trimotor, an obsolete plane but it still occurs in news stories. In railroading, power plants are locomotives—electric, steam, diesel. Diesels also may be called units, or engines.

6.2 Jet planes are driven solely by turbine engines. If the jet engine turns a propeller, it is a turboprop. True jets include the Boeing 707, Douglas DC8, Convair 880, de Havilland Comet, French Caravelle and numerous military (naval) planes. Turboprops include Lockheed Electra, Fairchild F27, Bristol Britannia, Vickers Viscount.

Propeller-driven planes include Super Constellation C, Douglas DC6B, Boeing Stratocruiser.

Flier is an aviator, flyer is a train.

6.3 A wife becomes a widow on the death of her husband. It is redundant to say "widow of the late."

"John Jones is survived by his widow" (not wife).

6.4 Include in first reference the first name and initials, or names or initials according to preference of person: Sen. Theodore Francis Green, D. H. Lawrence. (See 1.33, 9.7)

Correct spelling: Randolph McC. Pate. Howard McC. Snyder.

6.5 Long titles: (See 1.6)

International Brotherhood of Teamsters, Chauffeurs, Warehousemen and Helpers is shortened to Teamsters Union, and in subsequent references to Teamsters.

Cemetery Workers and Green Attendants Union of the Building Service Employes International Union is shortened to Cemetery Workers Union.

6.6 An automatic is not a revolver and vice versa, but "pistol" describes either. A bullet is the metal projectile of a cartridge which includes the propellant powder, casing and primer.

Shell describes military and naval or shotgun ammunition.

6.7 Weather: See Webster for Weather Bureau wind scale which has replaced the Beaufort wind scale.

Be certain in the use of tornado, cyclone, typhoon, monsoon, hurricane, etc. The U.S. Weather Bureau defines a blizzard:

"Generally when there are winds of 35 m.p.h., or more which whip falling snow, or snow already on the ground, and temperatures are 20 degrees above zero Fahrenheit, or lower.

"A severe blizzard is where winds are 45 m.p.h. or more, temperatures 10 degrees above zero or lower, and great density of snow either falling or whipped from the ground."

Neither is a hard and fast rule, the bureau says, because winds and temperatures may vary but blizzard-like conditions may prevail.

Rule of thumb: Do not call a snowstorm a blizzard unless the Weather Bureau describes it as such.

In weather stories, with addition of Alaska and Hawaii as states, it is incorrect to refer to highest or lowest temperatures "in the nation" if figures from those two states are not included. The Weather Bureau has a phrase to cover the omission: It refers to minimums and maximums in the "48 contiguous states."

6.8 There are policemen, detectives, deputies, investigators, etc., but not "lawmen."

6.9 Avoid making verbs out of nouns: shotgunned to death, suicided, etc.

Avoid trite phrases of dialect, especially "Sure and it was" and "begorra" etc., in March 17 stories.

If a record is set it is new—"new record" is redundant.

6.10 In describing someone or something from Washington, make clear it is the state or District of Columbia.

6.11 Fahrenheit is used most frequently to measure degrees of heat and cold. If centigrade occurs in foreign, or scientific, copy conversion to Fahrenheit is nine-fifths times centigrade plus 32.

The Kelvin scale of temperature will come into use oftener. Temperatures are referred to in this scale as "degrees absolute" or "degrees Kelvin." Absolute zero in the Kelvin scale is 460 degrees below Fahrenheit zero; 273 degrees below centigrade zero.

6.12 A knot is a unit of speed and is equivalent to 6,076.10 feet an hour. The knot is a nautical mile computed as the length of one minute of the meridian. To convert knots into approximate statute miles per hour, multiply knots by 1.15. It is incorrect to say "sailed 14 knots an hour."

6.13 Gross tonnage is a necessary part of any story dealing with commercial shipping as the accepted basic measurement of size. Naval vessels list "displacement tonnage."

6.14 Red-headed means a red head; red-haired means hair of that color. A person may be called a "redhead" jocularly but is not properly described as "red-headed."

6.15 It is not necessary to bracket time zones in ordinary happenings such as accidents, shootings, etc. It is sufficient to say something occurred at 11 p.m. (See 4.1)

Zone should be included in earthquakes, radio and TV broadcast times. Convert to EST.

Informative notes to editors giving times should include the zone.

6.16 G, G-force, is gravitational pull equal to about 32 feet per second, a second, in acceleration. Thus a flier (plane, rocket, etc.) subjected to a force of 5 G's is accelerating at five times the force of gravity at the earth's surface, or roughly at a 160-foot-a-second, per-second, rate.

6.17 Mach numbers refer to the speed of a body (aircraft, missile, etc.) in relation to the speed of sound. Mach 2 would be twice the speed of sound. A rule of thumb for speed of sound is 750 miles an hour at sea level, and 660 miles an hour at 30,000 feet.

6.18 Thrust is the measure of a driving force, or power, expressed in pounds. Jet engine and rocket powers are expressed in pounds. Thrust in pounds times speed in miles per hour divided by 375 converts thrust to horsepower.

Markets VII

7.1 Commodity routine consists of quotation material, stripped to barest essentials with most punctuation omitted. Dollar signs are not used in this routine. When quotations are less than a dollar, the decimal is not used. Range is indicated by the hyphen. The form:

Salable hogs 8,000; active and uneven, generally 75-1.00 higher on all weights; sows 50-75 higher; top 23.75 for short load; most good and choice 180-240 lb 23.00-23.50; 250-275 lb 22.00-22.75.

Wheat 1,534 cars; 1 lower to 3 higher; No 2 hard and dark hard 2.20½-2.30 (new) No 3 2.21-2.27 (new); No 2 red 2.19½-2.25N.

7.2 In newspage stories, the dollar sign is used, also decimal:

Stock advances ranged from $2 a share to more than $5.50 in brisk trading. At the opening, some shares were down $1 to $1.25 but a surge of buying which put the ticker several minutes behind trading sent prices up.

Market page leads do not use the dollar sign. Increases or losses are told in points as: Brown Bros. was up 1 at 82¼.

Bonds are designated: 3s, 4½s, etc.

7.3 Abbreviations in routine, but not used in newspage, roundups or market leads:

pt qt gal pk bu bbl lb

Letter designations in routine do not take periods: N (nominal); No (number); B (bid); A (asked).

7.4 Stories are carried when there is a change in dividend declarations — increased or decreased, passed or declared after having been passed. However, regular dividends of the large corporations are news — AT&T, U.S. Steel, General Motors, Ford, etc.

7.5 In reporting dividends, use the designation given by the firm (regular, special, extra, increased, interim, etc.) and show what was paid previously if there is no specified designation such as regular, quarterly, etc.

The story should say if there is a special, or extra, dividend paid with the regular dividend and include amount of previous added payments. The form:

Directors of the New Way Products Corp. voted a special dividend of $1.90 a share, in addition to the regular $1 dividend, both payable Sept. 15 to shareholders of record Aug. 25. A special dividend of 75 cents was paid June 15. (See 4.6)

When the usual dividend is passed, or reduced, some firms issue an explanatory statement, the gist of which should be included in the story.

7.6 News of corporate activities, and business and financial news should be stripped of technical terms. This does not apply to routine.

There should be some explanation of the firm's business (plastics, rubber, electronics, etc.) if there is no indication in the name of the nature of the business. The location of the firm should be carried.

Names of corporations are as important as those of individuals. Check New York Stock Exchange lists or Standard & Poor's Directory of Directors for correct names and spelling.

7.7 Corporate earnings are interesting chiefly because of net earnings, or losses. Net per common share always should be carried with comparison to the previous period specified. The form:

The ABC Co., automotive parts makers of Detroit, reported its net income for six months ending June 30 was $18,456,301, equal to $1.67 a common share. In the similar period last year net income was $12,412,006 or $1.03 a share.

Newsworthy earnings are carried in tabular form where several are available (after a dateline introduction). The form:

XYZ Corp. for six months ended June 30:

	1960	1959
Net income	$ 1,378,933	x-452,881
Share	74 cents	
Sales	24,114,396	16,513,662

x-net loss

Religious VIII

There is only one way to refer to confessions of faith and members and officials of them—the correct way. While general usage and correct titles of some of the faiths are listed in this section, some are not. In case of omission, or doubt, consult authoritative sources.

8.1 Members of communions of the National Council of the Churches of Christ in the United States of America—the official title which may be shortened to National Council of Churches—and others:

African Methodist Episcopal Church
African Methodist Episcopal Zion Church
American Baptist Convention
Antiochian Orthodox Catholic Archdiocese of Toledo, Ohio, and Dependencies
Armenian Church, Diocese of America, Diocese of California
Christian Churches (Disciples of Christ), International Convention
Christian Methodist Episcopal Church
Church of the Brethren
Church of the New Jerusalem
The Episcopal Church
Evangelical United Brethren Church
Exarchate of the Russian Orthodox Church of North and South America
Friends United Meeting
Greek Orthodox Archdiocese of North and South America
Hungarian Reformed Church in America
Lutheran Church in America
The Methodist Church
Moravian Church in America
National Baptist Convention, U.S.A., Inc.
National Baptist Convention of America
Philadelphia Yearly Meeting of the Religious Society of Friends
Polish National Catholic Church of America
Presbyterian Church in the U.S.
Progressive National Baptist Convention, U.S.A., Inc.
Reformed Church in America
Romanian Orthodox Episcopate of America
Russian Orthodox Greek Catholic Church of America
Serbian Eastern Orthodox Church
Seventh Day Baptist General Conference
Syrian Antiochian Orthodox Church
Syrian Orthodox Church of Antioch
Ukrainian Orthodox Church of America
United Church of Christ
United Presbyterian Church in the U.S.A.

8.2 Other communions:
Roman Catholic Church
Church of Jesus Christ of Latter-day Saints (Mormon)
Church of Christ, Scientist
The Lutheran Church—Missouri Synod
Seventh-day Adventists
Southern Baptist Convention
Churches of Christ
Jehovah's Witnesses
Unitarian Universalist Association
Unity of the Brethren
The American Lutheran Church

8.3 Jewish groups are:
Union of American Hebrew Congregations (Reform)
United Synagogue of America (Conservative)
Union of Orthodox Jewish Congregations of America (Orthodox)
Rabbinical groups:
Central Conference of American Rabbis (Reform)
Rabbinical Assembly (Conservative)
Rabbinical Council of America (Orthodox)
Union of Orthodox Rabbis (Orthodox)

The Synagogue Council of America represents both congregational and rabbinical groups of Reform, Conservative and Orthodox Judaism.

Terminology of each group should be followed, also in naming the place of worship as a temple or synagogue. The generic term: Jewish house of worship.

8.4 In general, in writing of clergymen, the form:
The Rev. John Smith, the Rev. Mr. Smith. Do NOT use Rev. without "the" preceding it.
The Rev. Dr. John Jones, Dr. Jones.

8.5 Roman Catholic usage:
The Rev. John Smith, Father Smith.
The Rt. Rev. Msgr. John Jones, Msgr. Jones.
The Most Rev. John Jones, bishop of the Denver diocese: Bishop Jones.
Francis Cardinal Spellman, Cardinal Spellman.
A sister whose name is Jones is called by her church name, Sister Mary Joseph (or whatever) and never referred to as Sister Jones.
Mass is celebrated, said or read. High Mass is sung—never held. The Rosary is recited or said—never read.

8.6 Episcopal usage:
A deacon or priest is referred to as the Rev. John Jones or the Rev. Mr. Jones.
A dean is the Very Rev. John Jones, the Rev. Mr. Jones, or Dean Jones.
A bishop is the Rt. Rev. John Jones, the Rev. Mr. Jones or Bishop Jones.
Note: An Episcopalian is a member of the Episcopal Church. Some priests use the term "Father" which is permissible but not generally used.

8.7 Jewish usage:
Rabbi James Wise, Rabbi Wise, Dr. Wise (where degree is held).
Cantor Harry Epstein, Cantor Epstein.
Do not identify a rabbi as a "Reverend Doctor."
See dictionary for spelling of Jewish holidays.

8.8 Christian Science usage:
Practitioner, Lecturer, Reader. Do not use Rev. in any form.
Reader John Jones of the First Church.
The Mother Church (Boston church only).

8.9 Methodist usage:
Pastor, Minister, Preacher, Bishop. Mr. with surname is acceptable. (See 2.15)

8.10 Lutheran usage:
In the United States: Pastor John Jones, Pastor Jones, Mr. Jones.
Scandinavian Lutheran usage follows the Episcopal form.

8.11 Latter-day Saints (Mormon) usage. (See 8.2 listing)
President David O. McKay, President McKay.
Elder Harold B. Lee, Elder Lee.
Presiding Bishop LeGrand Richards, Bishop Richards.
Bishop Joseph L. Wirthlin of the Presiding Bishopric, Bishop Wirthlin.
Members of the church may be called Mormons.

8.12 It is incorrect to apply the term "church" to any Baptist unit except the local church. The organization of Southern Baptists is the Southern Baptist Convention.
Other faiths have diocese, archdiocese, area, synod, presbytery, etc. Check official source for accurate designation.

8.13 Check, rather than follow listings in 8.1, 8.2.

8.14 Abbreviations of the Bible:

Gen.	1 and 2 Kings	Song of Sol.	Obad.
Exod.	1 and 2 Chron.	Isa.	Jonah
Lev.	Ezra	Jer.	Mic.
Num.	Neh.	Lam.	Nahum
Deut.	Esther	Ezek.	Hab.
Josh.	Job	Dan.	Zeph.
Judg.	Ps. (Psa. plural)	Hos.	Hag.
Ruth	Prov.	Joel	Zech.
1 and 2 Sam.	Eccl.	Amos	Mal.

New Testament:

Matt.	Rom.	Col.	Heb.
Mark	1 and 2 Cor.	1 and 2 Thess.	James
Luke	Gal.	1 and 2 Tim.	1 and 2 Pet.
John	Eph.	Titus	1, 2 and 3 John
Acts	Phil.	Philem.	Jude
			Rev.

Sports IX

9.1 BASIC SUMMARY:

Name of event—athlete's full name, his affiliation, performance (given in time, distance, points scored, or whatever performance factor is appropriate).

Observe punctuation. It calls for dash after event and commas. Semicolons are not used. Time follows the colon usage, but the word "time" is not used. The word "points" should be used with first listing only, where applicable to the event.

Example:

Mile—1, Ron Delany, Ireland, 4:06. 2, Derek Ibbotston, Britain, 4:05.5. 3, Don Bowden, United States, 4:08.2.

Include the colon before seconds in times of less than a minute, :10.2 or :50.6.

Condensed summary:

100—1, Jones, SMU. 2, Brown, Rice. 3, White, Texas. :09.7.

In the condensed summary, performance is given at end of listings of each event. If a record is broken, the former record is given immediately following the record performance in the expanded summary—but at the end of the condensed summary.

Tabular Summary:

Yacht	Elapsed Time	Corrected Time
1. Seagull	12:05.00	9:21.13
2. Comanche	11:18.20	10:12.12
3. Etc.		

Match Summary:

Althea Gibson, New York, N.Y., defeated Sally Moore, Bakersfield, Calif., 8-6, 2-6, 6-0.

9.2 BASEBALL:

The box score:

MINNESOTA	ab	r	h	bi
Oliva rf	4	0	1	0
Ward lf	1	0	0	0
Rollins ph	1	0	0	0
Hall cf etc.				
Totals	**30**	**3**	**6**	**3**

LOS ANGELES	ab	r	h	bi
Piersall cf	3	0	1	0
Smith lf	4	0	1	0
Rodgers pr	0	1	0	0
Totals	**31**	**1**	**7**	**1**

Minnesota	000	000	201—3
Los Angeles	000	000	001—1

E — Clinton, Satriano. DP — Los Angeles 1. LOB—Minnesota 7, Los Angeles 5. 2B—Oliva. 3B—Torres. HR—Hall (12). SB—Piersall. S—Knoop. SF—Hall.

	IP	H	R	ER	BB	SO
Pascual W 15-11	8 2-3	7	1	1	1	6
Worthington	1-3	0	0	0	0	0
Newman L 13-10	8	5	2	2	2	5
Latman	1	1	1	0	1	0

Newman faced 2 men in 9th.

HBP — By Pascual (Rodgers). Balk — Worthington. WP — Pascual. T—2:09. A—15,615.

In a game where the home team scores winning run in final inning, the explanation is given just before the linescore.

The above box is the standard used for all regular season games. It is transmitted in half-column agate in Teletypesetter. Longer player names are abbreviated, and only one position is shown for any player.

For All-Star and World Series games, headings may be expanded to full-column measure:

AB R H BI PO A

Footnotes are listed separately instead of being run together:
a—Flied out for Spahn in 4th.
b—Singled for Narleski, etc.

The summary starts with DP. The hitting summary, starting with 2B (or whatever extra-base hit) should include description of any score that is not batted in:
SF—Aaron. Musial scored on a wild pitch in 1st; Fox scored on a double play in 6th, etc.

The pitching summary is reduced to four categories:

IP H R ER

Bases on balls and strikeouts are listed and paragraphed:
BB—Turley 2 (Thomas, Spahn). Narleski (Aaron). SO—Turley 3 (Banks, Mazeroski, Jones). Spahn 2 (Mantle, Williams).

Umpires in final paragraph carry league designation:
—Rommell (A), Gorman (N), etc.

Bare linescore form:
Detroit   241 200 003—12 13 0
New York   000 000 221— 5 10 0
Lary, Aguirre (8) and Wilson; Monroe, Trucks (3), Sturdivant (8), Kucks (9) and Howard. W—Lary, 4-3. L—Monroe, 8-1. HRs—New York, Mantle (24). Detroit, Kaline 2 (16).

Schedule, result, standings, probable pitcher summary form:

**BASEBALL
AMERICAN LEAGUE**

	Won	Lost	Pct.	GB
New York	48	26	.649	—
x-Kansas City	38	37	.507	10½

etc.
x—late game not included.

Monday's Scores
Chicago 7, Boston 4
Cleveland 12, New York 2, night
Detroit at Baltimore, rain.

Today's Games
Cleveland (Grant 6-6 and Bell 3-2) at New York (Ditmar 3-1 and Maas 4-7), 2, Twi-night.

Wednesday's Games
Cleveland at New York
Chicago at Boston, night
Only games scheduled.

Afternoon paper headings say "today" and spell prior and subsequent days. Morning paper headings spell all days.

Standings are moved separately after afternoon games and repeated after night games.

The baseball forms should be followed on minor leagues.

In lists of results give winner first, except:

Where there are line, period, inning or box scores, home team is last, win or lose.

9.3 FOOTBALL:

All football games, whether using the two- or one-point conversion, will use the same summary style.

Army   8   6   15   6—35
Stanford   16   7   3   2—28

Army—John 6 run (Chambers run)
Stan—Temple 2 run (Central pass from Temple)
Stan—Powers 26 run (Powers run)
Army—Tennyson 11 run (kick failed)
Stan—Lutz 22 pass from Chambers (Chambers kick)
Stan—FG Lutz 23
Army—Tennyson 34 pass interception (Lutz kick)
Army—Brandt 22 punt return (Lutz pass from Tennyson)
Stan—Safety Doaks tackled in end zone
Army—Halmark 16 pass from Tennyson (run failed)
A—26,571.

Field goal is abbreviated to FG. Safety is spelled. It is not necessary to give any symbol for touchdowns or conversions.

In both college and professional football, the distance of a field goal is from the point the ball was kicked—not the line of scrimmage. Also, goal posts in college football are 10 yards back of the goal line. That distance must be included.

Football Statistics:

STANFORD, Calif. (logotype)— Statistics of the Army-Stanford football game:

	Army	Stanford
First downs	7	5
Rushing yardage	153	172
Passing yardage	71	62
Return yardage	69	51
Passes	4-9-0	4-7-1
Punts	4-37	5-44.2
Fumbles lost	2	3
Yards penalized	60	30

(Note—Return yardage includes punt returns, pass interception returns and fumble returns, but not kickoff returns.)

EASTERN CONFERENCE

           W   L   T   Pct.   Pts.   OP
New York   5   2   1   .714   205   105
Ties do not figure in percentage.

9.4 BASKETBALL—The box score form:

SEATTLE

	G	F	T
Taylor	8	2-4	18
Totals	**22**	**12-19**	**67**

KENTUCKY
Beck, etc.
Halftime: Seattle 30 Kentucky 27.

Note—In both NBA and ABA score by periods is carried in place of halftime score as follows:
Seattle   10   17   15   14—56
Kentucky   15   15   15   15—60

No positions are given after player name, but five starting players should be listed first and substitutes in order of appearance.

Add after linescore:
Fouled out—Seattle: Jones. Kentucky: Green.
Total fouls—Seattle 42, Kentucky 37.

(Note—In the American Basketball Association which has both 2-point and 3-point baskets, footnotes are used to explain as follows:
(3-point goals: Brown 1, Smith 2, etc.)
A—15,601.

Expanded football standings are headed by the name of the conference. The form then:

	Conference					All Games			
	W	L	T	Pts.	OP	W	L	T	Pts.	OP
Michigan	6	0	0	126	34	9	1	0	141	48

The form for basketball:

	Conference				All Games		
	W	L	Pct.	W	L	Pct.	Pts.	OP
Bradley	5	0	1.000	14	1	.933	1260	975

Basketball box scores in TTS are moved in half-column measure and carry only G F T headings.

Standings are the same as football except that points column is not carried. The headings are Won, Lost, Pct. The form for standings:

EASTERN DIVISION

	W	L	Pct.	GB
Boston	30	15	.667	—
New York	25	25	.500	7½

9.5 HOCKEY—The lineups:
New York—add NHL
Toronto: Goal—Bower, Smith. Defense—Stanley, Horton, Baun, Brewer, Douglas. Forwards—Bathgate, Keon, McKenney, Armstrong, Pappin, Shack, Kelly, Mahovlich, Pulford, Stewart.
New York: Goal—Plante, Greene. Defense—Howell, Neilson, Brown, Johns, Seiling. Forwards—Gilbert, Goyette, Henry, Nevin, Ingarfield, Duff, Mikol, Marshall, Hadfield, Ratelle.
Referee—Udvari. Linesmen—Papelich, Hayes.

(Both goalies are listed under goal. Starting goalie is listed first.)

(Please note we list the entire front line as forwards, and therefore no spares are listed. Do not use first names of officials).

Where the lineups are held until after the first period is completed, the first period scoring summary should be attached to the lineups. Otherwise it is sent separately. It takes this form:
New York—add NHL
First period—1, New York, Henry 21 (Goyette) 2:15. 2, Toronto, Bathgate 16 (Keen, McKenney) 8:19. Penalties—Duff 2:43; Mikol 7:26.

(Please note that each score is numbered, and that the figure after a man's name represents his total goals for the season to date. This, however, applies only to the National Hockey League. Shots on goal are sent with period summaries and at the end.)

Example of summary:
Third period—None. Penalties—Baum 4:15; Neilson, major, 17:00; Duff 18:12.
Shots on goal by:
New York   8   9   4—21
Toronto   6   8   6—20
A—14,520.

(Only major penalties are so designated.)

The final score is sent as a bulletin.

Standings:
NATIONAL HOCKEY LEAGUE

| | W | L | T | Pts. | GF | GA |
| Montreal | 50 | 9 | 1 | 101 | 245 | 113 |

9.6 HORSE RACING.

NEW YORK (logotype)—The field for Saturday's $75,000-added Wood Memorial, 1⅛ miles, at Aqueduct:

PP	Horse	Jockey	Prob. Odds
1.	Sacred River	Sellers	10-1
2.	Traffic	Adams	4-1
3.	Chieftan	Rotz	8-1

Owners—1, Mrs. Ethel Jacobs. 2, Rokeby Stable. 3, Cambridge Stable. etc.

Weights—All carry 126 pounds. Gross value—$89,250 with nine starters; $58,012.50 to winner, $17,850 to second, $8,925 to third, $4,462.50 to fourth. Post time—4:50 p.m. EST.

(If weights are not all same, weights should be included after the name of horse.)

Results:

THISTLE—9

9th—$1,600 clmg 4 & up 1 1-16 mi off 547½ time 1:48 3-5.

        a—Mr Action 118 R. Borg   4.40   3.20   2.60
        Blimey 116 T. Fortune   —   5.20   3.80
        Pirro 120 G. Smithson   —   —   5.80

Also: Gem Cutter, f-Baseball, a-Paris Fleet, Geo K.
f-Field; a-Jones entry.
(after final race)
A—6,256
Total handle $420,071.
After a second race, if there is a daily double, the form:
Daily Double:
Commendation and Lucky Ballot—9 & 11—paid $36.20.

HARNESS RACING—Same as running race results except where trotting or pacing events are in heats, when position and finish of each heat is required. Where there is betting, prices precede the heat tabulation.

9.7 BOXING—Match style summary:

Eddie Lynch, 152, New York, outpointed Johnny Saxton, 154, Philadelphia, 10.

If a knockout, use "knocked out." If a technical knockout, use "stopped."

If two officials vote for one boxer and the third votes for the other, it is a split decision.

If two officials vote for one boxer and the third votes a draw, it is a majority decision.

In championship fights, "Tale of The Tape" form:

	Olsen	Langlois
Age	26	29
Weight	160	160
Height	5-10½	5-9
Chest (normal)	39	40
Chest (expanded)	42	42
Reach	70	68
Biceps	13	14
Forearm	11½	12
Waist	32	33
Thigh	22	22½
Calf	16	13
Fist	12	11½

Facts and Figures:

SAN FRANCISCO (Logotype)—Facts and figures of the world middleweight championship fight between champion Carl "Bobo" Olson of San Francisco and Pierre Langlois of France:

Date—Wednesday, Dec. 15.

Place—San Francisco Cow Palace, capacity 18,000.

Distance—15 rounds.

Television—Nationwide, CBS, with blackout 100-mile radius of San Francisco.

Radio—Nationwide, CBS.

Time—10 p.m. EST

(Other pertinent information may be included such as estimated attendance, estimated gate, shares of the purses, etc., as available.)

When a fight is scored by rounds, the form:

NEW YORK (logotype)—Scorecards of the Carmen Basilio-Billy Graham 15-round welterweight title bout:

Rd.	Ref. Tom Swift	Judge John Jones	Judge Phil Cook	Logo.
1	B	B	B	B
2	B	B	B	B
3	B	B	B	B
4	G	E	G	G
5	G	G	G	G
6	G	G	G	G
7	B	B	B	B
8	B	B	B	B
9	B	B	B	B
10	B	B	B	B
11	B	B	B	B
12	G	G	G	G
13	G	G	G	G
14	G	G	G	G
15	B	B	B	B
	9-6	9-5-1	9-6	9-6

Scoring by points:
(Basilio-Graham)

Rd.	Ref. Phil Harris	Judge Dick Smith	Judge Joe Hunt	Logo.
1	10-10	10-10	10-10	10-10
2	10-9	10-9	10-9	10-8
3	etc.			
Totals	147-132	145-134	etc.	

9.8 GOLF: Summaries are medal or match play.

Medal play: At the end of each day's play, low scores and ties are cumulatively given:
Ben Hogan   70-70-66—206
On the final day when money winnings are reported, the amount is inserted:
Ben Hogan, $2,800 70-70-66-64—270

Home towns are given only in major amateur tournaments with home town on second line.

Match play:
Ben Hogan defeated Gary Player 4 and 3.
Arnold Palmer won from John Snow by default.
The form for pairings—Match:
8 a.m.—Ben Hogan vs. Gary Player.
Medal:
8 a.m.—Ben Hogan, Gary Player, Arnold Palmer.
The form for cards:

Par out	454	343	454—36
Par in	443	545	344—36—72
Hogan Out	444	333	etc.
Hogan In	444	445	etc.
Snead Out	434	343	etc.
Snead In	444	454	etc.

9.9 TRACK AND FIELD—Use basic summary, either condensed or expanded, depending on value.

Where the winning time, or distance, is a record, the form:
Mile—1, Ron Delany, Ireland, 3:52, world record; old record 3:53.6, Herb Elliott, Australia, Dec. 15, 1958. 2, Don Bowden, etc.

In summaries, record is given in the same form.

Team standings are given at the end of summaries in conference meets. The form:

TEAM SCORING—Michigan 97, Illinois 67, Iowa 63½, etc.

Use yards or meters as indicated in summaries in listing track events and include "hurdles" and "relay" after distances as indicated.

Full names of relay team winners should be listed:
Mile relay—1, Manhattan: Vern Jones, Joe Dixon, Lou Carty, Ed Thomas, 3:15. 2, Syracuse, 3:16. 3, Brown, etc.

9.10 SWIMMING—The same form as track summaries except events are identified by distances and style and points are included in diving: 100 freestyle, breaststroke, backstroke, individual medley, medley relay. Distance precedes each style.

Platform diving—1, Bob Clotworthy, Ohio State, 60.41 points. 2, Bob James, Yale, 59.71. 3, Tom etc.

9.11 TENNIS, badminton, table tennis—Use match summary form. The form for scores: 6-4, 6-3, 6-2.

9.12 ROWING—Basic summary.

9.13 FENCING—Match summary for dual and small meets and divide into epee, foil and saber classes.

In major meets where competitors meet in round-robin competition and divided into "pools" the form:

EPEE—First round, four qualify for semifinals:

Pool 1	W	L
Smith, U.S.A.	4	1
Lopez, Chile	3	2

Footnotes may be needed where a tie is decided on number of touches, or some such means.

9.14 CROSS COUNTRY—(Marathon) Tabular summary in meets giving 10 or more places; basic summary for less than 10 places.

9.15 DOG SHOWS—Summaries by groups have five places. The form:

SPORTING GROUP—Pointers: 1. Ch Magic of Mardomere, owned by Mardomere Kennels, Glen Head, N.Y. 2, etc.

The same form applies if judging is by breeds.

9.16 LACROSSE (soccer, polo, water polo)—Give scores by chukkers (periods) and list goals scored by individuals in paragraph form by teams.

9.17 AUTO RACING — Tabular summary with driver, car make, owner and average speed. Basic summary will suffice on lesser contests or where there are few drivers.

9.18 SHOOTING—(rifle, pistol, etc.)—Tabular summary with name, hometown, hits, handicap and total.

9.19 SKIING—Tabular summary for jumping, cross-country, downhill and slalom races. Jumping table should give distance of each jump and point total. Cross-country table should give time and handicap if used in event.

9.20 BOBSLEDDING — Tabular summary.

9.21 BOWLING—There are several forms. They are:

Jones	161	161	174
Smith	208	etc.	
Totals	802	903	887

In singles matches a fourth tabulation is added, giving the bowler's total for the three games. Handicaps are figured with the totals.

The Peterson summary:

	W	L	Pins	Pts.
John King, Cleveland	20	8	5886	137.36
Carmen Salvino, Chicago	16	12	5816	132.16
Tony, etc.				

9.22 WEIGHTLIFTING—Tabular summary with table for each weight class, giving name, affiliation, pounds lifted in each of three lifts, and total pounds lifted.

9.23 FIGURE SKATING—Tabular summary.

9.24 SPEED SKATING—Basic summary.

9.25 GYMNASTICS—Basic summary, events by name (sidehorse, horizontal bar, etc.) with points scored.

9.26 CYCLING—Basic summary.

9.27 WRESTLING—Match summary. Key words are "pinned" and "outpointed." Point scoring should be given after name and affiliation of loser if a decision match.

Teletypesetter X

Teletypesetter copy must meet requirements of conversion to metal.

Revision of material must retain, or regain, line justification. It is preferable to transmit an entire paragraph where a revision means casting several lines.

See current directives for transmission of material that is not to be cast, or changing type fonts.

All material must be transmitted in justified lines. Informative material, not for publication, must be justified but quads may be dropped instead of dividing words.

Numerical sequence and continuity must be observed.

10.1 Datelines are capitalized, light face, and except for major cities should carry the state. (See 2.7) There is no spacing in state abbreviations. Abbreviations should not be divided at the end of a line.

10.2 Dates are omitted from datelines. Days of the week are spelled throughout the AMS report. In the PMS report, the use is "today" and spell prior and subsequent days.

10.3 Notes to editors take several forms.

Nonpublishable: EDITORS—The following dispatch contains material which may be objectionable to some readers.

EDITORS—developing, top expected about 11 a.m. EST.

Such nonpublishable notes are followed by a 3m dash.

10.4 Current cycle advances, where release time is not fixed by source, carry only: Adv for 6:30 a.m. EST, or Adv for 6:30 p.m. EST. In Daylight Saving Time the slug is EDT.

Advance for a subsequent cycle carries a slug: Adv Tues PMS May 24. It also carries a closing note: End Adv Tues PMS May 24 (or AMS).

Current cycle advances do not require visible caution in tape.

Subsequent cycle advances carry in visible tape: MAY 24 at start of each take.

10.5 Identify leads, inserts, adds, revisions plainly. Give understandable pickup lines and precise location in story. Avoid duplicating key subject words in slugs where more than one story deals with the same field. This insures proper matching of leads, adds, etc.

10.6 Absence of parentheses on monitor printers requires special handling of parenthetical matter.

Where parenthetical matter occurs it must be indicated. In stories, where part is embargoed for later use, it either is separated in the story by 3m dash (in its proper sequence) and boldface caution **Adv for 00.00** time and **End Adv** followed by 3m dash, or may be sent as add at end of story under 3m dash with advance slugs and notation where to insert.

Within paragraphs, a parenthetical word or phrase usually is evident by the extra spacing which occurs on the monitor in place of the parenthesis.

10.7 Where a name is unusual and occurs only once, add note under 3m dash repeating name and saying it is correct. Check monitor to insure correctness.

10.8 In long lists of names, or similar compilations, break into paragraphs (with appropriate punctuation) after each six or eight lines, with next to last paragraph including the word "and" without punctuation after "and."

10.9 In textual matter, the signature should be flush right. Title, date and other descriptive matter are on a second line. Where signatures are multiple and of equal importance, set one flush left and other flush right and if names are too long to permit spacing, divide name and run over (right or left) under each.

10.10 In Teletypesetter, put addresses in separate paragraphs.

Instead of saying John Doe of 125 W. 71st St., Kansas City, Mo., was among those cited, make separate paragraph read: Doe lives at 125 W. 71st St., Kansas City, Mo.

That form permits deletion of the address by a distant or uninterested point without having to set a paragraph over.

10.11 Avoid transitional paragraphs except in introduction of lists, introduction to statistics or recital of events.

"Production," he said, "will equal, if not exceed, that of the past year." He added:

"The current outlook indicates a better growing season."

The above form means setting over if last paragraph is deleted.

In the following form, the paragraph may be deleted without new composition:

"Production will equal, if not exceed, that of the past year." he said.

"The current outlook indicates a better growing season."

10.12 Time zones are needed only in informative notes, release time of advances, radio or TV programs, or stories in which a time zone is part of required information. Where mention is made in a story that a conference, session, meeting, etc., is to be held at a certain hour, that information should be in a separate paragraph.

When zone is included it should be converted to EST or EDT.

It is NOT necessary to include time zones in accidents, fires, etc. A wreck at 3 a.m. gives the reader the clear picture without a time zone.

10.13 Weather table:
Temperature and precipitation in inches for the 24-hour period ending at 7:30 a.m., March 20:

	Temp.		Precip.
	High	Low	(T-trace)
Aroostook	80	70	T
Beaumont	92	72	.30

Aroostook and vicinity: Generally fair and warmer today. High 80-85. (Form for AMS would spell the day.)

Short form:
NEW MEXICO: Partly cloudy and warm today, mostly cloudy and continued warm with showers and possibly thunderstorms Sunday. (Change "today" to "Saturday" for AMS report.)

10.14 Play listings:
FABLE
"Rashomon": Music Box—A Japanese fable of brutality as seen by four witnesses. Clair Bloom and Rod Steiger head the cast.

10.15 Land description:
SE¼NW¼, Sec. 2 T. 10 S., R2E. Lot 3, NW¼ Sec. 2, T. 9S, R2W. S½ Sec. 10, T. 9S, R6E, sixth principal meridian.

10.16 Book review:
I WAS THERE. By John Doe, Scranton, Pa. County Press. $4.50.
John Doe has been around and his observations have been put into a readable volume. Travelers will find many things in this book that they have overlooked in their travels and will give them a guide for their return.

John Henry

Bylines and credit lines follow several forms, bold face and center in all cases, with the name capitalized. The "y" in "by" is lower case.

Forms:
By ALTON BLAKESLEE
Identification is up and down:
AP Science Writer
Where the byline replaces logotype (use only one or the other, not both):
By THE ASSOCIATED PRESS
If copyright, add up and down:
Copyright 1965
Where a story is written for The Associated Press:
By CASEY STENGEL
Manager New York Mets
(Written for Associated Press)
When a substitute column is sent for a regular fixture, it should be labeled "Sub for Thomas" or may take this form:
By SAUL PETT
(For Hal Boyle)
Include reason at end under 3m dash.

Information slugs of "PMS in" or "AMS in" are not used in TTS.

The TTS numbering and slugs vary. The numbers, visible in tape, may be preceded by "D" or "N" or some other letter, identifying the circuit. The monitor copy will show the same thing. The visible material in tape will appear as gibberish on justified line monitor printers. On circuits which change regularly from body to agate and back the letter "A" in visible tape and on monitor printers after the number indicates agate.

A115wyyf
Ike lead
The "wyyf" on the monitor printer is the "115" visible in the tape; the "Ike Lead" identifies the material.

The publishable form of editor's note:
EDITOR'S NOTE—Trapped in a cave, Donald Ames scribbled notes in the darkness describing his wait while rescuers cleared rock slides to reach him. "It was tough," he said, "to write without being able to see. I couldn't read some of the notes when I got out."

Here is his story as he could decipher:
By DONALD AMES
Written for Associated Press
or, the underline may read:
As Told to Associated Press
Stories which run 100 lines or more of monitor copy should be slugged "MORE" and subsequent takes should carry the heading the first carried (whether current cycle without visible advance, or subsequent-cycle advance with tape visible caution). The first take also should say how many takes there will be.

It is not necessary to repeat datelines on subsequent takes but clear subject connection must be indicated in the slug.

Where future cycle advance is broken into takes and does not move in entirety in one cycle, additional guidance for desks is needed:
TA316 MOONSHOT May 24 take 3. Previous TA315 moved May 10.

Filing Practices XI

There are three forms for fast handling news:

The FLASH—seldom used.

The BULLETIN—for prime news, kill notes, releases.

The URGENT—for just under prime news.

The form for the "FLASH"

A153 FLASH
    WASHN—Men land on moon.
                      (signoff)

The flash is followed immediately by a publishable bulletin.

Flashes and bulletins are written as the result of an event or an announcement. Pre-punching in tape either a flash or a bulletin in anticipation of a major story is strictly forbidden.

The BULLETIN should be one terse paragraph. Subsequent matter does not carry the former "bulletin matter" slug.

A bulletin may start with a byline. If not, and a byline is to be used, the byline is added under dash after end of an add:

The form:
A123 Bulletin Draft
    WASHINGTON (AP)—The November draft, etc.
                      signoff

A124 draft
Washn—draft add A123: men.
    The call was one, etc.
                      dash
    By WALTER P. MEARS
    Associated Press Writer
                      signoff

An underline may identify the writer as AP Special Correspondent, AP Science Writer, or whatever, instead of "Associated Press Writer."

The URGENT may be so slugged, but preferably is offered in a 95 schedule. Before breaking the wire for an unscheduled URGENT, check to determine what remains of matter being sent. There may be little wordage left so it is preferable to wait for the finish to avoid chopped up report. The editor controlling the wire will determine movement of the scheduled URGENT, whether to make a moving item more or wait.

Stories are to be laid down on member desks, and in tape, with the minimum breaks and short takes.

Stories of 150 or more carry the wordage count (and it must be accurate) at the start, as:

A150 Draft 350

If wordage exceeds 500, and all the story is in hand, it is broken into "takes":

A145 Draft 400, 2 takes Total 800

A147 Draft, take 2 400 age.

Takes should not exceed 500 words, but need not necessarily be that precise length. An 800-word story may be broken at 350 and 450—300 and 500—just so continuity is preserved. Also a thoughtful division may provide members with a choice of length.

Leads or revisions require clean pickups. In a story where a number of paragraphs start, or end, with the same word, more than a one- or two-word identification is needed, as:
The subcommittee delayed
The subcommittee heard

Also a lead may pick up in one paragraph, delete one, and then pick up balance. As an example: The lead picks up in 2nd graf, then eliminates 3rd graf, and picks up again in 4th graf, the lead should include the 4th paragraph (deleting the 3rd, of course) and then pick up in 5th paragraph. A lead should be written far enough down to make a clean pickup.

A story wrapping up angles from many places may carry the line:
By THE ASSOCIATED PRESS
at the start of the story. Some newspapers prefer a dateline. In some instances, it will be necessary to repeat at the end of such an item the first paragraph with the dateline, logotype, and pick up in the second paragraph. Adjust the dated paragraph to eliminate name of city if repetition is undesirable.

Where a story originates in one place, but may have a precede from another, avoid "here" and "there" in it, just as the words are avoided in material which does not have a dateline.

To avoid parentheses, where material from another area is included in one dateline, the form:
LONDON (AP)—Prime Minister Harold Wilson said he had learned of efforts in Washington circles to aid Britain's entry into the European Common Market.

In Washington, there was no comment.
Wilson did not, etc.

Do not use "Pick up previous at start" on a datelined story.

DEVELOPING STORIES

A key, or tag, word is used after the book number on a story, regardless of brevity, where there is obviously a developing situation. As:
A150 ships (followed by the item). As the story develops, the slug includes (after tag, Ships, "lead" and 2nd lead, and so on. If the story carries over into the AMS cycle, the slug would be Ships, 1st NL, and so on. "Bjt" would be included if the story is listed in the digest.

A story breaking in the AMS cycle and carried over has only the tag, or "lead" as any other PMS story.

The same form applies to a story where there may be sidebars or related material. For example:

If there is a plane crash in Lebanon and a prominent passenger (Zilch) is aboard and there is a London story about Zilch, the slug "Plane" on the original story then includes Zilch."
A150 Plane Zilch
LONDON (AP)—A. A. Zilch, etc.
To revise the London sidebar:
A150 Plane Zilch
London Zilch A145 sub 6th graf changing destination: trip.
Zilch was en route to London.
Traveling 7th graf
(signoff)

The key words, or tag, show topic—some thought must be given to avoiding duplicate tags on unrelated stories as fire, wreck, etc.—and are used in leads, adds, inserts, sub, revisions, with those identifications following the key word, locations, pickup, or whatever.

The key, or tag, follows the book number and gives the wordage: A150 Health 250, A150 Smoking 300, A150 Taxes 500, etc.

On AAA wire stories do not attention pickups to side, or regional, wires. Instead, send that information on those wires, as on BBB for example:

B125 Atomic

Editors: Washn atomic A150 may pick up B101 at 4th graf "Earlier" etc. The wire designations would be changed to fit wires involved.

A developing fire story on a side, or regional wire, may have several leads there before the story moves on the AAA. When it does move AAA the slug merely is "FIRE" without reference to earlier matter on the side wires. However, a later add to the AAA story might move on the side wires, and pick up into earlier side wire material:

B121 Fire
New York fire A150 add: stories.

Seven departments answered the alarm.

Police were, 6th graf 3rd lead B100.

ADVANCES

Advance material requires fullest identification, both in the slugs and in the visible tape.

There are several forms of advances: for use in current cycle, for a specified hour, on a hold for release basis, for a future cycle, and the Sunday ams advances. The automatic release time for the wire services is 6:30 a.m. or p.m., EST or EDT. Sources may fix certain hours, or material (presidential message) may have a fixed release time either in the current, or a future, cycle.

Slugs vary according to the advance.

Advances not originated by The Associated Press and where the release is designated by the source for AMS or PMS, carry a 6:30 p.m. (or a.m.) EST (or EDT) slug. The form:

adv for 6:30 a.m. EST

Where the source fixes an exact time, the form:

adv for 1 p.m. EST (or whatever the time)

The "hold" for release slug:

adv HOLD, release due 11 a.m. EST.

Such advance is released by a bulletin, either when a speech (for example) is delivered or when a release is broken. Editors should be advised if a "hold" advance has not been released, and also should be told (in a succeeding cycle) if a release has been broken ahead of the specified time.

No tape visible is required on current cycle advances, and no closing line is needed. Both tape visible at start and a closing line are needed in future cycle advances.

AP Newsfeatures budget stories for Sunday AMS will start at the first of each month numbered A300 and continue in sequence to the end of the month. At the first of the next month, the A300-series is begun again.

Where advances are more than 500 words in length they are divided into takes, the same as in spot copy. If advances are to be a series, the number of parts should be included.

Example:
A321 FEB 26 (the book number 321 and date FEB 26 are translated into tape visible)
adv Sun AMS Feb. 26
Thai, Part I, 800, 2 takes
 EDITOR'S NOTE—The growth and industrialization of Thailand have been impressive. In this, the first of five articles, William L. Ryan explains the background.
By **WILLIAM L. RYAN**
AP Special Correspondent
 BANGKOK, Thailand (AP)—The substance
(signoff)
A322 FEB 26 (322 and FEB 26 again in tape visible)
adv Sun AMS Feb. 26
Thai, Part I, take 2
 close with descriptive of next part, avoiding use of day of week:
Next: Thai farmers.
end adv Sun AMS Feb. 26 moved Feb. 10
(signoff)
 Other future cycle daily advances require the book number and date in visible tape. The form:
A150 FEB 28 (150 and FEB 28 in visible tape)
adv Tues PMS Feb. 28
 following that line, any descriptive (length, takes, number of parts if series, byline or overline, dateline).
 The closing line:
end adv Tues PMS Feb. 28 moved Feb. 20
(signoff)
 Revision of future cycle advances follows the same form of slugs that the original had. Example:
A103 JAN 17
 New York mayor moved as A153 Jan. 3 adv for Tues PMS Jan. 17 insert after 3rd graf:
 (the insert, then)
While the 4th graf
end adv Tues PMS Jan. 17, moved Jan. 5
(signoff)

ADVISORIES

There are two forms: Editor's Note and Note to Editors.

The Editor's Note precedes publishable material (see example in Teletypesetter section for one form, in "Advances" in example A321 for another.

A Note to Editors may call attention to something in the report, something expectable or helpful in planning, that a report is being investigated, or staffers are en route to a disaster, a "hold" advance has not been released or released prematurely, explanation of upcoming series, or advise of outstanding photos or when leads are expected.

Editors should be kept fully informed.

REVISIONS

Corrections, reruns of garbled matter, developments, need dateline, topic word, book number and location in previous. An example:
A123 Taxes
Washn Taxes A101 repeating garbled 3rd graf from end fixing garble:
 The debate attracted one of the largest crowds in recent years.
Although 2nd graf from end

The example "2nd graf from end" is for quicker and easier location than 17th graf (from start).

The same form would apply to corrections which would include the entire paragraph (if a substantial change—ordinary typographical errors or letter-transpositions are not corrected UNLESS meaning is changed, or incorrect word reads but doesn't make sense).

Where a correction makes a VITAL change, a separate note to editors (or inclusion in the revision itself) should be sent giving the dateline, book number, topic and explaining the radical change. For example:
 Editors: In Paris De Gaulle A105 please note that correction A131 inserts negative "not" in his remarks.

THE KILL

When it is mandatory to kill a story to remove possibly libelous material from the report, this is the form:

A123 BULLETIN KILL

New York—Kill story John Doe arrested, A105. Doe NOT jailed.

Editors—New York story John Doe jailed, A105, has been killed. A kill is mandatory. Make certain the story is NOT published.

sign off

The kill note should say why the story is being killed and, if possible, say whether there will, or will not, be a sub. If that information is not available and cannot be included in the note, a later, separate, note to editors is sent.

The kill note explains why, but avoids general terms such as "dangerous" or "libelous."

The kill note is repeated in the following cycle.

CORRECTIVE

The corrective, where there is a delay between the original and the corrective, carries the dateline, subject matter, book number and date of the previous story. The form:

A153 Corrective

Papers which printed the New York story of Feb. 10 on the rail merger, A105 at 10:15 aes, are requested to print the following:

The corrective story then moves.

The corrective should not say "The Associated Press regrets" or "is glad to correct" or similar.

To kill a paragraph, or paragraphs, of a story that has had adds, leads, or other revision, identify the part, or parts, to be killed by more than the paragraph number, as:

Killed paragraph starts "The court initially" and ends "yet to be heard." Or:

Killed paragraphs start "The count initially" and end "not earlier."

Both start and end identifications should have enough words to clearly locate the parts, in case other paragraphs start or end with one or two of the same words.

Biographical sketches are released in simple form under dash at the end of first take:

release sketch 1234567.

Notice of a sketch release is included in the next cycle of the death.

Identify corrections for photos, mailed pages or other material not carried on wires. The form (as applicable to whatever segment):

Editors—In mailed pages "Stamps" for Tues PMS Jan. 17 mailed from New York Jan. 10 in 6th graf change name to Bolivia instead of Brazil. AP Newsfeatures.

NOTE: That is a form of wire correction which does not repeat a whole paragraph.

ALL-AMERICA

There is only one All-America football team. This is Walter Camp's selection through 1924, and The Associated Press selections after 1924. Do not call anyone an All-America player unless he is listed either on the Camp or AP roster.

Similarly do not call anyone an All-America basketball player unless on AP selection. This selection started in 1948.

The same rule applies to the Little All-America teams in both football and basketball.

WIDE WORLD

Wide World is a supplementary service for feature and special assignment pictures, and a commercial service department. It operates in conjunction with AP Newsfeatures.

MISCELLANY

The Associated Press usually does not carry denials of stories not by AP, but editors may be informed by wire note of circumstances. Denials are carried, however, when they make news.

All wire notes, messages and publishable information—as well as stories—carry time and date as part of the operator signoff.

Messages of urgency are slugged 95.

"All Points" messages have replaced the "17" of the past. "All Points" messages calling for roundups or other material must be cleared with New York first.

The 97 message continues for markets and the financial department, but for the tabular department, the messages are slugged "TAB."

Messages must be clearly identified for departments: AP World, AP Newsfeatures, Wide World, Sports, Cables, etc.

Messages going through relay are addressed to the control bureau for the eventual recipient and signed by the sending bureau, i.e.:

AX for Athens (information) NY

Identify message content. "Referring our 6:03 PES yesterday, any answer?" means research and time wasted. Include essentials for quick identification as: "Referring bids Arcania stadium, our 6:03 PES Jan. 10, any answer?" If there is delay answering an inquiry, another message is sent.

Make schedules short and informative and give CORRECT wordage. Include names in schedules of deaths.

WORLD SERVICE

AP World Service requests and replies should be slugged plainly as dealing with that department to insure delivery. Time and messages will be saved by remembering to include home towns and addresses of foreigners in AP World Service copy.

WIREPHOTO

Bureaus and sending stations on the Wirephoto network schedule pictures verbally to the New York monitor, who controls the network.

In scheduling a picture, it is essential to describe the picture and give a brief sizeup of its value—whether the picture is worth general distribution or only regional movement. Pictures of value or interest for the greatest number will be transmitted first. Periodically, there are regional network splits during which prime regional or state network pictures are moved.

Captions must be accurate and complete so that no question is left unanswered. Captions should be complete enough to stand on their own without having to depend on a news story.

First names, initials, titles and identifications are basic. Nicknames should be avoided except for widely known sports figures. Unusual circumstances under which a picture is taken are pertinent and should be included in the caption. Where a picture is outstanding, the name of the photographer whether he's an AP staffer or on a member paper should be carried in the caption.

Any copyright notice must be included.

Kills, eliminations and corrections are handled on the same basis as they are in the news report except that Wirephoto matters are channeled through the New York Photo Desk.

Notices involving kills, important corrections, reverse prints, etc., are handled on the news wires and backstopped by transmission on the Wirephoto network. The New York Photo Desk should be consulted promptly on all such matters prior to sending any wire note or network transmission.

Eliminations are handled by a transmitted note both on the news wires and on the Wirephoto network. Regional eliminations are handled on a network split after consultation with the New York Photo Desk by the bureau involved.

Index
to the AP Stylebook

Abbreviations:
  Associations 2.1
  Business 2.3, 8.3
  Christmas 1.17
  Degrees 2.13
  Geographic 2.7, 2.10, 2.12, 2.19
  Military 2.21
  Months 2.17
  Names 2.20
  Organizations 2.11
  Titles 2.14, 2.15
Addresses 2.4, 3.11, 10.10
Advances 10.4
Ampersand 2.3, 3.40
Animals 2.6
Apostrophe 3.13, 3.14, 3.15
Army 1.14, 2.21
Auto racing 9.18
Awards 1.35
Avenue 2.4
Aviation 6.2, 6.3

Baseball 9.2
Basketball 9.5
Bible 1.22, 8.14
Blond, blonde 5.4
Bobsledding 9.21
Books 1.30, 10.22
Bowling 9.22
Boxing 9.8
Bullet 6.6
Business firms 2.3, 7.4, 7.7

Cabinet 1.9
Capitalization:
  Abbreviations 1.11, 1.21, 2.1, 2.2, 2.9, 2.11, 2.14
  Animals 1.26
  Associations 2.1
  Buildings 1.25
  Council 1.9
  Courts 1.12
  Executive 1.1, 1.2
  Flowers 1.27
  Geographic 1.25
  Highways 4.5
  Historic 1.6, 1.23
  Institution 1.25, 3.15
  Legislature 1.9
  Names 1.24
  Organizations 1.32
  Political parties 1.20
  Proper names 1.29
  Religious 1.31, 8.1
  Titles 1.1, 1.2, 1.3, 1.4, 1.6, 1.7
  Trade names 1.28
  Military 1.14, 1.15, 2.21
Capitol 1.9
Cartridge 6.6
Caucasian 1.24
Centigrade 6.11
Chinese 1.24, 5.3
Christmas 1.17
Churches, Section VIII
Coast Guard 1.14
Colon 3.16
Colored 1.24, 2.1
Compounds 5.5, 5.6
Comma 3.7, 8.9, 11,16
Committees 1.10

Congress 1.9, 1.20
Council 1.9
County 1.25
Courts 1.12
Cross country 9.15
Cycling 9.72

Dash 3.28, 3.29, 3.30
Datelines 10.1, 10.2
Dates 2.9, 2.17, 2.18
Deaths, widow 6.3
Decimal 3.4, 4.6
Decorations 1.35
Deity 1.22
Departments 1.11, 1.13
Diagonal 4.8
Dimensions 4.1
Directions 1.19, 2.4
Distances 4.1
Dividends 7.7, 7.8
Dog shows 9.16
Dollar sign 3.4, 4.6, Section VII

Ellipsis 3.2
Ex- 5.7
Exclamation point 5.7

Fahrenheit 6.11
Fencing 9.14
Figures:
  Abbreviation 4.12
  Casual 4.3
  Division, political, etc. 4.2
  Decimal 4.6
  Fractions 4.8, 8.2
  Highways 4.5
  Metric 4.10
  Money, 4.6, Section VII
  Roman numerals 4.4
  Serial 4.11
  Time 3.7, 4.9
Firearms 6.6
First, second, etc., 4.2, 4.12
Flowers 4.8
Football 9.4
Fowl 1.26
Fractions 4.8, 7.2
Fraternal orders 1.21

G, G-force 6.16
Geographic 1.18, 2.19
Golf 9.9
Gymnastics 9.26

Halloween 1.16
Highways 4.5
Historic events 1.16
Hockey 9.6
Holidays 1.16
House 1.9, 1.10, 1.25
Hyphen:
  Adjectival 3.32
  Compound 3.31
  Like, unlike 3.31
  Prefix 3.37, 3.38
  Spelling 3.36, 3.39
  Suspensive 3.33
  Vowels 3.34, 3.35

Index to the AP Stylebook

Identification 3.22, 3.23, 6.10
Initials 1.21, 1.33, 3.3, 6.4
Indian 1.24, 2.6
Integer 3.4

Jet 6.2
Jewish 8.3, 8.7
Jr. 2.14

Kelvin 6.11
Knot 6.12

Lacrosse 9.17
Leads 10.5
Legislature 1.9
Livestock 1.26
Lower case abbreviation 2.5

Mach 6.17
Marine 1.14, 2.21
Markets Section VII
Mass 8.5
Midwest 1.18
Military:
  Divisions 1.14, 1.15, 2.2
    Abbreviation 2.21
Miscellaneous Section VI
Mothers Day 1.16
Motor 6.1
Mr. 2.15
Multi 5.7

Names:
  Foreign 1.33
  Lists 10.8
  Preference 1.33
  Titles, 1.11, 1.7, 3.22
  Unusual 6.5, 10.7
Navy 1.14, 2.21
Negro 1.24
Nicknames 1.34
Non 5.7
Notes to Editor 10.3
Numbered streets 2.4, 3.11, 10.17
Numbered succession 3.1, 3.24
Number, abbreviation 4.12, 7.3
Numerals, Roman 4.4

Obituaries 6.3
Occupational titles 1.7
Officials 1.5
Organizations 1.32

Pan, Pan- 5.7
Paragraphs, transitional 10.11
Parentheses:
  Appellation 3.21
  Identification 3.22
  Paragraph 3.26, 10.6
  Punctuation 3.25
Per cent, percentage 5.4
Period:
  Abbreviation 3.3, 3.25
  Decimal 4.6
  Ellipsis 3.2
  Omission 3.5
Play listings 10.14
Pistol 6.6
Pope 1.3
Pound sign 4.7
Prefixes 5.7
Provinces 2.8
Punctuation:
  Apostrophe 3.13
  Colon 3.16

Comma 3.6
Dash 3.28
Exclamation point 3.19
Hyphen 3.30
Parentheses 3.21, 10.6
Period 3.2
Question mark 3.20
Quotation mark 1.31, 3.26, 3.27, 3.21
Semicolon 3.12

Races 1.24
Racing 9.7
Religious 1.3, 1.4, Section VIII
Revolver 6.6
River 1.25
Roman numerals 4.4
Rowing 9.13

Semicolon 3.12
Senate 1.9
Ships 2.2, 6.13
Shooting 9.19
Signatures 10.9
Skating 9.24, 9.25
Skiing 9.20
Social Security 1.13
Speed 2.5, 6.12
Slang 6.8, 6.9, 6.14
Spelling:
  Chinese 5.3
  Compound 5.5, 5.6
  Geographic 5.1
  Names 1.33, 2.20, 3.5, 6.4
  Prefix, suffix 5.7
Sports Section IX
States 2.7
Streets 2.4
Suffixes 5.7
Summaries 9.1
Super 5.7, 6.2
Suspensive hyphen 3.33
Swimming 9.11

Telephone numbers 3.11
Teletypesetter Section X
Temperatures 3.30, 6.11
Tennis 9.12
Thoroughfares 2.4
Thrust 6.17
Time Zones 2.2, 6.15, 10.12
Titles:
  Section I, 3.22
  Long 6.5
  Religious Section VIII
Track, field 9.10
Trade names 1.28, 6.2
Turboprop 6.2

Ultra 5.7
Union 1.8, 6.5
United States 1.8, 2.2, 2.12
U.S.S.R. 2.10

Versus 2.5

Ward 1.23
Washington, D.C., state 6.10
Weather 3.30, 6.11, 10.13
Weight 3.27
Weightlifting 9.23
Widow, wife 6.3
Wrestling 9.28

X ray, X-ray 5.4

Yellow 1.24

272

Copy Markings

¶	ATLANTA—When organization of	paragraph
or	is over. Now it will be the first	paragraph
	the last attempts.	
	With this the conquering is to	no paragraph
or ⌒	according to ~~the~~ this compendi-	elisions
	the Jones Smith firm is not in the	transpose
	over a period of sixty or more in	use figures
	there were 9 in the party at the	spell
	Ada, Oklahoma, is in the lead at	abbreviate
	the Ga. man is to be among the	spell
	prince edward said it is his to	capitals
	accordingly This will be done	lower case
	the acc user pointed to them	join
	in these times it is necessary to	separate
	the order for the ~~later~~ devices [stet]	retain
BF/c or BF ⎦	By DONALD AMES ⎣	bold (black) face centered
	J. R. Thomas ⎦	flush right
	⎣ A. B. Jones Co.	flush left
	president ∧is in a fine situation	caret
#	space (also 30 at end of item)	
ʾʾ ʿʾ ʿ	quotation marks, apostrophe	
∧	comma	
⊗ or ⊙	period	
=	hyphen	
⊢⊣	dash	
	a̲ u̲ n t (underline a u)	
	d o̅ n̅ e (overline n o)	

273

THE Associated Press Stylebook has been mailed to all newspaper members of The Associated Press and schools of journalism.

Additional copies are available to members, schools and libraries at the following charges which cover production, handling and mailing:

Single copies $1.00; three copies $2.00; ten copies or more 35 cents each.

Limited quantities will be available to other organizations at $1.00 each.

For copies or information write Traffic Department, The Associated Press, 50 Rockefeller Plaza, New York 20, N. Y.

Index

(The Associated Press Stylebook index is on pages 271 and 272.)

Abstraction, ladder of, 33-37
Accident stories, 93-97
Accident and disaster stories,
  elements of, 95
Accuracy, 37-38
"Add", 219, 221
Adversary relationship, press and government, 20
Advocacy journalism, 214
Alternative journalism, 213
Attribution, 54-58, 105, 113-116, 146
    Clarity of, 206-208
    Euphemistic-source, 115-116
    Freedom of, 113-116
    "Ladder" of, 115
    Location in sentence, 55-56
    Punctuation of, 57-58
    Rules of, 113-117
    Words of, 56-57

Backgrounding, 109
Balance in news, 18
Beat organization, 147
Beat reporting, 142-155
Behaviorism and press theory, 196
Broadcast journalism,
  law effecting, 192

Certainty, 15-16
City government organization, 150
City government reporting, 149-151
Clarity, 15-16
Cliches, 48-49
Commission on Freedom of
  the Press 196, 198-199
Completeness, 38-40
Concluding the story, 82
Concreteness, 27-28, 33-37

Confidential sources and
  information, 191-192
Conflict, 14, 17, 20
Connotative meaning, 30, 32-34, 210
Consequence, 12-13, 17, 205-206
Co-opting, 20-21, 145
Copy format, 218-221
Copyreading symbols, 221-223, 273
Copyright, 188-189
County government reporting, 151
Court reporting, 152-153, 189-190
Crime stories, 97-98

Darwinism, social, 196
Dead-level abstracting, 34-35
Delayed reward, 16
Denotative meaning, 29-30, 33-34, 210
Departmentalization, 17-18
Disaster stories, 93-97
Double-meaning words, 31-32, 127-128

Editing, purpose of, 61-62, 156-157
"Editorial game," 18-19
Editorializing, 30-33
Election coverage, 154-155
Emotional appeal, 14, 16-17, 167-168
Emphasis, factual, 71-72
Equal time, 192
Event versus issue reporting, 199

Faction, 214
Fair comment, 184
Fairness Doctrine, 192
Fairness in news, 198-199, 201-205
Fair Trial-Free Press, 189-190
Feature language, 176-177
Feature leads, 174-176

Feature story organization, 175, 181
Feature treatment, types of, 169-173
Featurizing, examples of, 169-173
Feedback, 8-9
Five W's and H, 69-75, 83-84
Foreign words, 47-48
Freedom of the press, 30-31

General assignment reporting, 89, 142
Ginzburg v. U.S., 187
Goals for the press, 198-199
Grammar, 44-47

"Hard" news, 16-17
Hood, Red Riding, 83-86
Hostile news sources, 132, 144-145
Human interest, 14-15, 167-181
Humanizing techniques, 174-181
Humanizing the news, 167-181

Identification in news, 16, 53-54, 76
Immediate reward, 16
Incongruity as news value, 11, 167-168
Inserts, 166
Interpretation, tools of, 200-206
Interpretive reporting, 199-209
Interview, 118-137

    Cooperation and rapport in, 120-123, 130-131
    Man-on-the-street, 107-108, 136

Interview questions, clarity of, 127-128

    Filter, 128-129
    Open-ended or structured, 123-126
    Probe, 130-131
    Sequence of, 122, 125-126, 128, 129

Interviewer bias, 117-120, 124, 126, 129-130, 132-133
Interviewing, preparation for, 109, 111-112, 120-123, 137-139
Interview stories, 108-110
Inverted pyramid, 64-69

    Variations of, 77-81

Jargon, mastery of, 48, 153

Language of news, 43-63
Law, 182-193

Leads, backing into, 72
    Feature, 81-86, 174-176
    Narrative, 81-82
    Speech story, 103-104
    Summary, 69-75

Lead-to-body connection, 75-77
Libel, 182-187
Libertarian theory, 194-195
Library, use of, 137-139
Lindley Rule, 116
Loaded words in interviewing, 118, 126
Loaded words in writing, 30-33

Meaning, types of, 28-30
Miller v. California, 187
Mishkin v. New York, 188
Mr., use of, 91

Neiman-Marcus Co. v. Lait, 185
Neutral wording, 126-127
New Journalism, 212-215
New leads, 166
News conferences, 111-113
News, defining, 2
News elements, 10-19
Newsfeatures, 170-173
Newshole, 19
News judgment, in choosing stories, 1-26
    In organizing stories, 66-67
News leak, 116
New York Times v. Sullivan, 183
Nonpurposive communicator, 3-4, 7
Note taking, 102-103, 133-135
Novelty, 11-13, 17, 167-168

Obituaries, 90-93
Objectivity, 27-33, 196-197, 212-215
Obscenity, 187-188
Off-the-record, 114, 145-146
Open meetings, 190-191
Organization of story, 64-86, 181, 201-206

    Humanizing approaches, 181
    Interpretation, 201-206
    Narrative, 82
    Suspended interest, 82
    Traditional, 64-86

Panel discussions, 113
Paragraphs, 52
Pentagon Papers, 191
"Play" theory, 18
Police reporting, 147-149
Political campaign coverage, 210-212
Postal regulations, 188
Precision journalism, 209-212
Press conferences, 111-113
Press responsibility, 19-23, 37-41, 194-199
"Printed debate" format, 201-205
Privilege, qualified, 186-187
Prominence, 15
Proximity, 10, 17
Psychoanalysis and press theory, 196
Public records, 190-191
Purposive communicator, 4, 9

Question-and-answer story, 109, 200-201
Questions, types of, 123-126
Quotation, direct and indirect, 105-107, 113-115, 133-134

Racial coverage, 32-33, 198, 209-210
Redundancy, 49
Reluctant news source, 132-134, 144-147
Reportage, 214
Resource materials, 137-139
Rewriting, 156-166
   Examples of, 5-8, 158-165
   Other reporters' stories, 159-165
   Own stories, 156-157
   Public relations releases, 157-158
   Readers' contributions, 158-159
   Telephoned notes, 165-166
Role reversal, 21-22
Rosenblatt v. Baer, 184
Rosenbloom v. Metromedia, Inc., 185

Sampling, 136-137
Saturation reporting, 214
School reporting, 153-154
Scientific language, 48
Scientist-reporter conflict, 19-20
Sensationalism, 14, 17
Sentences, 50-51
Shield laws, 146, 191-192
Slug, identifying, 219-221

Small newspapers handling spot news, 89, 198
Social responsibility theory, 195-199
Social science techniques, 32-33, 136-137, 209-212
"Soft" news, 16-18
Source-reporter relations, 19-23, 142-145
Specialization, 142-155, 208-209
Speech coverage, 101-107
Speeches, advance copies of, 103
Speed, 40-41
"Sports slanguage," 49
Spot news, 88-100
Stereotyping by interviewer, 119-120
Structural meaning, 30
Style, Associated Press, 224-273
Style, news in general, 52
Style, office, 53
Style, personal, 52
Suburban reporting, 151-152
Suspense, 15
Symbols, 28-29

"Take," 219, 221
Telephone interviewing, 135-136
Time, Inc., v. Hill, 185
Timeliness, 10-11, 17, 88
Transition, types of, 58-61
   From lead to body of story, 75-77
   In complex stories, 77-81, 85-87

Weather stories, 99
Westley-MacLean Model, 3-5, 8-9, 19
Word choice, effective, 47-49, 176-179
Words, 33-37
Writing style, feature, 177-181